ROGUE STATE

Also by T. D. Allman

Unmanifest Destiny

Miami: City of the Future

ROGUE STATE

AMERICA at WAR ☆ ☆ ☆
☆ ☆ ☆ with the WORLD

T.D. ALLMAN

NATION BOOKS
NEW YORK

ROGUE STATE: *America at War with the World*

Published by
Nation Books
An Imprint of Avalon Publishing Group
245 West 17th St., 11th Floor
New York, NY 10011

Nation Books is a co-publishing venture of the Nation Institute and Avalon Publishing Group Incorporated.

Library of Congress Cataloging-in-Publication Data is available.

ISBN 1-56025-562-5

9 8 7 6 5 4 3 2 1

Book design by Simon M. Sullivan
Printed in the United States of America
Distributed by Publishers Group West

This book is dedicated with passion and respect to

JOYCE JOHNSON *Great Writer,* *Incomparable Friend*	*and*	PETER CURTIS *Ambassador Extraordinary,* *Paterfamilias Extraordinaire*

Never forgetting NEAN STODDART
Who painted the portrait while I read Plutarch

CONTENTS

Prologue

The Most Dangerous Man in the World

LIFE IS A COMEDY for those who think, a tragedy for those who feel. That's why the spectacle of the George W. Bush presidency makes you want to laugh and cry at the same time.

The reasons this unelected president has given us to cry are as numberless as the sands of the Iraqi desert. He's done more than Osama bin Laden or Saddam Hussein to endanger America. All by himself, he's destabilized a fragile, emerging world order. He's poisoned alliances; he's torn up treaties. He has convinced foes they had better get nuclear weapons, and get them quick. He's made America the global enemy of law and order. No enemy of human rights, or of the environment, or of a realistic approach to dealing with the problems of living sanely on this planet is friendless so long as George W. Bush is in the White House.

George Bush has destroyed belief in America's goodness and America's wisdom among hundreds of millions of people. Gratuitously, with his trademark smirk, he's turned a friendly world into a hostile world. Nations and people who once saw America as a global protector now see the United States as the greatest threat to civilized human values currently at large in the world.

Important, worthwhile allies, people whose help we need and whose judgment we should respect—the Canadians, the Germans, the Turks, and, yes, the French—have complete contempt for the president of the United States, as do the Russians and Chinese. Every nation in Africa explicitly opposed his attack on Iraq. Every one of Iraq's neighbors—Kuwait, Saudi Arabia, Jordan, Syria, Turkey, Iran—warned that catastrophe would be the result. But George W. Bush, a C student at Yale and Harvard, sneers at wisdom. Facts don't matter. Reality can take a walk. You're either for us or against us, he announces. Among those George Bush has turned against us include Nelson Mandela. According to Mandela, "the president of the United States does not know how to think. His attitude is a threat to world peace."

In a world where the technology of death is a mouse-click away, it's the hatred Bush has sown in countless unknown hearts that, sooner or later, may harm America most. Right now, in many places—including, it is reasonable to assume, inside the United States itself—smart, angry kids are on the Internet, amassing information on nuclear fission and biological warfare. In the world they know, George W. Bush, not some swarthy terrorist, personifies evil. Meanwhile, intelligent people everywhere ask themselves: How can the American people go on supporting this peculiar man? Why did they let him grab the presidency in the first place? Why, now, of all times—when the world truly needs sane, measured, constructive and patient US leadership—is an American president running wild?

The world was dangerous when Bush took office. He's made it much more dangerous. Every day he stays in office it gets even more dangerous. Bush's recklessness creates the danger. His bungling incompetence multiplies it. Americans today have a president who can invade Afghanistan—but after three years still can't bring back Osama bin Laden, dead or alive. American power is in the hands of a president who invades Iraq in order to rid the world of Saddam Hussein and weapons of mass destruction—and then takes eight months just to find Saddam, never unearths the weapons of mass destruction, and treats the death trap he's created there for our National Guardsmen (and women) as some kind of victory. The Bush bungling isn't limited to foreign wars. He is also the president whose Administration, years later, still hasn't managed to track down, right here in the United States, whoever it was who sent anthrax to some of George W. Bush's more unfavorite people, including Senator Tom Daschle and Dan Rather, as well to many quite average Americans, who died.

A willful, prideful ignorance completes the circle of incompetence and reckless endangerment. Why did the US "intelligence" community—with its thousands of analysts, and multibillion dollar secret budgets—fail so utterly to warn us about the impending attacks of September 11, 2001? Why is it that the Bush Administration did not foresee the catastrophe in Iraq it was creating for us, and for the Iraqis, when it plunged so blindly into war? Hans Blix, the astute and philosophical head of the UN inspectors, afterward remarked that before it invaded Iraq, the Bush Administration had "100 percent certainty that Iraq had weapons of mass destruction, and zero percent knowledge as to where they were."

That's George W. Bush: 100 percent certainty, zero percent knowledge. He is the President who doesn't know, doesn't care, and doesn't care to know. That's why America's President has stymied impartial investigations into the 9/11 intelligence catastrophe. It's why he opposed the creation of the Department of Homeland Security, and then, when it became politically impossible not to create it, left out both the FBI and the CIA. It's why, even now, Bush and his crowd never ask themselves: Could it be that others oppose us not because they are evil, but because we are wrong? Could it be that those uppity French and craven Germans, and all the others on the Security Council did not support us because invading Iraq was a dreadful, stupid idea? Could it be we are the problem? Could it be we have some explaining to do?

Now ask yourself a question. Are you safer now than you were four years ago? The reason why you and your family are not safer—and probably are in greater danger—is that George W. Bush, for all his talk about fighting terrorism, has no aptitude and no interest in running the kind of government that might protect you and me from another 9/11. He prefers to sneer at the UN, insult NATO, and pick grudge matches with unsavory, faraway dictators who, nasty as they are, had nothing to do with 9/11, instead of doing his duty as president, which is to protect our lives and our property. George W. Bush starts wars as a kind of diversion from the real responsibilities of his office. And why shouldn't he? Very few wealthy white Republicans die in his wars.

All this is a crying shame for America yet, when you stop to think about it, there's also something deeply comical about George W. Bush's performance as president. You don't find him funny? That's because you're feeling, not thinking. Suppress your emotions for a moment. Wrap your intellect, and only your intellect, around what Bush said on May 1, 2003, in the course of a political appearance as lavishly choreographed as a Michael Jackson video. As he stood at taxpayers' expense on the deck of the US aircraft carrier, the "Abraham Lincoln," George W. Bush announced: "In the battle of Iraq, the United States and our allies have prevailed."

In the same speech, scripted by the White House to be a triumphant overture to his 2004 presidential election campaign, he also declared, "major combat operations in Iraq have ended." He at least had that right. Two months after Bush had defied the UN Security Council, defied world public opinion, and defied reality by invading Iraq, "major combat operations" were indeed over. The drip-drip phase of Americans getting killed—on patrols in Baghdad; at the wheels of Humvees in the Iraqi countryside—had begun. George Bush's videogame Iraq war had given way to the war in which young men and women from Hometown America—mostly with high school diplomas, and disproportionately working-class, black, and Latino—were being bludgeoned in the head, shot in the back, and left bleeding to death by their Iraqi attackers who included women in addition to violent young Iraqi males, and in one documented case, a twelve-year-old little girl.

George W. Bush is the president who, while all this is happening, stands beneath a banner proclaiming MISSION ACCOMPLISHED, and announces, "Iraq is free." Why, then, are so many Americans being killed in what Bush described as "liberated Iraq"? "Decades of lies and intimidation could not make the Iraqi people love their oppressors or desire their own enslavement," Bush proclaimed on the aircraft carrier. When the American occupation started running into resistance, however, he had a different explanation. The "evil agents of terror" were "making war on democratic Iraq." Wasn't his invasion supposed to have put a stop to all that?

Except when his knees are bothering him, George W. Bush runs around the world making trouble for himself, and even more trouble for others, the way Larry David runs around Beverly Hills in the cult comedy *Curb Your Enthusiasm*. Each new

George W. Bush–generated disaster, just like on TV, is propelled by the supercharged superego of a spoiled middle-aged narcissist who, having willfully and bizarrely misconstrued reality, gets himself ensnared in a series of weird yet initially avoidable misadventures of his own making. In each case, what escalates a minor misjudgment into a major crisis is the protagonist's refusal to conceive of the possibility that it might be he, not reality, that's to blame when things go wrong.

In February 2003, nearly two months before Bush ordered the Iraq invasion. George W. Bush and his Secretary of Defense, Donald Rumsfeld, were so fixated on attacking Iraq that in spite of all the diplomatic scurrying at the United Nations, it was beyond doubt that there would be an invasion. Given that Saddam Hussein was a tinpot torturer and that the United States, militarily, was the mightiest nation on earth, the outcome of the invasion also was not in doubt. However—to use a medical metaphor much favored by politicians and the press—a good surgeon always takes pains to make sure everything is just right, even when the patient on the operating table is undergoing minor surgery. How many troops would it take to make sure that the Iraq strike truly was surgical—and that once the surgery was finished, the patient not only survived the operation but got better?

It would take "something on the order of several hundred thousand" ground troops to defeat Saddam and then secure the country, former US Army Chief of Staff Gen. Eric Shinseki pointed out. This figure, as events in Iraq soon showed, was correct, just as one would hope it to be, coming from a highly-experienced, senior military commander. However, Rumsfeld—who's never fought in a war, walked patrol in a hostile city, or spent the night in a foxhole—had already decided that he knew better than the professionals. A mere 140,000 US troops, he informed the Joint Chiefs, was the magic number sufficient to impose democratic tranquility on Iraq, while simultaneously scooping up Saddam Hussein and his weapons of mass destruction for exhibit in the ensuing Bush Administration victory parade. While military men who had actually experienced the reality of war tried to keep their faces expressionless, Rumsfeld made a further prediction even more wildly defiant of reality. By Christmas 2003, he announced, the Bush Administration's triumph over evil in Iraq would be so total that the US occupation force there would be down to a mere 30,000 Americans, about the same size as the New York City police force.

Events on the ground soon proved that General Shinseki's judgment on the force levels necessary in Iraq had been, if anything, low. Maybe not even half a million ground troops could pacify Iraq. At the rate things were going, American soldiers, unless the United States scuttled and ran, would be celebrating Christmas beside the Tigris and Euphrates forever. Troop levels were not Rumsfeld's only error of judgment. When it came to counting the dollars necessary to occupy Iraq, his powers of clairvoyance had also failed him. Initially, Rumsfeld and other Bush officials treated the costs of occupying Iraq as incidental. There was talk of a mere billion a month sufficing to get "free Iraq" up and running; once US troops reached Baghdad, the Bush-Rumsfeld soundbite number edged up to two billion a month. Even this great sum, as it turned out, was not nearly enough just to hang on in Iraq, let alone actually end the chaos—and the killing of Americans there. Under congressional quizzing, Rumsfeld was forced to concede that "estimated" US expenditures in Iraq were actually running at about four billion dollars a month. This is nearly fifty billion dollars a year to maintain a US military presence that had brought neither peace to the Iraqis nor success to the United States. How much would it cost actually to win the guerrilla war George W. Bush had started in Iraq? Ten billion dollars a month? Twenty billion? And how many more Americans would have to die? While the American death toll crept higher, the cost to the US taxpayer kept soaring. Eighty-seven billion dollars turned out to be the number—provisional, and only for the first year following the invasion—that George W. Bush eventually pulled from a hat.

There was another little detail they had not foreseen. All that Iraqi oil that was supposed to have paid for Iraq's construction (and made US construction companies, including Vice President Cheney's Halliburton Corporation, megabucks)? It wasn't flowing. Secretary of Defense Rumsfeld, as always, was as unalarmed by reality as his boss. Once free-market forces took hold, he predicted, all Iraq's ills—including the drive-by murders of Americans—would disappear. This was Rumsfeld's prognosis for the country that invented the bazaar, and yet in spite of its 5,000–year experience with free markets, has never enjoyed the delights of democracy or known peace except while under the heel of some tyrant.

While neither the hemorrhage of blood nor of money in the war zone shakes Rumsfeld's virtually autistic serenity, even a brief stopover in "old Europe" can unnerve him, as was demonstrated during his June 2003 visit to the tidy constitutional kingdom of Belgium. The horrendous problems of Mesopotamia were but bagatelles to Rumsfeld, compared with the shocking discovery that tiny Belgium should be so presumptuous as to try foreign war criminals in its courts. Outraged that the perpetrators of genocide, as well as dictators who had tortured their own people, to say nothing of the perpetrators of illegal, unprovoked wars of aggression, might under certain circumstances be subjected to the ordeal of Belgian justice, the Secretary of Defense presented our Belgian allies with an ultimatum. Chuck your laws against war crimes and genocide or forget about getting any US dollars for the new NATO headquarters in Brussels. Unfortunately for him, Rumsfeld's threat to unleash dollar diplomacy carried considerably less weight than it once would have—about twenty percent less. That was how much value the once-mighty US dollar had lost in Europe since the Bush Administration started frightening away foreign tourists and investment in the United States with its "for us or against us" insults. Thanks to George W. Bush's continuing fiscal wizardry, the dollar has fallen even further since then.

As she traverses the world, Condoleezza Rice, Bush's National Security Adviser, evokes a different kind of laughter—the snortling and snickering that comes when a third-rate, irredeemably conventional intellect pretends to elucidate important global complexities to an audience made up of people more intelligent, more experienced, and much better informed than she is. Such scenes are never pleasant. The unease rises to the level of embarrassment when the speaker is both a representative of the president of the United States and oblivious to the fact that she is making a fool of herself.

Such was the distressful scene at London's International Institute of Strategic Studies when, a little after Rumsfeld let loose on the Belgians, Condoleezza Rice delivered her latest lecture to the Europeans on how they should comport themselves. Earlier Rice, in her self-assumed role as homeroom enforcer of the Western alliance, had pronounced the Europeans guilty of "appeasement"—that is, of being the same kind of people who condoned Hitler's aggression and excused the crimes of the Nazis—because they disagreed with US policy. In her monologue, Rice lectured the British foreign policy elite on the perils of another great threat to global security about which they were, in this case also, in her opinion, insufficiently vigilant. This latest menace so obvious to Condoleezza Rice yet, mysteriously, hitherto invisible to otherwise perceptive people on the other side of the Atlantic, wasn't Saddam. Nor was it hunger, global warming, or even militant Islam. This time the threat was what Rice called "multipolarity."

The snares and evils of "multipolarity," which Rice abjured her audience to avoid like the plague, were, in her presentation, contrasted with the beauties and benefits of "multilateralism." In her lengthy exegesis, Rice never explicitly defined her terms. But by question time it was clear what they meant. "Multipolarity" was bad because it was a term the French liked. It therefore violated Rule Two in the Bush instruction manual for the new Europe: "Always thwart anything the French suggest." "Multilateralism," conversely, was highly desirable because, as Rice used the term, it consisted of obeying the Bush Administration's Rule One: "Do exactly what we tell you to do, when we tell you, whatever it is."

"Multipolarity," Rice warned her distinguished audience in conclusion, "would take us back to the Concert of Europe." Had she been a member of Parliament, and had this been the House of Commons, Rice's sermonette would have been hooted down. Had she been an Oxbridge doctoral candidate defending her thesis, her examiners would have cut her to shreds. But since Condoleezza Rica was an adviser to the President of the United States, there was silence. Eventually, one member of the audience did ask Rice if she thought "six percent of the world's population," that is, the Americans, should always be the ones who decided what's best for "the other ninety-four percent of us."

"We want multilateralism," George W. Bush's chief confidante on war and peace reiterated, "but it must be a multilateralism that produces solutions, not delays and inaction." To everyone in the room except the speaker, it was already sadly evident that the Iraq war was no "solution." Even the London cabbies driving past the International Institute of Strategic Studies understood what eluded her: Far from providing a solution, invading Iraq had created a vast new international problem which was now going to torture the Middle East, the United States, and the rest of the world for years, maybe decades, to come. Like Rumsfeld, Rice wasn't merely oblivious to this disturbing new reality. She still regarded the failure of others to have supported the US attack as the result of some character flaw—evidence of lack of moral fiber among the effete Europeans. It simply did not occur to her, any more than it did to her President, that so many people disagreed with US policy because their understanding of this major international problem was superior to her own. Holding up the Iraq fiasco as a model of US leadership, she informed the distinguished audience that "Iran and North Korea are serious threats to security which require a multilateral solution." Not since Lyndon Johnson's emissaries, during their London and Paris transits to Saigon, had lectured the obtuse Europeans on the self-evident verities of the domino theory had such geopolitical hokum been so solemnly presented to them by an American official enjoying the confidence of a president of the United States, several members of the audience afterward noted.

Then there are the Two Stooges of the Bush comedy team, Richard "The Magician" Perle and Kenneth "Cakewalk"

Adelman. Both have been prominent agitators for a shoot-now-think-later US foreign policy since the 1980s, when they were cheerleaders for the disastrous Iran/*contra* operation. It was Perle who predicted that Saddam Hussein and his henchmen would disappear, as if by magic, in a puff of smoke. "Support for Saddam, including within his military organization, will collapse at the first whiff of gunpowder," was Perle's exact prognosis. Adelman—who likes to compare George W. Bush to Winston Churchill favorably while wearing an American-flag tie during his TV performances—was the one who predicted that conquering Iraq would be like dancing at an old-fashioned cotillion.

More than a year before the Iraq invasion, at a time when the difficulties and risks of such a complicated and dangerous military operation should have been seriously debated by serious people, the *Washington Post* lent Adelman its editorial columns. He used them to deride the findings of two researchers at the Brookings Institution, one of Washington's most respected think tanks. The two Brookings experts, Philip H. Gordon and Michael E. O'Hanlon, unlike those within the Bush entourage, had tried to assess what level of forces actually would be necessary to mount a successful invasion of Iraq. They concluded that the United States would "almost surely" need "at least 100,000 to 200,000" ground forces to defeat Saddam and secure the country.

The Brookings assessment, as we know now, was overoptimistic. But it was not nearly unrealistic enough for "regime change" true believers like Adelman. Instead of pondering the implications of their findings, Adelman treated the Brookings report as a joke. "I believe demolishing Hussein's military power and liberating Iraq would be a cakewalk," he wrote.

Even those who agreed with him considered Adelman a

lightweight in comparison to Rice (which, if true, would make him, intellectually speaking, lighter than hydrogen). However, he shares with George W. Bush himself, as well as with Rice and Rumsfeld, a capacity which is highly regarded in the Washington world of TV soundbites and op-ed sloganeering. This is the ability to deal with evidence that totally refutes his claims by shouting: See! I told you so! I told you I was right, and this proves it!

Bush launched his Iraq invasion on March 19, 2003. Within days it was clear to anyone capable of turning on a TV that the George W. Bush administration, as one US military man put it, had made a "serious strategic miscalculation" in not sending enough troops to Iraq. Though the full consequences of this miscalculation were only beginning to accumulate, conditions from the first day of the invasion were worse on the battlefield than either the administration or the American media had previously considered possible. The dark shape of worse things to come quickly became visible. This was an invasion without enough boots on the ground to prevent looting in Baghdad, or even direct traffic there, but worse quickly followed. Saddam's timely escape, along with the futile search for weapons of mass destruction, would tie down tens of thousands of US troops from the start. Thanks to hit-and-run low-intensity resistance to the Americans, the US occupation force never would be able to pacify the country. By April Fool's Day, it was clear, the cakewalkers had danced into a quagmire. What was Adelman's reaction?

"Now we know!" Adelman exulted on April 10, 2003—even as Saddam slipped out of America's grasp and Iraqi forces regrouped for the coming guerrilla war against the American occupation. What did we know? "I always said it would be a cakewalk," Adelman exulted, yet again in the pages of the *Washington Post*.

Vice President Dick Cheney, though far less frequently, can also cut loose with a memorable one-liner. The last time was actually in 1989; it had to do with the future vice president's military record or, rather, lack of one. Cheney has spent his career in Washington promoting wars for others to fight. Yet he himself, like Bush and virtually all Bush's closest advisers with the exception of Secretary of State Colin Powell, avoided fighting in the Vietnam War. In fact Cheney, the fiercest hawk in the Bush Administration, has never carried so much as a slingshot in his nation's defense. Along with Adelman and Perle, he escaped the draft altogether.

Even Cheney's boss and President, George W. Bush, had, in the end, to serve in the Texas Air National Guard—the martial arts equivalent of majoring in bartending at Party Animal State U. How did the Vice President, one of Washington's master maneuverers, manage to maneuver himself out of military service of any kind? Cheney has never answered that question. However, once, back in 1989, when pressed on the subject of why he—unlike the three million Americans of his age who did go to Vietnam—never fought for his country, Cheney grabbed the chance to show that he, too, if he so chooses, can be funny. "I had other priorities than military service in the sixties," he shot back, as though getting maimed or killed in Vietnam had ever been anyone's priority.

Within George W. Bush himself, as within many comics, there seems always to gurgle, and frequently to surge, a wellspring of anger. A kind of rage at somehow being shortchanged by life seems to animate his worldview. Though it's hard to figure out why a person as privileged as he should feel that way, it's not an uncommon syndrome. Many of us have known the rich kid, the son of the famous father who goofs off a lot, makes fun of the wonks and weirdos, and then, when he hits the trifecta—the Ivy League degrees, the pretty girl, the big job—still has a chip on his shoulder.

Whatever the reason for his peculiarly deficient approach to the world, it certainly is not that Bush is stupid. Far from being a "moron," as a Canadian government official erroneously suggested, Bush is quick-witted and has a very resourceful political mind. Think how adroitly, for instance, he used the vileness of Saddam Hussein to distract attention from the fact that he himself had gone AWOL from the real war on terrorism. Until he diverted attention from his failures in the war on terrorism by beating the Iraq war drums, it was starting to become clear that on every front of the real war on terror, Bush was a loser. Even his biggest victory—Afghanistan—had turned out to be hollow. Osama, unlike Saddam, was never caught. True, American techno-power did overthrow the local government, in this case the Taliban. But to what effect? The result was not "regime change" but merely, and disastrously, as in Iraq later, "regime elimination"—the creation, by US firepower, of a power vacuum. Not even after Mohammed Karzai was installed in Kabul did Afghanistan have a national government—let alone the kind of human and institutional infrastructure that could prevent it from being used as a terrorist base again, once US forces, under George W. Bush's direction, bugged out, this time to invade Iraq.

Fighting a real war against terrorism would have required wisdom, not just smart bombs—and, in Afghanistan, Bush didn't even try. He had sneered at "nation-building" in the 2000 presidential debates. Now it wasn't even a case of Shoot Now, Think Later. It was Shoot Now, Then Start Another War, So We'll Never Have to Think. The result? Even as Bush bungled into a self-inflicted guerrilla war in Iraq, Afghanistan once again was being abandoned to warlords, heroin producers, and political outlaws.

Bush's failure is larger than Iraq and Afghanistan: He and his administration have not done anything effective anywhere to solve the problem of failed states being used as terrorist bases for attacks on innocent civilians, including you and me. He has blocked meaningful, indeed even token reform of the FBI, CIA, and INS. He's tried to keep even the facts of the 9/11 intelligence catastrophe secret, especially where they concern relations with his Saudi friends.

Bush's domestic "antiterror" policies mirror his economic policies. When it comes to jobs and incomes for the American people, Bush's objective isn't to "revive the economy." It's to make the rich richer, however much doing that enfeebles the economy, and deforms the US tax system. Similarly, his domestic "antiterror" measures serve to protect the agencies, politicians, and paper-pushers who made 9/11 possible in the first place, not the American people.

Under Bush's leadership, the US government remains, on the whole, simply uninvolved in protecting our lives and our property from future attack. But who noticed, once Bush's big buildup to the Iraq war began? Launching a new war to distract attention from failure in an old war—like manufacturing a foreign crisis to conceal a domestic hidden agenda—is a tactic older than Machiavelli. The tactic worked for Ming emperors and for Medicis, and it certainly worked for Bush in the 2002 midterm election, when he used the danger of war he himself had manufactured to make the Democrats seem iffy on national security. Yet as our last president from Texas, Lyndon Johnson, learned, the war you start overseas can come home and devour you. In the event George W. Bush is ever undone, it may be the result of him having been too clever. That, in turn, would be an oddly humorous denouement both for Bush, who often has pretended to be less clever than he really is, and for his critics—who all too often fall for the idea that some slowness of mental process explains why George W. Bush acts as he does.

The problem with Bush is not his IQ, but his emotional intelligence—along with what Martin Luther King Jr., would have called "the content of his character." Something is missing in the quality of Bush's temperament, and temperament, as Justice Oliver Wendell Holmes memorably observed, is far more essential to presidential greatness than intellect. George W. Bush's meanness of spirit is at the heart of the mystery. Why does someone with such a sunny background surround himself with dark souls? Why has he turned a world that wanted to be pals with him into a world that finds him the most dislikeable US President in living memory—a far worse pill of a president than Nixon was? He himself sometimes claims that the attacks of 9/11 made his aggressive, violent, and hostile chip-on-the-shoulder approach to the world necessary. Not since Pearl Harbor, he likes to remind us. He forgets that after Pearl Harbor President Franklin Roosevelt united America and filled it with hope. He won the respect and love of the world by treating the world with love and respect.

George W. Bush in contrast has used 9/11 to divide, and divide, and divide. He has turned his constitutional responsibility to defend the United States into the biggest of all his wedge issues. In the Bush presidency, 9/11 is used to excuse everything, and justify anything, but it explains nothing. George W. Bush—and those whose advice he chooses to follow when he makes life-and-death decisions—regarded the world and its possibilities with dark contempt long before 9/11.

Not since Coolidge has a president kept his inner self so remote from the American people, but in Bush's case too, sometimes a little window opens. This happened two months after he announced that the United States had "prevailed." It was just before the July 4 holiday. Every night, on TV, Americans were watching other Americans dying in Iraq. There are moments when Bush reveals he has a soul, and this was one of them, and what a dark, insensitive one it turns out to be. The Bush soul-window opened when he was asked for his reaction to the drip-drip of American dead in Iraq. Even some Republicans were startled by George W. Bush's response. He delighted in these deaths. He reveled in them. They made him gleeful. "Bring 'em on!" he challenged the killers of Americans. Bush's July 4 speech, delivered a few days later, was also a revelation.

It is current White House practice to conscript members of the US armed forces to serve as extras in Bush disinfomercials. George W. Bush made his July 4 speech at a US Air Force base in Ohio to an audience from which the public was excluded. He spoke, instead, to an audience of Americans in uniform who had been ordered to provide the human backdrop for his patriotic remarks, along with their families. This Independence Day—July 4, 2003—was the first since the Iraq invasion. The nature of the holiday, the composition of Bush's audience, above all the disturbing events in Iraq, all legitimately posed the question: How many more Fourths of Julys would see Americans being killed in Iraq?

On this occasion Bush—enveloped by the banners and symbols of American patriotism—once again did something that, when you stop to think about it, was laughable. In his July 4 speech to this military audience he did not mention the Iraq war or the Americans being killed there, not once.

In the previous few days, as if responding to his "bring 'em on" dare, Iraqis had killed and wounded nearly thirty Americans. Bush's carefully selected audience knew that. They knew something else: It could have been me, or my son, or husband, or my wife. Yet on America's most patriotic holiday, in spite of these special circumstances, the painful sacrifices being made in Iraq were not in the script. George W. Bush did not so much as mention Iraq, or the American dead there, just as the word "Afghanistan" is seldom heard anymore to emerge from his lips. However, to the cheering, flag-waving crowd he did say the following: "The enemies of America plot against us, and our people in uniform do not have an easy duty." This was his closest allusion to the dying.

Admit it. All this is funny when you think about it—though it has to be understood from the start that when George W. Bush performs, it's not *Brady Bunch* humor you're getting, or even a riff suitable for *Seinfeld.* You can imagine a George W. guest spot on *The Simpsons.* Those Simpson kids, you can be sure, would put his hypocritical address to the student body in its proper moral perspective. But it is really Richard Pryor territory George W. Bush is working most of the time, as he flies from aircraft carrier to Air Force base, orating about the plotters. Richard Pryor, that is, in the case of his lighter riffs: The next time you watch him talking about some situation that, with him handling it, is going to lead to Americans getting killed, consider the possibility that the ghost of Lenny Bruce is head joke writer in the White House.

An American was shot dead in downtown Baghdad just

before Bush began his speech in Ohio. His name never made the news reports; such deaths were hardly news now. He had been killed while guarding the wrecked antiquities museum, so on July 4 an American death shaded into metaphor. Having arrived too late and in insufficient numbers to save civilization and its artifacts in Iraq, Americans now were bringing tragedy down upon themselves. A few days earlier, the decomposing bodies of two other GIs had been discovered, dumped in the countryside outside Baghdad. This time names were attached to the deaths. Sgt. Gladimir Philippe, 37, had been from Roselle, New Jersey, and Pvt. Kevin Ott, 27, had hailed from Orient, Ohio—and as soon as you attach the names of real human beings to the dark hilarity it stops being funny, of course. If you have any human compassion—and if, before George W. Bush entered the White House, you were proud of your country, and if even now, in spite of all he's done, you still love America—it makes you want to cry for America, when you stop to feel about it.

Ott had owned a Harley-Davidson back in Ohio. Philippe was the son of Haitian immigrants who, acting out their version of the American Dream, had already made it to the suburbs. Ott's family, as nonethnic Americans of his background often do, asked to be allowed to grieve in private. "Please don't bother us at the moment and thank you very much for respecting our wishes," the voice answering the Ott telephone told a reporter. In New Jersey, Philippe's kid brother Fedlyn, 16, said: "I looked up to him a lot. He always told me not to join the military. He told me to play basketball and keep my head strong and don't worry about girls, and to do good in school."

Philippe, the Haitian with the exotic name who liked to go bowling when off-duty, had died with Ott, the biker from the

Cleveland suburbs whose family knew how to fend off the press. Such details only seem to make the dead live: Gladimir Philippe and Kevin Ott were killed on guard duty at a town called Balad, about twenty-five miles north of Baghdad. Their bodies were found stripped of their weapons. Their Humvee was recovered before their bodies, at a different location.

Such deaths were beginning to become normal in Iraq, which was why in this instance they attracted unusual attention. The killings of Philippe and Ott were among the first to demonstrate unequivocally what the Bush Administration denies to this day: The invasion of Iraq all along had been based on a calculus of fantasy. The disturbing deaths of Americans like Philippe and Ott, happening all over Iraq, were not, as US officials were still trying to claim, "isolated incidents." These deaths were the first casualties in a war the American occupation force would have been unprepared to fight even if Bush and those around him had possessed the courage to admit the extraordinarily dark reality their arrogance and blundering had created for America in the Middle East.

Thanks to the Bush invasion, the United States now faced the prospect of fighting an imperial war in the same land that, in the end, has consumed every superpower that has ever presumed to hoist its pennants in the shadows of Babylon. The British, the French, the Ottomans, Genghis Khan, Alexander the Great: Every one of them had come, seen, and eventually been conquered. Just how unprepared the America of George W. Bush was to follow in the footsteps of either the Western "civilizers" or of the Mongol Horde was illustrated by the deaths of Sergeant Philippe and Private Ott. Historically, you could say their deaths were inevitable, but as a practical matter they were the product of what, in civil law, would be called criminal negligence. Had the government of the United States listened to the voices of reason and not invaded Iraq in the first place, they would never have been killed. Had the Bush Administration, having determined to invade Iraq whatever the cost, listened to the voices of reason when it came to assessing the cost, they might never have been killed.

But George W. Bush had chosen to be reckless on the cheap. So just before July 4, 2003, a guy from New Jersey and another from Ohio found themselves alone in an Iraqi town that, prior to their arrival, had been ruled by Saddam Hussein for more than twenty years. They were approached by some Iraqis and persuaded to get out of their vehicle—to investigate something, to help someone?

How were they lured out of their Humvee? Why didn't they fire in self-defense? We'll never know. As always with the Bush blunders, there was no backup and there would be no follow-up. What we do know is that if George W. Bush had paid attention to the Pentagon force estimates, and not preferred to rule though people like Rumsfeld—if he had bothered to read the Brookings report on troop strength, not watch people like Adelman gesticulate on the cable news channels—these two American citizens might never have found themselves so alone in such a dangerous place.

Was there an additional reason they died? Someone who actually knows war firsthand could speculate that perhaps some fundamental misapprehension caused Ott and Philippe to fatally misconstrue the nature of the danger they faced. One could speculate—and it would only be speculation—that they died because, like most Americans, they believed what their President had told them about his invasion of Iraq: Following the cakewalk to Baghdad, a rapturous and grateful

Iraqi population would welcome them as liberators. Not Bush or anyone else, including the free press of America, had told people like the Philippe family and the Ott family the truth, unvarnished and straight-out: "Your loved ones are being sent on a mad adventure. God help them."

It was all lies. It always had been all lies—and not just the specific lies, for example, about the weapons of mass destruction. The lie was the entire false construct spun and respun with such expertise by Bush and those around him that had convinced a majority of Americans—though no one else—that invading Iraq was, if not absolutely essential to America's self-defense, then certainly a plausible and desirable thing to do.

Now that the drip-drip war was underway, it was time to spin new lies—this time, about who was killing Americans in Iraq and why. In addition to Saddam Hussein's loyalists and "common criminals," a US official spokesman told the Associated Press, when asked about the two soldiers' disappearance, "outside agitators" were responsible for the mounting American death toll. These American deaths in Iraq resonated with the long, tragic history of the Middle East. In fact they were a continuation of it, but this latest official explanation for why Americans were being killed came straight out of America's own past. "Outside agitators" had also been the ones blamed by officials in the Deep South for the freedom marches of the 1960s, as they dispersed the demonstrators with truncheons, attack dogs, and water cannons.

It was in reaction to the disappearance of Philippe and Ott, and a cluster of deaths like theirs, that Bush had unleashed his dare: "Bring 'em on." Once their bodies were recovered, they were flown from Iraq to the military mortuary at the US Air Force base near Dover, Delaware. So it happened that on the same July 4, as they lay dead at one Air Force base, George W. Bush was orating about plotters at another. Americans as well as foreigners like to think of the United States as a new country, but this was America's 227th Fourth of July. For nearly a quarter of a millennium now, Americans have been celebrating July 4. Thanks to Bush this "Glorious Fourth," as it's sometimes called—was different from all previous ones.

What made it different was that all over the world ordinary people as well as national leaders were troubled by questions that, until recently, never would have occurred to them to ask: What might America do next to disrupt and endanger the world? What was to be done about the threat America posed? This was the first July 4 when it fairly could be said that the United States, not some foreign power, was the most dangerous country on earth.

It was all part of George W. Bush's transformation. Without really noticing it, an entire nation—and not just any nation—had been dragged along by George W. Bush's presidential transformation. On September 12, 2001, if you asked, most people everywhere would have told you Osama bin Laden was the world's most dangerous man. But by July 4, 2003, most people outside the United States would have given you a different answer because they could see what, to millions of Americans, was still invisible.

Had he betrayed America's trust or only taken advantage of the American people's startling indifference to the realities of the world? Whatever the case, George W. Bush had displaced bin Laden as the focus of the world's anxiety and fears. He was now the most dangerous man on earth.

HIJACKED

☆ ☆ ☆

I

The Omen

George W. Bush's transformation of America began with a hijacking, though not the hijackings of September 11, 2001. The planes with their passengers vaporizing into the Twin Towers; the faces at the windows of the trapped people, gesticulating to us before they died—all would come ten months later. The primordial hijacking of the Bush presidency—the one that turned the millennial possibilities of Y2K into a rehash of some of the stupider, triter, and nastier themes of American nationalism—happened on December 11, 2000. It happened in Washington, and the perpetrators waited until after dark.

September 11 would be seared into America's consciousness by the images of Americans dying live on TV, but who remembers 12/11? That was the date Chief Justice William Rehnquist and four other Republican judicial activists on the US Supreme Court intervened to make George W. Bush, the losing candidate for President in the 2000 election, president of the United States. This was not the first time politicians in judicial robes had thwarted democracy in America. Back in 1876—during the robber baron age in America—the winning candidate for president, Samuel Tilden, also had victory snatched away from him.

In a partisan power grab, the Republican candidate, Rutherford B. Hayes, was made president even though he had lost the election. The key player in that degrading electoral travesty was a judicial nullity from New York, US Supreme Court Justice Joseph P. Bradley. In 2000, the decisive figure would be another Republican member of the US Supreme Court, Chief Justice William Rehnquist.

The similarities of the 2000 presidential election to the stolen 1876 election are many and instructive. In each case, the constitutional separation of powers broke down. The supposedly impartial judiciary was used for party-political purposes, in order to gain control of the executive branch of the federal government. In each case, the outcome hinged on Florida's disputed electoral votes, though in 1876 the votes of three other states—Louisiana, South Carolina, and Oregon—were also in dispute. On both occasions the tiniest political advantage was ruthlessly pressed in order to gain the biggest prize in American politics. In 1876, Republicans had a one-vote majority on the Electoral Commission charged with adjudicating the balloting in Florida and the other disputed states. In 2000 they had a one-vote majority on the Supreme Court. They used it on both occasions to make the winner the loser—and the loser the winner—in the race to be President of the United States.

In 1876 as in 2000, the key to the Republican "victory" was finding a way to ensure that the will of the American people was disregarded. In 1876 as in 2000, this was achieved by the expedient of steamroller politics. Rather than investigating the disputed electoral returns in order to determine who actually had won the election, Republicans simply used their one-vote margin to award all the disputed electoral votes to their guy. There is an even more striking similarity. In each case, the single vote of a single party-politician-turned-Supreme-Court Justice made the difference. On both occasions, the figure in question chose political expediency over democratic, and constitutional, principle.

Both the Tilden-Hayes and Gore-Bush elections took place on November 7. In 1876 as in 2000, the balloting left the government in Washington very evenly divided. Republicans won control of the House of Representatives; Democrats controlled the Senate. In the presidential race the Democratic candidate, Tilden, was the clear leader, winning 51 percent of the vote to Hayes's 48 percent. Newspaper headlines proclaimed Samuel Tilden America's next president. Then news reached Washington, over the newfangled telegraph cables, that voting irregularities in Florida, Louisiana, South Carolina, and Oregon had left those states' electoral votes in dispute.

At first these disputed returns did not seem very important. Even without a single additional electoral vote from the four contested states, Tilden already had 185 out of the 186 electoral votes necessary to make him president. It was clear, too, that Tilden had won some, if not all, of the disputed states. Any one of the disputed electoral votes, numbering twenty in all, would suffice to assure him victory in the Electoral College. It seemed inconceivable at the beginning that none of the disputed electoral votes would go to Tilden, formalizing his election as president. Nonetheless, the combined total of disputed electoral votes was just enough to keep Tilden one tantalizing vote shy of formal victory in the Electoral College.

Who would get the disputed electoral votes, and who would decide who got them? That was the question that first gripped the political elite in Washington, and then the whole nation. Under the US Constitution, Congress—not the Supreme Court—has the duty to resolve electoral disputes of this kind.

The normal way to have resolved the presidential election dispute in 1876, as in 2000, would have been for Congress, not a Supreme Court justice, to determine who actually had won in each of the four disputed states, and then to have awarded the states' electoral votes accordingly. But the 1870s were an epoch of fat cigars and political pork. Instead of offering leadership in 1876, Congress offered a profile in spinelessness. No senator or representative wanted to be tarred and feathered by his constituents in the public outrage that was expected to follow selection of the President, whichever candidate actually got the presidency, so Congress devised an ingenious way to pass the buck. It quickly invented an electoral commission responsible for resolving electoral disputes. This commission then proceeded to do nothing. Weeks, then months passed, with no resolution. A presidential election that had not seemed exceptionally close was turning into a constitutional crisis. The danger grew that, come Inauguration Day, there would be no President to inaugurate—or worse, that two men would show up at the inaugural ceremonies in Washington, each demanding to be sworn in as President of the United States.

As the country watched in disbelief, the failure of Congress to resolve a handful of disputed election results turned into the worst constitutional crisis involving the selection of a President since 1800. Back then, an unintended tie in the Electoral College had almost caused the unstable Aaron Burr, not the revered Thomas Jefferson, to be chosen president. The Tilden-Hayes impasse, coming so soon after the Civil War, risked unleashing an even greater national crisis. Some even predicted the outbreak of a new civil war.

Why didn't the Electoral Commission simply do its job, and in the manner of an impartial board of inquiry, make sure that each candidate got the electoral votes to which he was entitled? Party politics, pure and simple, provides the answer. The membership of the newly created Electoral Commission, an extraconstitutional body unique in American history, had been split right down the middle, seven-to-seven, between Republicans and Democrats, party men all. Politicians being politicians, not one of these appointees was willing to trade party preferment for a place in history by letting the actual election results, rather than party loyalty, determine how he voted. The result was a built-in deadlock on the Electoral Commission between Republican supporters of Hayes, and Democratic supporters of Tilden. Within the Electoral Commission, responsibility was further diffused by dividing membership equally between senators and representatives as well as between Democrats and Republicans. The waffling hadn't stopped there. Congress had also named four Supreme Court Justices—two Republicans, two Democrats—to this Congressional body charged with exercising Congress's own power. This highly dubious move spread political responsibility even thinner, further engorging the political deadlock on the commission.

The four Supreme Court Justices in turn were charged with choosing a fifth, supposedly non-partisan Supreme Court Justice to sit on the Electoral Commission, in order to provide a fifteenth, tie-breaking vote. This is where Justice Joseph P. Bradley entered the scene, to become the first US citizen ever to choose a president all by himself. Following a series of fitful attempts to select the fifteenth member, it was Bradley who was named to be the crucial, tiebreaking member of the commission.

Although Republican, the hitherto obscure Justice Bradley, unlike all the fourteen other members of the Electoral Commission, had been chosen for the supposed impartiality he would bring to the unique historical responsibility that now faced him. He, unlike all the others, was supposed to be nonpartisan, independent-minded, and fair.

As the crisis deepened, the dispute, as often happens in politics, had modulated away from the original question—Who won the presidency?—to a more fudgeable issue: What powers did the Electoral Commission actually have anyway? In this matter, as well, Congress had weaseled, transferring its "powers, if any" to resolve the dispute to the commission. This failure to define the Electoral Commission's powers opened the way for the Republicans to make an ingenious argument. The Electoral Commission, they declared, had no power to adjudicate the electoral dispute it had been specifically created to resolve.

Why create a commission to resolve an electoral dispute with no powers to resolve an electoral dispute? Wasn't the whole purpose of creating the Electoral Commission to determine which candidate actually had won the election, and who therefore was entitled to the disputed electoral votes? To these questions the Republicans offered no answers. They simply went on arguing that the commission was powerless to adjudicate the voting disputes in the four contested states. Since in all four states it was the Democrats who were contesting the decision of Republican state officials to award votes to the Republican candidate, this meant that if the Republican argument prevailed, every one of the twenty disputed electoral votes would go to Rutherford B. Hayes. Yet, as everyone—even the Republicans—knew, Hayes had not won the presidential vote in all four of those states. It was possible he had not won in any of them. However you counted the votes—so long as you did count them, honestly—Tilden was the winner, both of the popular vote, which not even the Republicans disputed, and of the electoral vote as well.

Both democratic principle and constitutional procedure dictated that Tilden the Democrat be the next president. To deny him the presidency, and make the Republican loser, Hayes, President, would amount to a coup d'état.

The genius of the Republican argument was that it made the will of the American people, along with the way they had voted, irrelevant. It did away with the rights of political freedom guaranteed by the US Constitution as well. All that mattered, they contended, was that the Electoral Commission had no power to investigate whether there had been fraud at the polls or not. Since the Electoral Commission, according to the Republicans, had no right to question the decisions of state officials, no matter how dubious or fraudulent they were, the decision of local officials to award the electoral votes to Hayes, whether justified or not, must be allowed to stand, even if it meant reversing the will of the people, and making the loser of a free election president of the United States.

The Democrats, for their part, took a position similar to the one Democrats did 124 years later on behalf of Al Gore in Florida. They argued that the commission's job was to find out which candidate had actually won the election, not simply to rubber-stamp disputed state electoral returns, especially in cases where they quite likely were fraudulent. In order to do that, they urged, the Electoral Commission should examine the voting in the disputed states and correct any injustices it found.

Republicans rejoindered with an argument that made even some Republicans gasp, and others blush. Any attempt to make sure that the candidate who had won the most votes in the disputed states actually was awarded those states' electoral votes was entirely impermissible, the pro-Hayes Republicans announced. Why? Making sure that the votes in a particular state had been honestly counted, they declared, would "invade" such a state's sovereignty—as if the federal government in Washington, under a Republican president, Abraham Lincoln, had not already invaded the Southern states' sovereignty during the recently ended Civil War.

The Republican argument, if accepted as constitutionally valid, would have meant the abolition of democracy in the United States. Authorities in each of today's fifty states would be free to disregard how their citizens voted in presidential elections. They would be empowered to give their state's electoral votes to whomsoever they pleased, whether he had won the election or lost it. Under such circumstances, the presidency itself would pass out of the hands of the American people into the clutches of whichever gang of party politicos happened to control the ballot boxes at the state level. This brings us to another parallel between the 1876 and 2000 elections. It was just such a strange claim—in effect, that how American citizens voted didn't matter—that resurfaced in Florida 124 years later, in Republican arguments that George W. Bush, not Al Gore, should get Florida's electoral votes.

Would Justice Bradley accept the Republican argument, in spite of its patently partisan motivation? Would he decide, on the contrary, that the duty of the Electoral Commission was, as its name and the circumstances of its creation certainly implied, to make sure the disputed election results were honestly tabulated? Or would he perhaps tailor his response to each of the separate situations prevailing in each of the four separate states? Upon the answer to those questions depended the outcome of an American election for president.

Politically, Bradley was a Republican, but he was the kind of activist Republican whose principles, had he been faithful to them, would logically have led him to make a series of decisions which almost certainly would have resulted in Tilden the Democrat, not Hayes the Republican, becoming president. Back then the positions of the two major parties were virtually the reverse of what they are now when it came to federal power. The Republicans were the party of "big government," the Democrats opponents of interference from Washington. Bradley himself had been named to the Supreme Court on the understanding that he would uphold the federal government's power in monetary affairs.

A Supreme Court Justice philosophically committed to the principle that the federal government had the power to decide how money was used in every state of the United States might be supposed, also, to support the principle that the federal government had the power to ensure that its most powerful officer—the President—was fairly elected in every state. Bradley was also expected to bring probity, dignity, and wisdom to his responsibilities as the only person capable of breaking the presidential deadlock. Instead, finding himself at the pivot of one of the greatest constitutional crises in US history, he chose to act as though it were a New York patronage dispute.

At the heart of what now had become a grave national crisis lay the same questions that in 2000, during the Gore–Bush dispute over Florida's electoral votes, also tended to get obscured by the political maneuvering: How had the American people actually voted? Tilden, as everyone by then knew, had without any doubt won the election on a nationwide basis by the small though clear margin of some 250,000 votes. A dispassionate investigation into the voting in the four disputed states quickly could have determined which of those four states Tilden had won, and which, if any, had gone for Hayes. But since no one, not even the Republicans, doubted that Tilden had won in at least one of those states, and since the Democratic candidate required only one more electoral vote to get a majority in the Electoral College, there was no doubt, either, that Tilden was entitled to be the next president of the United States.

What about Rutherford B. Hayes, the candidate who actually became president? A way had to be found to award all the electoral votes of all four disputed states to Hayes, regardless of how the people of those states had voted. Justice Bradley provided that way. All that was really required, after all, to turn the loser into the winner of the 1876 US presidential election was for the Electoral Commission to award each and every one of the disputed votes to Hayes the Republican, whether he was entitled to them or not. And all that was needed to do that was for Justice Bradley to betray democratic principle and judicial ethics—as well as the principles of his own Republican Party. This he did not once, but four times, breaking the tie each time, as the commission voted 8–7, 8-7, 8–7, and 8–7 to give the electoral votes of all four disputed states to the man who had come in second in the race to be president. What compounded the scandal was that the Republicans, over and over, used the same argument to justify their partisanship that the slave states had used to justify rebellion against the US government during the Civil War. To make sure the votes of the American people were counted honestly, they claimed, even as they hijacked the presidency itself, would violate state sovereignty—something the Republicans had considered it their duty to do with bayonets and cannon only eleven years earlier, in order that "government of the people, by the people, for the people shall not perish from the Earth."

Though American historians, politicians, and civics teachers have glossed over it ever since, the result was a violation of the US Constitution, especially of the recently enacted Thirteenth, Fourteenth, and Fifteenth Amendments, which specifically prohibited states from violating the "privileges or immunities of citizens of the United States," including their right both to vote and to have their votes honestly counted. Hayes's installation as president was also a betrayal of the principles for which hundreds of thousands of Americans, including the first Republican president, Abraham Lincoln, had died during the Civil War.

There was another parallel with the future. Like the installation of George W. Bush as president in 2000, the installation of Rutherford B. Hayes as president in 1876 was a disaster for America. It ushered in a period of racist political domination in the South that would warp American national life for generations. It also marked the definitive transformation of the Republicans from the party of reform and equality, of Lincoln, into the party of privileged special interest—the party whose heart, in the end, always belonged to the Howard Tafts, not the Teddy Roosevelts, to the tycoons and big contributors—to what today are called the "special interests." In countless, almost entirely unperceived ways, Americans are still living with the consequences of the betrayal of democracy that followed the 1876 presidential election, just as they will be living with the consequence of 2000 election long after George W. Bush has joined Rutherford B. Hayes on the roster of America's failed, forgotten presidents.

II

The Renchburg Choice

CHIEF JUSTICE WILLIAM REHNQUIST was the Joseph Bradley of the 2000 presidential election. A diligent chief justice, faithful to his duties as supreme guardian of the rights of the American people, would have assured that the people's votes were honestly counted. Instead, using the Supreme Court as a political tool of the Republican Party, Rehnquist engineered a judicial coup d'état. Al Gore, the Democratic candidate for president, had won the popular vote nationwide by the same kind of small but clear margin Tilden had. A scrupulous count in Florida would have shown Gore to have been the winner there too. But, to paraphrase baseball philosopher Yogi Berra, with Rehnquist as umpire it was Rutherford B. Hayes all over again.

Thanks to Rehnquist, a Republican Party political operative originally appointed to the Supreme Court by Richard Nixon, attempts to find out which candidate had actually won in Florida were stopped dead in their tracks. No meaningful recount would ever occur. Even the partial recount the Supreme Court of Florida had authorized was stopped on Rehnquist's orders from Washington. He and the other Republican activists on the Supreme Court simply awarded Florida's electoral votes, and with them the presidency of the United States, to the loser of the 2000 presidential race, George W. Bush. How could a Chief Justice be so contemptuous of the right of Americans to elect their president? Rehnquist himself explained why: In his august opinion, they had no such right.

"The individual citizen has no federal constitutional right to vote for electors for the President of the United States," he declared, in the second of two Supreme Court orders making an accurate recount in Florida impossible—that is to say, making George W. Bush President. This was the most disgraceful utterance by a chief justice since 1896, when Chief Justice Melville W. Fuller, in a notorious case known as *Plessey v. Ferguson*, had ruled that racial segregation did not violate the Fourteenth, Fifteenth, and Sixteenth Amendments of the Constitution. Brazen as it was, Rehnquist's disregard for the most fundamental right in a democracy, the right to vote, did illustrate a point Americans usually forget. Proportionately, just as many hacks, knaves, and cretins have populated the benches of the US Supreme Court as have sullied the floor of the Senate and disgraced the cloakrooms of the House of Representatives.

Some Americans—and not only those irresponsibly foolish enough to have voted for Ralph Nader—still claim it makes no difference whether the president is a Republican or a Democrat. Rehnquist's usurpation of American democracy proves otherwise. The United States not only might have had a different president, it might be a different country today had not one Republican president (Nixon) named Rehnquist to the Supreme Court, a second Republican president (Reagan) made him chief justice, then a third Republican president (George W. Bush) been installed in office thanks to Rehnquist. Rehnquist's use of the Supreme Court for partisan purposes was one of the greatest acts of judicial chicanery in American history; it was also Richard Nixon's ultimate dirty trick. The win-at-any-cost tactics and the enemies-list ethics of Nixon and his plumbers, Rehnquist showed, had not been purged from the American political system back in 1974, when Nixon resigned to avoid impeachment. Like sleeper cells, they had been lurking in the Supreme Court. Only this time it wasn't merely political documents that had been stolen; it was the presidency of the United States.

Until he was named to the Supreme Court, Rehnquist had been a nullity in national affairs. That high office came to him, unexpectedly, as part of Nixon's "Southern strategy" of appealing to white voters angered by racial integration and the social disruptions it unleashed following the Supreme Court's 1954 decision ending segregation in public schools. Appealing to such voters was the key to the historic breakthrough that transformed the Republican Party from a permanent minority into the party that, by both hook and crook, had gained control of both houses of Congress, as well as the Supreme Court, by the time George W. Bush was made president. The key to this Republican reversal of fortunes was winning white votes in places, notably the former Confederate states of the Deep South, where Republicans had not won elections since the days of Hayes and Tilden. In part, precisely because Republicans had stolen the presidency in 1876, Democrats won the states of the Deep South in every presidential election for the next eighty-eight years. Then, in 1964, the Republican candidate for president, Barry Goldwater, turned American politics on its head. Goldwater swept the Deep South—while losing the rest of the country, except for his native Arizona.

Goldwater's defeat revealed the outlines of a winning strategy for future Republican candidates. If Republicans could orchestrate their political appeal in such a way as to keep winning big in the South, while also winning back the states they normally carried in the rest of the country, they could become America's new majority party. But how to keep winning in the South—where, into the 1960s, Republicans were remembered as the party of freed slaves, scalawags, carpetbaggers, and General Sherman?

First under Nixon and then, with utter mastery, under Ronald Reagan, Republicans adroitly changed their spots. Deliberately, as part of a well-executed strategy, they made themselves the party of the fears and resentments, though not of the social and economic well-being, of middle- and working-class white Southerners. They became what earlier the Dixiecrats and Democrats had been, the party of white supremacy. However, nomenclature as well as the times had changed. Explicit exploitation of race hatred was no longer permissible. To be successful, this Republican appeal to what no longer could openly be called the "anti-nigra" vote had to be coy as well as calculated. In 1980, for example, Ronald Reagan could have launched his presidential campaign anywhere, and California would have been the obvious choice. Instead, he kicked off his run for the presidency in Philadelphia, Mississippi, where in 1964 white racists had murdered three civil rights workers—"outside agitators"—from the North. Reagan did not have to condone the murders that had made this part of Mississippi infamous. By simply not condemning the racial hate crimes during his visit to that notorious town, he gave racially motivated voters the signal they needed. That November white Southerners overwhelmingly rejected Jimmy Carter, a white Southerner, and voted to elect the Illinois-born Republican movie actor from Hollywood.

When Nixon named him to the Supreme Court, William Rehnquist was hardly one of the 5,000 most eminent jurists in the United States. But mediocrity was part of the political message Nixon wanted to send with his Supreme Court appointments. No federal act had angered whites more than the 1954 Supreme Court decision, under a Republican Chief Justice, Earl Warren, to end racial segregation in America's public schools. What better way to woo the "Impeach Earl Warren" crowd than to name nonentities, even closet racists, to the Court? Other presidents have spent months pondering who their Supreme Court nominees should be, comparing the qualifications of America's most distinguished jurists. Nixon might as well have picked Rehnquist's name from a hat—a grease-stained thrift-store hat stuffed with the finger-marked names of some thirty politicos and mediocrities which Ehrlichman, Haldeman, and Nixon's other political henchmen had assembled. Nixon didn't even know Rehnquist's name. When he named him to the Supreme Court, he kept calling the future chief justice "Renchburg."

It was all part of Nixon's policy of turning Democrat and Dixiecrat supporters of "states' rights"—that is, white supremacy—into Republican voters, while avoiding documentable appeals to racism. Degrading the Supreme Court was an excellent way to do that, but the ploy required finesse. The trick was to nominate justices whose credentials on paper were just respectable enough to make opposition to them seem political. At first Nixon didn't get the formula right. In his early attempts to diminish the Supreme Court's standing, he nominated two candidates so laughably unfit their nominations had to be withdrawn. These failures led to Nixon finally selecting Rehnquist. He, unlike Nixon's previous Supreme Court nominees, was one of those useful figures who combines a respectable demeanor with unscrupulousness. As his most important Supreme Court decisions would show, Rehnquist had the steal-what-you-want-break-what-you-don't juridical heart of a Watergate plumber. Unlike Nixon's previous nominees he looked presentable in judicial robes.

Like George W. Bush and his crowd later, Rehnquist was labeled a conservative, but in terms of the judicial "mainstream" as it existed in the aftermath of the great legal and social upheavals of the 1950s and 1960s, he was simply off the wall. As his partisan meddling in the 2000 election showed, Rehnquist was never the "strict constructionist" Republican propagandists made him out to be. Nor was he one of the great activist chief justices in the tradition, stretching back from Earl Warren to John Marshall, of using the Supreme Court to expand Americans' rights and liberties. No, Rehnquist was the archetype of a sleazier, more banal, and quirkier variety of Supreme Court justice. He was a judicial reincarnation of the same Chief Justice Fuller who, back in the 1890s, ruled that American apartheid did not violate the equal protection clause of the US Constitution.

Fuller, like Rehnquist a century later, was an anomaly in his time and place: a Northerner with Southern sympathies, an Illinois politician who opposed Abraham Lincoln. Fuller's 1896 decision supporting racial segregation—that is, legalizing black exclusion and condoning white supremacy in the South—amounted to a judicial attempt to reverse the outcome of the Civil War. It was the most notorious Supreme Court decision since the court ordered Dred Scott, an escaped black American, to be returned forcibly to his white "owner" in the South in 1857—a decision that so divided the nation it helped lead to the Civil

War. For more than 200 years, both judicial activists and strict constructionists have sat on the Supreme Court of the United States. But as the dark stain that "jurists" like Rehnquist and Fuller have left on American legal history shows, they often have been outnumbered by the hacks, the mediocrities, and the opportunists. A biographical precis of Chief Justice Fuller, whom history has consigned to the despised oblivion he deserves, could with a change of name as accurately describe Rehnquist: "Senate confirmation took three months. There were objections about Fuller's sympathies for big corporations. In the end, however, Fuller was approved. Fuller presided over a Court that was barraged by constant criticism." There was another similarity: "Both Courts actively injected their value preferences into the legislative arena."

From the beginning, Rehnquist's value preferences also ran counter to the prevailing themes—greater equality and opportunity for all Americans—of his region and time, in his case, Midwestern, twentieth-century America. President Franklin D. Roosevelt, so far as millions of Americans were concerned, was to this period of increased liberty and bigger government what Abraham Lincoln had been to the Civil War era. Rehnquist was a child of the Great Depression, as well as the beneficiary of many federal programs—including the government support that paid his way through law school. He nonetheless grew up revering Herbert Hoover, the Republican President who presided over the Great Depression.

A native of Wisconsin and descendant of Swedish immigrants, Rehnquist was also somewhat out of place geographically at first. During the nineteenth century Wisconsin, along with neighboring Minnesota, attracted many German and Scandinavian immigrants. Partly as a result of these northern

European links, it was also a hotbed of American progressivism. Then, in the 1950s, Wisconsin startled America by producing the infamous Senator Joseph McCarthy. Many in Wisconsin were appalled by McCarthy's tactics, but if he had any qualms about Wisconsin Senator Joe McCarthy's abuses of the civil liberties of Americans, Rehnquist never made a political or legal issue out of it, either then or later.

Going back to the earliest attempts to abolish slavery, Wisconsin had been a stronghold of activism on behalf of racial justice. Here, too, Rehnquist was a contrarian, as he proved in 1952 when, just out of law school, he landed a job in Washington as law clerk to Robert Jackson, an associate justice of the Supreme Court. Even when it condoned racial segregation back in the 1890s, the Supreme Court had affirmed the principle that all US citizens, whatever their race or color, must be equal before the law. If a state excluded blacks from white schools, the Supreme Court decreed in *Plessey v. Ferguson*, it had to provide "separate but equal" educational facilities for what, back then, were called colored people. For more than fifty years, this doctrine provided the rationale for restricting the rights of black Americans in everything from admission to movie theaters to admission to hospital emergency rooms. Yet even by the race-tainted standards of the time, these restrictions continued to be manifestly unconstitutional, because the "equal" in this "separate but equal" system of racial separation was always a lie. One only had to look at "colored" restrooms, "colored" railroad cars, to say nothing of "colored" hospitals and schools, to see that the facilities blacks were obliged to use were always inferior, the facilities reserved for whites, from which they were excluded, invariably superior. As the Supreme Court itself would ultimately decree, when it repudiated the Fuller decision, "separate but equal" was inherently unequal, hence a violation of the Constitution, and therefore illegal, from the start.

By the early 1950s Rehnquist—who had come of age during World War II—was beginning his law career. To most Americans of his generation that old 1896 Supreme Court decision legalizing racial segregation seemed an embarrassing legacy of a bygone era. A consensus had emerged among lawyers and judges that the time had come for the Supreme Court to end the system of racial discrimination that the Supreme Court itself had created.

"I realize that it is an unpopular and unhumanitarian position, for which I have been excoriated by my 'liberal' colleagues, but *Plessey v. Ferguson* should be reaffirmed," Rehnquist wrote in 1952, while working for Supreme Court Justice Jackson. He also argued in favor of preventing black Americans from voting in primary elections. Since, in most Southern states at that time, the primary election was the one that determined who actually was elected governor or got to go to Congress, excluding "Negroes," as they were called, was tantamount to denying them the right to vote, a clear violation of the Fourteenth Amendment to the US Constitution. What legal grounds did Rehnquist cite for such a blatant abridgment of democratic rights? "The white people of the south don't like the colored people," he wrote—as though race hatred was entitled to trump the US Constitution when it came to deciding who voted.

Rehnquist continued to oppose legal equality of the races. In 1964, he agitated against passage of a municipal ordinance permitting blacks to eat in restaurants in Phoenix, Arizona. Then, in 1970, while serving as an assistant attorney general in the Nixon administration, he wrote a proposed amendment to the

US Constitution which, if adopted, would have made de facto racial segregation in public schools legal in neighborhoods all over the country. These different geographical locales of Rehnquist's activities on behalf of racial injustice trace the trajectory of a political career that—via Arizona and the Nixon Administration—carried Rehnquist from Wisconsin to the Supreme Court, transforming him in the process from a man with "unpopular and unhumanitarian" views into the figure who could, and did, overrule the American people's choice of a president of the United States.

In *The Great Gatsby*, F. Scott Fitzgerald's classic novel of American illusion, the narrator reacts with delight, not anger, when Gatsby introduces him to "the man who fixed the 1919 World Series." Republican politicos, beginning in the 1960s, reacted the same way to Rehnquist, the man who would eventually fix the 2000 presidential election. When it came to legal substance, he might have been the local attorney for the White Citizens Council, but Rehnquist's great value lay in the fact that he didn't look, talk, or smell like a bigot. With his Wisconsin-Swedish looks and lawyerly banality of bearing, he appeared to be what George W. Bush later called himself, a "compassionate conservative." The reality was something else. Rehnquist was one of those ideological activists who in the 1960s started building the political organization that first would make Republicans like him dominant in the South and the Sunbelt, and then, thanks to the "Reagan Revolution," national masters of the Republican Party, and, finally, in the time of George W. Bush, dominant in all three branches of America's federal government. Rehnquist and the damage he would do to America's democracy epitomize one of the great ironies of modern American history: Precisely at the moment—the Sixties!—when most Americans believed their country was lurching into a new, freer era, other Americans were planning to impose a very different structure of power on the country, if they ever got the chance. Thanks to Rehnquist, George W. Bush would be that chance.

For nearly forty years, culminating in his 2000 intervention in the presidential election, Rehnquist's willingness to make legal-sounding arguments on behalf of undemocratic practices made him useful to politicians like Richard Nixon and Ronald Reagan, not to mention George W. Bush. The key political maneuver of his early political career, however, was geographical. Following his clerkship at the Supreme Court, he shifted his base of operations to a much more ideologically congenial locale, the Sunbelt state of Arizona, Barry Goldwater's own home turf. Rehnquist worked hard for Goldwater when he ran for President in 1964. Even though Goldwater was defeated, his proclamation that "Extremism in defense of liberty is no vice" helped make the views of men like Rehnquist politically acceptable for the first time. In between political campaigns, Rehnquist immersed himself in the struggle to keep blacks out of white schools in Phoenix.

In 1968, Rehnquist was a political organizer for Richard Nixon, who that year finally made it to the White House following his 1960 defeat by John F. Kennedy. Nixon named a better-known Arizona politico, Richard Kleindeist, to head the Justice Department. As a result Rehnquist got the middle-ranking post of assistant attorney general. It was a telling appointment, since the Justice Department is charged with enforcing civil rights legislation. Back in Arizona, Rehnquist's opponents alleged, he had used intimidation to prevent blacks from voting. Such allegations made Rehnquist even more useful to the Republican Party that, thanks to its Southern strategy, was already making gains nationally as well as in the South by attracting white voters angered by the Democrats' support of affirmative action and court-ordered busing. Like his later appointment to the Supreme Court, Rehnquist's appointment as assistant attorney general was a political wink to whites in the South, and other parts of the country as well. We can't say we're against racial equality, the appointment of figures like Rehnquist said, but—wink, wink—take a look at the guys we're putting in charge of civil rights.

As Assistant Attorney General in one of the most legally corrupt presidential administrations in US history, Rehnquist might have wound up in the rogue's gallery of the Watergate era, except that in late 1971, just as the dirty-tricks phase of his presidency was moving into high gear, Nixon plucked Rehnquist out of near-anonymity, and made him an associate justice of the United States Supreme Court. Immortality itself struck in 1986, when President Ronald Reagan promoted Rehnquist to chief justice. As with Nixon earlier, Reagan's decision to choose Rehnquist was political—and haphazard. The US Senate must confirm presidential appointments to the Supreme Court. Reagan calculated that the Senate, having already approved Rehnquist once as associate justice, would find it hard to reject him as chief justice a second time around in spite of concerns about Rehnquist's "conservative" ideology. Reagan, as usual in such matters, was right. Rehnquist was confirmed, though only after he had come up with a defense of his position on race worthy of the maneuverings of the Electoral Commission of 1876—and of his own, later, legal casuistry on behalf of George W. Bush.

The text of Rehnquist's 1952 "unhumanitarian" brief favoring racial segregation had surfaced during his first confirmation hearings. Rehnquist's opponents brandished it again when he was named chief justice. On both occasions, Rehnquist resorted to a lexicographical defense of his moral fitness to serve on the Supreme Court. It was beyond doubt that Rehnquist, *inter alia*, had written, "I think *Plessey v. Ferguson* was right." But what did the meaning of words matter, when it came to US law and the Supreme Court? Rehnquist would make George W. Bush president by changing the meaning of the US Constitution. He got himself approved as chief justice in 1986 by redefining the meaning of "I." As Rehnquist explained it, the pronoun "I," when he used it, had a special meaning not found in the dictionary. Specifically, Rehnquist informed the Senate, when he wrote "I think," it didn't mean that was what he thought, or even that he was the one doing the thinking. It meant that was what he was suggesting that his boss, Justice Jackson, thought, or should think.

Justice Robert Jackson is one of America's best-remembered jurists, though not by name. Following Hitler's defeat in World War II, Jackson presided over the Nuremberg war crimes trials. His historic role as the American judge who brought Nazi war criminals to justice was immortalized in the film, *Judgment at Nuremberg*. It would have been a nasty irony if the American judge who sent Nazi racists to the gallows had himself been a racist. Was there any truth to Rehnquist's allegation that in his memos favoring racial segregation, he had been expressing Justice Jackson's views, not his own?

Justice Jackson had been dead for more than thirty years by the time Rehnquist was named chief justice. Inconveniently for Rehnquist, he had not died soon enough. In 1954, shortly before his death, Jackson had set down his own views on *Plessey v. Ferguson*. "I am convinced that present day conditions require us to strike from our books the doctrine of separate but equal facilities." In the last great judicial act of his life, Jackson, though grievously ill, left his sickbed to vote to overturn *Plessey v. Ferguson*. Handed down by a unanimous, 9–0 vote, the ensuing Supreme Court decision—*Brown v. Board of Education*—declared that "separate but equal" was inherently unequal, and therefore unconstitutional. This decision banning racial segregation ushered in the tumultuous era of the civil rights revolution in the United States, and Justice Jackson was one of its founding fathers.

This was odd behavior for a jurist who, according to William Rehnquist, actually thought racial segregation "was right." It was odder still that Justice Jackson, in the course of a lifetime in the law, should never have expressed his supposed segregationist views with his own pen, in his own words, but only through the writings of a law clerk named William Rehnquist who worked for him for less than a year. There was something even odder in Rehnquist's redefinition of "I"—the context in which he had used it. "I realize that it is an unpopular and unhumanitarian position, for which I have been excoriated by my 'liberal' colleagues, but *Plessey v. Ferguson* should be reaffirmed," read the exact words. Yet no one remembered the late Justice Jackson as having been "excoriated" by liberals, though, throughout his career, William Rehnquist certainly had been.

People who had known Jackson throughout his lifetime were outraged at Rehnquist's allegations. Some went so far as to accuse the soon-to-be-chief-justice of perjury, but the "I" controversy turned out to be another fruitful wedge issue for the Republicans. While the politicians in Washington squabbled over the meaning of a pronoun, the real message got across loud and clear to the core constituency Rehnquist's nomination was meant to satisfy.

As Rehnquist himself had put it in one of his memos to Justice Jackson: "It is about time the Court faced the fact that the white people of the South don't like the colored people." By then, it wasn't just white people "of the South." Millions of normally Democratic-voting, working-class whites all over the country were angry at court-ordered busing, court-ordered affirmative action, and other judicially mandated attempts to achieve racial equality.

Rehnquist's opponents had aimed to discredit him. Instead, the "I" controversy transformed Rehnquist from a Nixon-era apparatchik into a Reagan-era icon. Precisely because he had expressed racial views which, until shortly before that time, would have been considered shameful for a chief justice, Rehnquist became a hero to the two "neocon" strains of Republican zealots—neoconservatives and neo-Confederates—who would eventually dictate the policies of the George W. Bush administration. In the process, the real issue was forgotten. This was that Rehnquist was a candidate for chief justice who was contemptuous of the rights of all Americans, not just blacks. Liberties that generations of Americans, going back to the Founding Fathers, had considered to be both self-evident and inalienable, so far as he was concerned, did not exist at all. As Americans of all colors would find out in 2000, Rehnquist's views on race were only part of a larger disqualification. He would be a chief justice for whom justice had no fixed definition at all.

From the beginning, the Rehnquist appointment had a baneful effect on American politics; it introduced a venomous pattern into the selection of America's most important judges. The confirmation of Supreme Court judges became part and parcel of Republican ideological coalition-building. Just as George W. Bush would promise the rich tax breaks and provide his favorite corporations with new weapons contracts and the wars to go with them in return for their millions of dollars in campaign donations, so Supreme Court justices became what the party of privilege and special interests offered the little guys in return for their votes. The Republicans weren't about give the people in the trailer parks and decaying old neighborhoods—or the families whose kids would do the dying in Iraq—decent health care or public education. But militant antiabortionists and religious fundamentalists could have Supreme Court justices to their heart's content, if they stood up for America, against the liberals, and helped the Republicans win. Such an approach brought political benefits, but it corrupted the very spirit of federalism by corrupting the independence of the judiciary. As Americans discovered in 2000, it also turned the supposedly independent judicial branch of the US government into a partisan weapon of political warfare.

This process of degrading the Supreme Court by degrading the process of choosing Supreme Court justices reached its most ludicrous point in the 1991 battle over the nomination of Clarence Thomas as associate justice. What had begun with the appointment of Rehnquist, a Northerner whose prejudices were those of a stereotypical white Southerner, culminated in the appointment of a black who, so far as his voting record on the Supreme Court was concerned, might in many cases just as well have been a cross-burning member in good standing of the Ku Klux Klan. Later, black Americans would joke that in the 2000 election, they finally made a difference: A single black vote—Thomas's—had made George W. Bush the winner.

The Supreme Court had fallen into peculiar hands by the time by the Republican politicians in Florida, having lost their battle to prevent a recount, ran to Washington in November

2000, asking Chief Justice Rehnquist to intervene. By then, the US Supreme Court was no longer an impartial tribunal. It was a rogue court. At least four of the nine justices regularly voted as partisan Republican judicial ideologues. The Rehnquist court was a court which, when it wished, defied the law, and when it so desired, disregarded democratic principle, as it applied an ideological-political test, not a legal or constitutional test, to the most important issues brought before it.

III

Hijacked

As the Internet seethed with speculation, the fate of the American presidency hinged on the partisanship of a chief justice with a nineteenth-century idea of how democracy should work. America's first president of the twenty-first century would be chosen by a jurist whose concept of liberty was lodged in a time before telephones, in the America that existed before women got the vote, when members of the Senate were still chosen by state legislatures—when, thanks to closed political primaries and the pervasive use of violence, the votes of white men like William Rehnquist were the only votes that had counted because they were the only votes that were counted.

Rehnquist's response to the Republican appeal for help in Florida was guileful. He set a trap for those who wanted a fair count of Florida's presidential votes. When a Florida judge authorized a recount, Rehnquist, from Washington, ordered the Florida recount "temporarily" suspended. Then, when the Florida Supreme Court, that state's supreme legal authority, ruled that the recount could continue, Rehnquist ordered it stopped for a second time—this time permanently, on the grounds that there wasn't enough time for the recount to take place.

It was a stunning piece of chicanery. Having deliberately delayed the Florida recount, Rehnquist then used the delay he himself created as the pretext for the legal decision that achieved his political end: making George W. Bush president. It was also a breathtaking piece of judicial usurpation. With his pre-emptory order from Washington to give Florida's electoral votes to the Republicans, Rehnquist, the supposed strict constructionist, nullified the right of an American state to govern itself according to its own Constitution. He also usurped the federal authority for dealing with such electoral disputes—thus engineering one of the most broad-ranging attacks on the rule of law in US history. For when a supposed court of law unilaterally overrules the voters, the states, and the other branches of the federal government, and arrogates to itself the power to choose the president, what is there left of federalism, or of the Constitution?

In the uproar that followed Rehnquist's order, the essential question was largely forgotten. Did the Supreme Court have any right to make such a decision in the first place? Or, to put the question in context: In a dispute within a state (Florida) over state election law, which authority should prevail—that of the Florida Supreme Court in Tallahassee, or of the US Supreme Court in Washington? Until the Rehnquist court, by its one-vote margin, decided to change the law for George W. Bush's benefit, the settled state of the law, so far as both "liberals" and "conservatives" were concerned, was that meddling by the federal courts in such internal matters was not allowed.

Until the 2000 election, it could have been argued that Rehnquist was a jurist of at least one principle—what might be called the Pontius Pilate principle of American injustice. However heinous the miscarriage of justice, this convenient, pharasaical doctrine holds, there is nothing to be done about it, except for the federal government to shake its head sadly, and turn away.

Rehnquist's long espousal of the Pontius Pilate principle, prior to the 2000 presidential election, had made him consistent. It did not make him admirable. Throughout American history few principles have been used to justify more injustice. It was states' rights, Governor George Wallace of Alabama had argued, that allowed state troopers to keep black children out of white schools at gunpoint. It was this same restrictive view of the federal government's powers that meant—during the Great Depression, when millions of Americans, including William Rehnquist's Wisconsin neighbors, were hungry, jobless, and homeless—that the federal government had no right, as President Hoover and those who supported him saw it, to help poor people, or the jobless, or those who had lost their farms and homes. Going back earlier, this same insistence by Rehnquist's philosophical predecessors on the Supreme Court on limiting the powers of the federal government had provided the rationale for the slave ships, the slave auctions, for "selling your brother down the river" (as white sons often did with their father's black sons, after they inherited their black half-brothers as slave property).

When it comes to the law, America has a dark past. Its legal history is essentially the story of the struggle to advance human rights against the defenders of preferential treatment for the privileged. Many of those controversies inevitably are appealed to the Supreme Court. Yet over the decades of Rehnquist's tenure, the legacies of slavery, poverty, and other kinds of injustice, including unequal treatment of women, as they shape the recurring legal controversies of modern America, had never caused him to reconsider his views. From the Rehnquist perspective, the government that did least to disrupt the special privileges of him, and people like him, was the government that governed best.

After decades of telling other people they could not have what they wanted because the federal government had no authority to give it to them, Rehnquist now answered a question that applied to him. Were there any legal limits on the use of federal power when Republican Party expediency was involved? Richard Nixon had given his answer to that question back in 1972, in the form of the Watergate break-in. Now Rehnquist and the other Republican judicial activists on the court gave their answer. Putting Republican political expediency ahead of democracy, country, and Constitution, they ruled that the most important thing was for their party candidate to be made president. This, along with *Plessey vs. Ferguson* and the *Dred Scott* decision, was one of the most shameful decisions in US legal history, yet it cannot be said that Rehnquist acted shamelessly.

To the contrary, he acted as though he understood full well that his act was shameful. With his Florida decision, Rehnquist had changed America's destiny. And what did Rehnquist do at this extraordinary moment? He hid. Having done their dirty work, he and the other pro-Bush activists slinked out of the Supreme Court building. They waited for night to fall. Only then were reporters beckoned into an empty room. There, stacked on a table, were copies of Rehnquist's decision. Rehnquist had been right to hide. The key phrase of his decision—and there could be no doubt this time that this extraordinary pronouncement actually did represent Rehnquist's own views—amounted to a unilateral abrogation of the fundamental rights of all Americans by the Supreme Court of the United States.

"The individual citizen has no federal constitutional right to vote for electors for the president of the United States," Rehnquist announced, "unless and until the state legislature chooses a state-wide election as the means to implement its power to appoint members of the Electoral College." In the forty-eight years since he had written his first "unhumanitarian" legal opinion, Rehnquist's vision of the rights of Americans, or rather the lack of them, it was clear, had undergone a vast enlargement. His contempt for the rights of "colored people" had expanded to include contempt for the rights of all Americans.

Taking his pronouncement that the "individual citizen has no federal constitutional right to vote" as his premise, Rehnquist went on to construct a temple of injustice, located on a legalistic hilltop of false syllogisms. Starting with the state legislatures' constitutionally mandated responsibility to establish the procedures by which its presidential electors are chosen, Rehnquist derived a legal doctrine in which it didn't matter if "the individual citizen" was excluded altogether from the process of choosing the president of the United States. Oh, there was another reason, Rehnquist added, why he was giving Florida's electoral votes to George W. Bush. Thanks to the delaying tactics employed by Republican Party activists, and abetted by Rehnquist himself, there was no time to recount the votes and find out who the real winner was anyway.

None of this was true. Or as President Harry Truman might have put it back when words had meanings in American politics, it was all a bald-faced, goddam bunch of lies, including the bit about there being no time to recount the votes. Rehnquist delivered his opinion on December 11, 2000. Congress was not scheduled to count the electoral votes until January 5, 2001, and the presidential inauguration would not take place until January 21.

Delays in the counting of electoral votes had occurred periodically in United States, without anyone purporting that such delays justified a federal court ordering that the counting of votes for president be stopped. As recently as 1961, the electoral votes of the state of Hawaii had not been determined until January 1961 following the November 1960 election. In 1876, the electoral votes of four states had remained undecided from November all the way into March 1877, which was when presidents were inaugurated back then. No one, until this moment, had ever purported that an electoral dispute inside a state was anything but a contingency bound to recur periodically in a nation with a 200-year history of electoral politics. No one, until Rehnquist intervened, had imagined that such an internal state dispute could justify the Supreme Court in Washington ordering that valid votes not be counted.

Like a lawyer tampering with evidence, Rehnquist entirely excluded the most important legal precedent for dealing with the 2000 Florida presidential election dispute. Astonishingly, he never mentioned the 1876 presidential election, though in her dissenting opinion Associate Justice Ruth Bader Ginsberg did. Following that dispute, she noted, Congress had made legal provision for dealing with another such crisis should one ever arise again—and it wasn't the Supreme Court that the law designated to deal with such problems. "The Electoral Count Act, enacted after the close 1876 Hayes-Tilden Presidential election," Justice Ginsberg pointed out, "specifies that, after States have tried to resolve disputes (through 'judicial' or other means), Congress is the body primarily authorized to resolve remaining disputes."

"The legislative history of the Act makes clear its intent to commit the power to resolve such disputes to Congress, rather than the courts," Justice Ginsberg continued, adding: "The Act goes on to set out rules for the congressional determination of disputes about those votes."

In his haste to make Bush the winner in Florida, Rehnquist had not only violated the spirit of federalism and contravened US law, he had also refused to face up to the real problem the 2000 presidential election crisis had placed in the hands of the Supreme Court: the lurking menace to American democracy posed by the US Constitution's most bizarre voting contraption, the Electoral College. Thomas Jefferson described the Electoral College as "the most dangerous blot on our Constitution," and by the time the Gore–Bush dispute arose, its dangerous unpredictability had been creating electoral crises in America for 200 years—in 1888, 1824, and 1800, as well as 1876.

Now, once again, in the year 2000, America's wacky presidential election system produced a situation in which the world's greatest democracy could, and would, wind up with a president who hadn't been democratically chosen. How could such a thing still happen in the age of microchips and supercomputers, in the country that considers itself the world's model democracy? It all went back to the darkest of America's original sins. While proclaiming freedom to the world, the framers of the US Constitution not only legalized human slavery, they accorded special rights to slaveowners that ordinary US citizens were not given.

When the US Constitution was written, slaveowners not only insisted that their right to own slaves be guaranteed. They insisted on being politically rewarded for practicing slavery. The Founding Fathers, the most eminent of them being slaveowners themselves, obliged. They created a federal system in which slaves were treated as property, not human beings, except for certain explicitly defined political purposes. In those cases, and those cases only, our Founding Fathers decided, would slaves be treated as human beings—though only partial ones. As the very first article of the US Constitution put it, each state's representation in the House of Representatives "shall be determined by adding to the whole Number of free Persons, including those bound to Service for a Term of Years, and excluding Indians not taxed, three-fifths of all other Persons."

That "three-fifths of all other Persons" provision of the US Constitution meant that the more slaves a state had, the more members of Congress it got. How many more? The US Constitution set up a mathematical formula right out of grade-school arithmetic class. Count up all your slaves, boys and girls. Now multiply them by three, and divide by five, and there is your answer. This grotesque calculus was the first of the great North/South compromises over slavery that, for more than seventy years, would defer the American Civil War, but never remove its causes.

Treating slaves as "Persons" when it came to representation in Congress complicated an even more nettlesome problem: How to select the president (and vice president) of the United States, under the new Constitution? The slave states wanted their slave property to confer on them added political advantages when it came to choosing the president, too. Again they got their way. Since the idea of letting slaves line up to vote for president, even if it was only three-fifths of a vote each slave would cast, was intolerable by the standards of the era, the framers, in Article II of the Constitution, sidestepped the question of a direct popular vote for president. They decided the President would be chosen indirectly, by an Electoral College.

This only rephrased the underlying question. Who would

elect the electors, and how many votes in the Electoral College would each state get? The number of electoral votes each state got, once again, was determined by a formula that rewarded slavery. The more slaves it had, the bigger the state's say in the choice of the president would be. Each state's number of presidential electors, it was decided, would be equal to its total membership in Congress—that is, the sum of its Representatives, which varied according to the population, including the slave population of each state, plus its senators, of which each state had two. This gave a decided political advantage to the slave states of the South in presidential politics—and it amounted to a bonanza for Virginia and its favorite sons when it came to electing America's first presidents. Virginia at the time was by far the most populous state. The extra representation it got in Congress as a result of its immense slave population made it even more powerful. At the time, Washington, Jefferson, Monroe, and Madison were indisputably the most esteemed public men in American. The added votes Virginia's slave property gave them in the Electoral College enhanced their political power even further. It also introduced an unpredictable wild card into the choice of the president.

One of the curiosities of the outcome of the American Civil War was that while it did away with slavery, it kept the most important American political institution designed to enhance the electoral power of slaveholders, the Electoral College. This meant that even when Constitutional procedure was followed faithfully and the presidential vote was counted accurately and honestly in each state, there still remained the possibility of an American president being elected constitutionally, but not democratically. This is exactly what happened only twelve years after the Tilden-Hayes standoff, in 1888. President Grover

Cleveland won the popular vote in his campaign to be re-elected, but his Republican rival, Benjamin Harrison, won in the Electoral College. Unlike the election of 1876, the election of 1888 created little controversy, and was almost entirely forgotten later, for two reasons. After four years, the 1888 election was re-run. This time around, Cleveland won the electoral as well as the popular vote. Cleveland's second term in the White House, it turned out, had only been deferred by the quirky discrepancies in the US presidential election system that had made Benjamin Harrison a parenthesis of a president. Second, it was assumed, as the twentieth century dawned, that such a strange thing simply could not happen again in modern times in America—and for a long time, more than 100 years, it didn't.

Then George W. Bush happened. Over the intervening twentieth century, the United States had become the greatest power on earth. During that century—the American Century—most of the world had been transformed by the appeal and power of democracy, as epitomized by the United States of America. Yet one thing had not changed. As it entered the twenty-first century, America still had an eighteenth-century electoral system that could, and now suddenly did, make it possible for the candidate who lost a democratic election to win the presidency. America's dangerously unpredictable, two-tiered presidential election system—not some hanging chads in Palm Beach County—was the problem the Rehnquist court faced in 2000.

The 2000 presidential election offered an opportunity for the Supreme Court to face the fact that "present-day conditions" required fundamental reappraisal of a US presidential electoral system that had become dangerously anachronistic. To do that, however, would have required the chief justice to transcend partisanship. He would have had to seek constitutional consensus—and William Rehnquist was a wedge-issue chief justice as much as George W. Bush would be a wedge issue president. By the narrowest of margins, he handed down one of the most divisive decisions in Supreme Court history.

Constitutionally and legally, the most prudent course for the Supreme Court—especially under a supposedly "strict constructionist" chief justice like Rehnquist—would have been for the court to do nothing. The Florida Supreme Court had already spoken concerning the matter of Florida state law which was involved. If the dispute continued after the Florida recount was finished, existing law provided for several courses of appeal—all of them leading ultimately to Congress, not to the Supreme Court. Instead, Rehnquist, superseding his own authority, rushed to impose a partisan result on the systemic meltdown of a dangerous, antiquated electoral system. His intemperate intervention was grievously harmful in another, broader way. It prevented both the American political class and the voting public from facing the fact that their election system didn't work.

In an era when public labels have no necessary meaning, it was left to the supposedly "activist" and "liberal" Justice Ginsberg to argue the strict-constructionist case. "What it does today, the Court should have left undone," she wrote, which may have been the most memorable understatement of the 2000 election crisis. Ginsberg was a Democrat appointed by a Democratic president. Was there not one unquestionably impartial Justice left on the Supreme Court? There was one: Associate Justice David Hackett Souter, a Republican, had been appointed to the Court by George W. Bush's own father. In his dissenting opinion, Souter drew attention to the most transparent and self-serving of Rehnquist's pretexts—that there was no time left to count the votes.

Recounting the votes, Souter conceded, "would be a tall order, but before this Court stayed the effort to do that, the courts of Florida were ready to do their best to get that job done. There is no justification for denying the State the opportunity to try to count all disputed ballots now," this Republican Justice pointed out, adding: "I respectfully dissent."

Election results are always revealing—all the more so, sometimes, when elections are stolen. By the time Tilden and Hayes contested the presidency, the focus of America's destiny had transcended North and South. The railroad had reached California; new immigrants were pouring into Ellis Island. As the Republican power-play approach to the 1876 election showed, the Republicans were no longer the party of Lincoln. They were the party of big business, of money, of the dawning Industrial Revolution in America. What did it matter to them that they'd lost the election? They'd grabbed the prize.

Even more than the 1876 usurpation of the presidency, the apathy in response to what happened was the revelation of how much America had changed following the Civil War. "Normalcy" was a phrase that would be invented, forty-four years later, by President Warren Gameliel Harding. But normalcy was what America wanted. After the Republicans stole the election of 1876, normalcy was what they got.

In 2000, the nationwide apathy was also a revelation. The 1876 election had at least produced important legislation—utterly ignored by the Rehnquist Court—designed to make sure such an electoral travesty never recurred. Following George W. Bush's installation as president, there was no significant effort to improve national election procedures—no movement to reform, let alone abolish, the Electoral College either. In 2000 the American people watched the courtroom drama that followed the election the same way they earlier had watched the O.J. Simpson trial. They were avid TV spectators of a legal drama whose outcome left them untouched. Judge Judy, not Chief Justice Rehnquist, was the jurist who mattered most to Americans.

Presidential politics had become something Americans watched, not did. About fifty percent of those eligible hadn't voted at all. Now, even to those who had voted, the outcome evidently did not matter enough for them to use their constitutionally indisputable rights of assembly and free speech to protest the usurpation of the American presidency. This was a response that understandably might be construed by a man such as George W. Bush, who had been installed in office in the manner he had, as a sign that once in the White House, he could do anything he wanted without fear of the law or rebuke from the American people.

"Although we may never know with complete certainty the identity of the winner of this year's presidential election, the identity of the loser is perfectly clear. It is the nation's confidence in the judge as an impartial guardian of the rule of law," Justice Stephen Breyer wrote, in another dissenting opinion. Breyer was wrong on both counts. The nation's confidence in the judge as an impartial guardian of the rule of law had vanished much earlier—and thanks in part to Florida's freedom of information laws, it eventually did become known with virtual certainty that in the voting of November 7, 2000, Al Gore had defeated George W. Bush in Florida, and thereby won the presidency.

As usual the media spun the story beyond recognition. Even when it became clear that a complete Florida recount—that is to say, an accurate count of how people in Florida actually had voted in the first place—would have shown Gore to be the winner, the news flashes and soundbites focused on the possibility that if only the votes in Palm Beach and Dade counties had been recounted, Bush still might have won, though, they conceded, Gore might have, as well. The revelation that Gore actually had gotten the most votes in Florida was spun into another Gore the Chump news day. In fact Gore had not only gotten the most votes in Florida, he'd won more votes for president—more than fifty million votes in all—than any other candidate in history except for Ronald Reagan in his run for a second term. Nationwide, he'd defeated Bush by nearly 600,000 votes. This was a lot wider than Kennedy's margin over Nixon in 1960, though slightly narrower than Nixon's own slender win over Humphrey in 1968. In the only thing that counts in real democracy—votes—Gore not only had bested both of the Bushes, historically speaking. He'd outpolled landslide winners like Johnson and Eisenhower.

Jeffrey Toobin was one of the very few journalists reporting the Florida dispute to show any appreciation for the tragedy of American values that was unfolding. "In the cynical calculus of contemporary politics," he later wrote, "it is easy to dismiss Gore's putative victory. But if more people intended to vote for Gore than for Bush in Florida—as they surely did—then it is a crime against democracy that he did not win the state and thus the presidency." He described Rehnquist's choice as "a Supreme Court opinion that is doomed to infamy," and concluded: "The bell of this election can never be unrung, and the sound will haunt us for some time."

Whatever would the Rehnquist Rogue Court do for an encore? A few months after he decreed that "the individual citizen has no federal constitutional right to vote for electors for the President of the United States," the chief justice ordained that handicapped golfers do have the right to use their wheelchairs in professional competition. Later, in another act of judicial activism, the Supreme Court startled both liberals and conservatives by announcing that the individual citizen's right to engage in homosexual acts was protected by the Constitution. What label can one put on a Supreme Court that holds that US citizens have a right to commit sodomy and play golf in wheelchairs, but "no federal constitutional" right to vote for president?

As the capricious sweep of its judicial meddling indicated, the Rehnquist Court isn't a conservative Court, let alone the "strict constructionist" Court Republicans pretended. It was an I-do-as-I-please-you-do-as-I-tell-you Supreme Court. The Rehnquist pattern of disregard for established practice, indeed of the law itself, was the latest judicial echo of the approach that Richard Nixon, who put Rehnquist on the Supreme Court in the first place, had taken to presidential governance.

Ronald Reagan is revered as the father of contemporary Republicanism. But what about its godfather? The Nixon legacy of disrespect for the law is the great unnoticed moral and ethical —or rather, immoral and unethical—theme dominating modern Republican politics. Better than any other factor, contempt for the law—American law, international law, all and any laws, including the laws of civility—helps explain the how, if not always the why, of what George W. Bush has done to the United States and its place the world. His constant reliance on radical unscrupulousness goes surprisingly unnoticed, at least within the United States, in part because of the Republicans' incontestable superiority over the Democrats when it comes to the fraudulent manipulation of political and patriotic imagery. But the main reason lying has served George W. Bush so well is that the American idiom of political discourse has become so debased. Terms with centuries of accrued political and philosophical significance have had the meanings soundbited out of them. So even when politicians like Bush show themselves to be the opposite of what they claim to be, it's like Rehnquist and his corrupted pronoun. They get away with their phony definitions—in George W. Bush's case, his unjustified use of the "conservative" label to describe himself, and what he has been doing.

In reality, George W. Bush, like the chief justice who made him president, is an ultraradical—his presidency a dangerous departure from previous norms of American behavior. A conservative is someone who, unlike George W. Bush, distrusts ideological notions and, whenever possible, respects customary norms of behavior whether he happens to like them or not. A conservative leader places established practice ahead of ideological concerns. A conservative adjusts himself to reality. He puts reality first, not himself.

A radical hates reality; a radical makes war on reality, which is what George W. Bush has done from Baghdad to Langley, Virginia, and from the United Nations to the US Capitol. Whether the issue is a nonexistent axis of evil, or illusory weapons of mass destruction, he and the ideologues surrounding him have been driven by the need to demonstrate the superiority of ideological presupposition over fact, whatever the cost to the American people in lives, money, security, and allies. This loathing of reality for its failure to correspond to their ideological requirements may explain their anger. It certainly helps explain why they fail in most everything except political spin control.

The definition of the true conservative is that, if forced to choose, he will always choose to work within an established system or framework such as the US Constitution or the United Nations Security Council, even if he finds it irksome. He will never destroy what is in a blind rush to replace it with some untried abstract idea of what reality should be. Or as that conservative Democrat, Bert Lance, once put it, "If it ain't broke, don't fix it." By the year 2000, the supposedly conservative Republicans had become the Party of Breaking Things. Thanks to the Rehnquist Court breaking the Constitution, the presidency of the United States fell into the hands of a radical, George W. Bush, whose overarching strategic impulse was to break things.

What happens in a world where things are so very easy to break, and so extremely difficult, often impossible, to fix, once you do break them? Thanks to the Rehnquist coup, that was the question the George W. Bush presidency would pose.

IV

Affirmative Action

George W. Bush belongs to that generation of Americans who came of age during the Watergate scandal, but his view of American democracy wasn't chastened by the revelations that came out of the Nixon White House. He is one of those millions of Americans who, even at the time, didn't see much of anything wrong in what Nixon did, just as they didn't see anything wrong in the Vietnam war, so long as they themselves didn't have to go over there, and get injured or killed.

Many authentic and unadmirable American traditions converge in the person of George W. Bush and his presidency. The single most prominent one is party patriotism—as in, "you die while I party." While 55,000 Americans of his age died in Vietnam, he partied with the Texas Air National Guard, when he wasn't AWOL. Thanks to this unearned exemption from having to endanger himself in Vietnam, George W. Bush could have learned to fly an airplane. He never bothered. George W. Bush's presidency, like his life, has been a series of variations on his May 2003 visit to that aircraft carrier, where contrary to reality, he proclaimed himself the winner. Someone else has to fly the plane, but George W. Bush is the one who gets to stand on the flight deck, claim victory, and get the applause. Meanwhile—far away, out of sight—something horrible is happening for which he denies all responsibility. As the 2004 presidential election approached, George W. Bush's party patriotism took the form of fundraisers. By now, Americans were no longer being killed in ones and twos. They were being ambushed, killed by car bombs, and shot down in helicopters every day.

In no other war had so many American women been killed, wounded, and permanently disfigured. The official bodycounts listed the Americans dead in the hundreds. However, medical evacuations reached 10,000 by the beginning of 2004 and kept rising. Male or female, the majority of the Americans killed and mutilated weren't professional soldiers. They were the kind of next-door Joes and Janes who join the National Guard partly out of patriotism, but also for the extra money and benefits too. Now, in faraway Iraq, they found themselves victims of an unnecessary war in which neither withdrawal nor victory was an option.

A president of courage would have faced up to the dreadful dilemma his own disastrous lack of judgment had gratuitously produced: All by himself, George W. Bush had created a vast, unsolvable military and foreign policy problem for the United States, with far-reaching consequences for the entire world, but he lacked the guts to admit a mistake. In any event, the killings of Americans in Iraq, for which he was entirely and personally responsible, had to take second place to his 2004 presidential election campaign. From the perspective of personal political expediency, which was his only constant standard, withdrawal was unthinkable, and so was escalation. So, while George W. Bush crisscrossed America fundraising, 140,000 Americas were left marooned in Iraq—hostages to his improvidence, his gutlessness, and his fear of losing the 2004 election.

In 2004, as always, life was a party for George W. Bush. At each stop, there was the staged-propped patriotic pep rally, followed by a fundraiser, where George W. Bush was enveloped in money. All his wealthy supporters wanted—and no one, least of all George W. Bush, was at all embarrassed about saying it—was for him to keep on doing for another four years exactly what he'd been doing ever since he'd been made president: Keep those tax cuts coming to us, Mr. President, while you send the daughters and sons of those other people over there to defend our freedoms in Iraq.

This is the story of George W. Bush's life, not just his presidency. First screw up. Then let the praise and money flow over you. If anyone claims you don't play fair, impugn their patriotism; at least accuse them of being a liberal. And when thousands die, and billions are thrown down a rat hole because of you, blame the terrorists, "evil," and Democrats. It doesn't matter who, so long as the buck never stops with you.

That he had turned out to be this kind of President was only natural. George W. Bush always had been a screwup, going back to his boolah-boolah days. It never mattered; he always got the trophy anyway. Other rich kids had private tutors; he had his own special affirmative-action program going for him. A lousy record at prep school (superelitist Phillips Academy, Andover)? No problem, young George, welcome to Yale! He'd been a C student at Yale, yet somehow the liberals at Harvard admitted him to Harvard Business School. (Harvard's little secret, the same as Yale's, was that the sons of ambassadors and politicians—and astronauts and billionaires—got extra admission points ages and ages before "affirmative action" for black kids ticked off so many "conservatives," and no one ever complained, let alone claimed it was unconstitutional. What if you weren't Teddy Kennedy or George W. Bush or, later, black? Tough luck, buddy. They have state universities for people like you.)

A Yale plus a Harvard degree normally makes a chap an Ivy League elitist, especially if he was born, as George W. Bush was, in Greenwich, Connecticut, and the family "summered" in Kennebunkport, Maine. But just as an oil company would come to him without him having to discover oil, and then a baseball team would come to him without him having to play baseball, so a good-ol'-boy political persona had been conferred on him like an honorary degree by the time he ran for President. George Walker Bush—in keeping with the upper-class WASP tradition of keeping the commonplace "junior" out of their names by giving the son the same first name, but not the same middle name, as the father—was the son of President George Herbert Walker Bush, that *Doonesbury*-perfect epitome of WASP political privilege. He was the grandson of Senator Prescott Bush of Connecticut. It's hard, outside a hereditary monarchy, to be better-born than that. Yet by the time George W. Bush ran for president, the Yale-Harvard prep-school boy with the New England social register ancestors had been rebranded. In the same exact sense in which Chief Justice Rehnquist had become "a strict constructionist," Bush was now the "outsider"—running against the elitist liberals of the Northeast. Even so, George W. Bush, as usual, came up short. Also as usual, it didn't matter. Except this time what he got from the admissions committee this time was extra electoral votes.

The American media reported George W. Bush's inauguration with a straight face, but how did it look to others? To get an idea, simply turn the tables. Suppose the same thing happened in some other turbulent, imperfect, gigantic democracy. Imagine the dateline to be Brasilia, as the news is reported: Another candidate gets the most votes, but the losing candidate, Jorge Busquito, is installed as president anyway. And guess what? The governor of the Brazilian state where the loser is declared the winner is the guy's brother! And the judge who fixes the election is a political crony of Jorge's father. Oh, those Latins! But what can you expect? It's not like they have our Anglo-Saxon traditions of fair play.

The rest of the world saw from the beginning what even now many Americans refuse to see. Affirmative action—also known as unearned privilege—had conferred upon George W. Bush the grandest preferment public life in America can offer. This latest unearned distinction automatically posed a question none of the commentators on entertainment-news TV ever thought of asking: What did it bode for the United States, now that it had a Commander in Chief who never once in his life had needed to fight for anything? Among other things, it meant that command of the US armed forces passed to a person with a juvenile and unrealistic view of war's realities and possibilities.

The circumstances of George W. Bush's privileged life answered another question about George W. Bush that, after it was too late, many Americans would begin to ask: Why on earth did he turn out to be such a disastrous president? The answer is easiest to understand, once again, if you simply turn the question around. Why on earth should anyone suppose in the first place that a guy who couldn't get into grad school without connections, let alone get into office without the US Supreme Court intervening, would be anything except a disaster as president? It only stood to reason that, along with electoral illegitimacy, incompetence would turn out to be the great characteristic of the George W. Bush presidency.

George W. Bush was no more competent to govern America, as events would prove, than he was to land a plane on the deck of an aircraft carrier, which posed another question as he took office: Who'd "co-pilot" the plane? Fatefully for Americans, this was a choice George W. Bush already had made, all by himself, even before he got sworn in as president, when he chose the weird, scary, and unhealthy Dick Cheney as his running mate. Put a loser in the White House, and one result is that he's more likely to surround himself with dangerous incompetent characters who'll menace our national well-being. George W. Bush's predilection for conferring unearned power on dark souls who like to destroy things would become one of the defining characteristics of his presidency.

Choosing Cheney was the prelude to all this. Bush delighted in his choice, calling it his "first presidential decision." Like his presidency as a whole, Bush's Cheney decision was not only bad for America but self-defeating too. Bush might actually have won the election fair and square had he chosen a vice presidential candidate with some genuine interest and real experience in running government for the benefit of real people—as opposed to corporate entities, like Cheney's Halliburton Corporation, and special interests, most notably the oil industry. Instead, in the form of Cheney, he chose to put one heartbeat away from the presidency a vice presidential candidate with a bad heart and no sense of public responsibility. Hundreds of notable Americans might have filled the post of vice president with distinction, yet Bush would have no one else. He insisted on picking a shadowy eminence with no national following from within the closed world of Republican power politics.

Cheney was Bush's first big losing decision. On Election Day, it showed. He lost state after state that might have gone Republican had a sunnier kind of candidate been on the ticket—if, say, he'd chosen an amiable Republican governor from one of the big northern states he lost. Winning only one of them—Pennsylvania or Michigan or Illinois—would have made all the miscounts in Florida a three-day story.

While campaigning for president, Bush presented himself as a practical man, impatient with abstract theorizing. He tailored his campaign persona to appeal to Americans who were tired of the Republican tactics of ideological confrontation personified by the former Speaker of the House of Representatives, Newt Gingrich. "Help is on the way," Bush would tell the cameras as, at each campaign stop, he delivered his stock speech to a selected crowd of Republican enthusiasts. (At most rallies, protesters could not get anywhere near him; admission to the Bush rallies, which were usually held indoors, was by ticket only.) But choosing Cheney indicated something else: Trouble was on the way.

Bush—the self-styled "compassionate conservative"—had chosen an ideological Siamese twin. No one would ever accuse Dick Cheney of compassion, and he was no more a conservative than George W. Bush himself. Cheney was an ultraradical—the first important appointee of what would turn out to be the most dangerously ultraradical administration in modern American history. Choosing Cheney was the act of a presidential candidate whose inner circle, when it came to vital decisions, would be as gratuitously defiant of the realities of the world and as hellbent on inflicting a preselected ideological agenda upon events as George W. Bush himself.

Choosing Cheney also provided an early clue as to how

power would be grabbed and used within the inner coterie of the Administration. Initially Cheney wasn't even in the running for the vice presidential nomination. He was so far out of the running, indeed, that Bush asked him to head his search committee for vice president. Ethics and custom required that Cheney therefore take a disinterested approach, remove himself from consideration and, after careful appraisal of potential candidates, present Bush with a short list of possible nominees.

Instead, Cheney orchestrated the search so that he himself got picked—just as, later, things would be arranged so that, so far as George W. Bush was concerned, the only choice was to repudiate the Anti–Ballistic Missile Treaty and to thumb his nose at efforts to reduce the effects of global warming. It wasn't that Bush was hoodwinked. Excellent political advice was available to him from people like James Baker, the politically savvy former secretary of state who would be sent in to save the situation in Florida for Bush during the postelection crisis there. The problem was that, like Lyndon Johnson, another Texas president who liked starting unnecessary wars, George W. Bush systematically disregarded the intelligent advice available to him. Countless people, for example, could have informed Bush that invading Iraq was a nutty, self-defeating idea. Many did. But again and again, Bush would disregard the voices of reason. Again and again, he would do what Cheney wanted to do for the same reason he had chosen him to be vice president. Cheney—secretive, dumpy, uncharismatic—is to the crinkly-grinned, kinetic George W. Bush what the portrait was to Dorian Gray. More than any other figure in the administration, Cheney would be George W. Bush's alter ego.

George W. Bush would be like the ship's officer in Conrad's *The Secret Sharer* and in the self-created crises to come, Cheney would be the dark id to his chattering superego: What drove them both, what made them partners in destiny, was an impulse to plunge America into a heart of darkness.

Choosing Cheney had the same dynamic—arrogance arcing into disaster—that would propel the other disasters of the Bush administration. Like the decision to invade Iraq, the Cheney decision was ideology- and not reality-driven. It showed clearly and early, to those who cared to look, the dark compulsions Bush would bring to his presidential choices. It also showed how inward-looking he was, how disinterested he was in searching for better options when faced with difficult choices. The promise of the Bush campaign was a promise of normalcy. Choosing Cheney revealed something else—how truly abnormal George W. Bush's approach to the world would be once he got his hands on the presidency.

V
The Wyoming Candidate

RICHARD CHENEY IS A native of Nebraska who, at the time Bush selected him as his running mate, was a multimillionaire executive who had long been residing in Dallas, Texas. The Cheney choice therefore was predictive in another way. It produced George W. Bush's, first deliberate breach of the US Constitution.

The Constitution, contrary to what many Americans believe, does not rule out the election of a president and a vice president from the same home state. However—and here the Electoral College, yet again, sows confusion and provides additional grounds for its abolition—it does forbid their state's electors from voting for both a president and a vice president. Although nothing forbids electors from Oklahoma or Maine for voting for two Texans, this provision means that an elector from Texas can't vote for a president from Crawford (Bush), and for a vice president (Cheney) from Dallas. Until George W. Bush came along, no major political party had ever nominated two candidates from the same state. They never did it because, unlike him, they recognized it was too risky, especially in close elections. In the exact words of the Constitution: "The Electors . ... shall vote by ballot for President and Vice President, one of whom, at least, shall not be an inhabitant of the same state as themselves." Inhabitant is the key word here. Its meaning is unequivocal, yet in the 2000 election the Republicans, having first chosen a presidential candidate from Texas, then chose, at George W. Bush's behest, a vice presidential candidate who also was "an inhabitant" of the same state, and then, in the end, Texas's electors voted for both of them, even though the Constitution forbids it.

The president and vice president are the only two US officials who are chosen nationally; the Founding Fathers' intention, in encouraging them to come from different states, was to promote a national view. This was one of the very first attempts by the government in Washington to encourage "diversity." The idea was that a variety of voices was preferable to uniformity at the top. Though they did not explicitly forbid it, the framers of the Constitution thought that, as a general rule, it would not be a good idea, for instance, to have both the presidency and the vice presidency concurrently occupied by two radical extremist multimillionaire oilmen obsessed with doing away with inheritances taxes for the rich inside the United States while enforcing regime change on faraway nations through unprovoked military attack, both of whom were from a single state, Texas.

The framers hoped that geographical diversity would encourage philosophical diversity when it came to choosing the two highest officials of the United States. They did not ban a situation like the Bush-Cheney run outright, however. The constitutional language just quoted only discourages the president and vice president from being from the same state. It is possible for the president and vice president to be from the same state provided they win by a big enough margin in the Electoral College. The state of Texas, for example, had thirty-nine electoral votes in the 2000 election. It takes 270 electoral votes to win. If the Bush-Cheney ticket had gotten 270 electoral votes plus 39, for a grand total of 309 electoral votes, both Bush and Cheney could have been constitutionally elected, even though Texas's thirty-nine electors would have been obliged by the US Constitution to abstain from voting for one or the other of them.

What happens in a very close election, when the two winning candidates are both from the same state? So far as the 2000 election is concerned, it meant that, had the US Constitution been respected, George W. Bush could have been chosen president by the Electoral College or Dick Cheney chosen vice president, after Rehnquist decreed they would get Florida's votes, but not both. Bush and Cheney could not both take office constitutionally because Texas's electoral votes could not under any circumstances go to both of them—and without Texas's crucial thirty-nine electoral votes, Bush and Cheney lacked a majority in the Electoral College.

If forced to choose, Texas's electors no doubt would have voted for the Republican presidential candidate, George W. Bush. But what about the vice presidency? Since Cheney would have lacked a majority in the Electoral College, the choice of vice president would have devolved, in keeping with the gratuitous electoral complexity favored by the Founding Fathers, on the US Senate, creating yet another constitutional crisis—a heinous complication US political parties have always sought to avoid. At least they had until George W. Bush made his "first presidential decision."

The obvious solution would have been for Bush and his spin doctors to think again, then choose someone from any one of the other forty-nine states. Surely every one of them, from glacial Alaska and palmy Hawaii to bluegrass Kentucky and plucky Rhode Island possessed at least one "inhabitant" capable of serving with agreeable distinction as George W. Bush's running mate?

No. Absolutely not. George W. Bush wanted Cheney. So Cheney it had to be—and let the US Constitution (like the United Nations charter later) be damned. As a result, Bush's media manipulators faced their first big test: Could they pass off a bald-faced lie as gospel truth, during a heated election campaign, to a nation of more than 250 million people? They could, and did, with flying colors! It was beyond dispute that Cheney was, in the words of the US Constitution, "an inhabitant" of Texas. The house where Cheney and his wife lived was located there, as was the company where he worked, and it wasn't just any company. With annual revenues of nearly $15 billion, some 100,000 employees worldwide, and with its immense subsidiary, Brown and Root, headquartered in Houston, Dallas-based Halliburton is one of the crown jewels of the Texas economy. Claiming that the CEO of Halliburton wasn't an inhabitant of Texas was like claiming the CEO of General Motors was not an inhabitant of Michigan. Cheney didn't just make his money in Texas. He was a registered voter in Texas—though as it turned out, he had not bothered to vote for George W. Bush in the 2000 Texas presidential primary election. His federal tax returns showed a Texas address. Cheney even carried a Texas drivers' license. No problem. The Bush media machine dealt with Cheney's presence in Texas the same way it later dealt with the absence of weapons of mass destruction in Iraq, though the spins went in reverse: They disregarded the reality of the situation.

Specifically, they asserted that Cheney, in spite of the many, constant sightings of him in the Dallas area, was actually "an inhabitant" of the state of Wyoming. Cheney owned property in

Wyoming, they pointed out. He had spent part of his youth there and had gone to college there, they added. But the US Constitution doesn't say a word about real estate or going to college. It does not establish a boyhood qualification for vice president of the United States. It specifies, unequivocally, that the candidate for vice president must be "an inhabitant" of a different state from the presidential candidate in order to avoid political complications. There was an additional problem. Even if he actually had moved out of Texas after being nominated for vice president, Cheney would still not qualify as a resident of Wyoming, even though he was listed as such on official ballots all over the country. Wyoming has a one-year residency requirement and Cheney had started calling himself a resident of Wyoming less than six months before the November 2000 election. Wyoming law further forbids using the state as a residence of convenience. You have to spend at least six months at a stretch in Wyoming in order to qualify as a resident—and Cheney hadn't done that in decades.

Legally and constitutionally, as well as in the daily circumstances of his personal and professional daily life, Cheney was no more "an inhabitant" of Wyoming than he was of the moon, but no matter. George W. Bush's affirmative action forces sprang into action. A complaisant Republican judge slapped down a legal challenge to Cheney's claim of Wyoming residency as blithely as Chief Justice Rehnquist, later, would deliver Florida to Bush. When the time came, Texas's thirty-nine electors—in clear violation of the US Constitution—voted for both the guy from Crawford, Texas, and the guy from Dallas, Texas.

Legally speaking, Dick Cheney today is not vice president of the United States since the votes Texas's electors cast for him were not valid. Constitutionally speaking, the post of vice president remains vacant since the US Senate, following Cheney's failure to get a valid majority in the Electoral College, did not fulfill its constitutional duty in this matter. But what do terms like "illegal" matter, anyway, when the law is applied one way to George W. Bush and those he selects for special treatment, and another way to everyone else?

Though Wyoming was not where Cheney lived, that remote and thinly populated Rocky Mountain state had been the scene of Cheney's only previous experience as a candidate for elective office prior to the 2000 election. From 1979 to 1989, Cheney had represented Wyoming in Congress. Then he'd quit electoral politics. Thereafter the face of the "inhabitant" was seldom seen in that state. Politically, Wyoming is one of the least consequential states in the Union. Normally, being an ex-congressman from Wyoming won't get you a lobbyist job in Washington, let alone the nomination of a major political party for vice president. Yet by 2000, Cheney was one of most influential men in the world so far as George W. Bush was concerned.

Cheney had acquired his great influence, along with his great wealth, by making himself an indispensable details man within the Texas and, especially, the Bush family sectors of the Republican elite. That world of political power and financial influence was in turn part of an even larger world of political power and financial influence stretching far beyond the skyscrapers of Texas to Saudi Arabia, the rest of the Middle East, and the many, many other places where oil is extracted from the earth as the result of political deals that make those who are in on them enormously rich.

Oil is the blood, but money is the soul, and war is the ultimate political implement in this world in which Cheney flourished after quitting Congress. It is a world in which religious extremism—Christian at one end, Islamic at the other—exists in symbiosis with the core obsessions of power and money. It is also a world of rigid moral codes and constant violation of them. It is a world, too, of what to others can seem like paranoid resentments—perhaps because, when the bottom line is oil, wealth and status, including dynastic and political status, are also extracted, rather than built or earned. This may help explain why, whether he's from Riyadh or Houston, the princely heir (whether George W. Bush or Osama bin Laden) flies into New York (or Cairo) and comes down the gangplank with a chip on his shoulder. The problem prince knows—or at least thinks he knows—that while he's richer and tougher than the denatured sophisticates of the traditional American (or Arab) elite, they will never accept him, ever. They will always be conspiring against him. George W. Bush is odd, even aberrant, in terms of America; he doesn't even fully work as a kind of National Lampoon travesty of the right-wing paranoid Sunbelt Republican. But take his peculiar meld of political anger, ideological fervor, and moral pharisaism, and apply them to this particular jigsaw puzzle, and a lot of the more jagged pieces start to fit.

Princely families need crafty henchmen. That's where Dick Cheney enters the picture. By the time he was nominated for vice president, there was scarcely an oil dynasty from Brunei to the Gulf to Texas itself that wouldn't send a private jet to give Dick Cheney a free ride. In the years since he had stopped being the lone congressman from the Cowboy State, Cheney had become a smooth world-class operator—one of those nearly invisible manipulators who appear to do almost nothing and yet seem privy to everything. He was one of many links, for example, between the Bush family and the bin Laden family, as well as the royal family, in Saudi Arabia.

With Cheney at the helm in Dallas, Halliburton and its subsidiaries made money in more than 100 countries. Almost all the profits were oil- or military-related, which meant that Cheney and Halliburton had close relations with scores of unsavory regimes. "You've got to go where the oil is. I don't think about it very much," Cheney told the Panhandle Producers and Royalty Owners Association's annual meeting in 1998.

Unlike George W. Bush, Cheney had not been born to privilege. Lincoln, Nebraska, his hometown, was on the northern fringe of the American Dust Bowl at the time he was born there, at the tail end of the Great Depression, just before US entry into World War II, in 1941. Cheney's background, like Rehnquist's, was within spitting distance of poverty. Whether or not this proximity explained anything, Cheney's gut reaction to the disadvantaged throughout his career has been dislike, not sympathy. As his voting record in Congress would show, Cheney's positions on race were those normally associated, however unjustly, with white male Southerners. Cheney's origins couldn't have more different from George W. Bush's, yet early on, they acquired something in common: Yale. After graduating from high school, Cheney was admitted to Yale as a scholarship student. The opportunity for someone like Cheney to mingle on an equal footing with people like Bush is how many an American success story begins. It would make a nice beginning to the tale of the Bush-Cheney partnership if one night, at a table down at Mory's, while the Whiffenpoofs assembled, Cheney the scholarship student and Bush the privileged preppie had raised their glasses on high, drinking to the partnership that would take them together to the two highest offices in the land. That would be a complete invention, however. This was the 1960s in America. While Bush scraped by with a little help from his friends, Cheney dropped out of Yale after less than a year.

Dropping out of college in the 1960s was a decision that for many a young American male had life-and-death consequences. But Cheney had no trouble avoiding military service in Vietnam. In a preview of his later knack for arranging things to his personal advantage at much higher levels of government, he extracted deferment after deferment from the local Selective Service draft boards. Like the constitutional residency requirements for the vice presidency, Cheney's military responsibilities as a draft-aged American didn't inconvenience him at all. After leaving Yale, he headed west back to Wyoming. There he attended college and got married, giving himself double grounds for deferment from being drafted to fight in Vietnam. After graduation, he stayed on another year in Wyoming to get a master's degree, and with it yet another military deferment. Then, showing a zeal for academic pursuits that never again would surface in the course of his remarkable career, Dick Cheney enrolled to study for yet another degree (and yet another excuse for not serving in the military), this time at the University of Wisconsin.

In those days, draft boards normally ceased calling up young men for military service once they passed their twenty-sixth birthday, though in cases of willful draft evasion that exemption did not apply. After turning twenty-six, Cheney dropped out of Wisconsin, as he had at Yale, without finishing work for his degree, in order to test his luck in Washington, D.C. Soon after he got there, Richard Nixon was elected President, and Cheney made the first of his many astonishingly successful career moves. After sending incoming Nixon appointees memo after memo, he landed a job as a staffer in the new Nixon administration at the same time William Rehnquist, along with many another Republican political operator who would be useful to Dick Cheney in the future, was moving into town.

Richard Nixon had won the presidency promising that he had "a secret plan" to end the war, but that was a lie. The Vietnam war would continue another six years. Longhaired Democratic antiwar protesters like Bill Clinton weren't the only ones who avoided fighting for their country as the Indochina conflict dragged on longer than most people imagined possible. The Nixon administration itself was a draft-dodger's haven—peppered with bright young men who wanted victory in the Vietnam war but no part in winning it. Draft boards in places like Nebraska, Wyoming, and Wisconsin were not in the habit of calling up for military service young men who worked for the president of the United States, and when it came to Washington's own draft boards, well-connected young men like Cheney were even safer. Washington had an inexhaustible pool of draft-age young blacks to send over to fight in the jungles. Besides, wasn't working for important politicians in our nation's capital as much a part of defending America as shooting at people in Asia? Thanks to their jobs with Nixon, Cheney and his ilk were virtually home-free when it came to avoiding military service. Even though their earlier "deferments," technically speaking, had not exempted them from military service and only postponed their obligation to their country, not one of George W. Bush's top advisers—with the sole exception of Colin Powell—ever fought in Vietnam.

In Washington Cheney found his vocation—gofer to the mighty. His first job was assistant to the director of the Office of Economic Opportunity, or OEO, a holdover agency from Lyndon Johnson's War on Poverty. Using the federal government to provide people other than themselves with opportunities was no more a priority for Republicans back then than it is now. The job of director, let alone assistant to the director, normally would have been a stepping stone to oblivion, except for one thing. The particular Republican director of the OEO who hired Cheney was an ex-congressman from the Chicago suburbs named Donald Rumsfeld. It was the start of a stunning rise to unelected power for them both. For the next thirty-five years their ambitions would intertwine, like the strands in a double helix, until both Rumsfeld and Cheney had risen almost to the top of the American power structure. They might, under certain circumstances, have risen all the way to the top, to the presidency itself—except that first one George Bush, and then another, got there first.

Even that early on, Cheney's career illustrated how much unaccountable power there is to be had in America—and how, if you know where it is and how to grab it, you can acquire influence officials who are actually chosen by the people almost never have. At the time Richard Nixon was elected President in 1968, Cheney was virtually unknown. By the time Richard Nixon resigned from office in disgrace in 1974, Cheney was one of the best-connected Republican operators in Washington. By 1975, he was about to rise even higher. Defeat in Vietnam and the Watergate crisis had not slowed Cheney's rise to power from within. To the contrary, as power vacuum after power vacuum opened up, Cheney filled them with his own bland, pervasive persona. A key adumbrative event of these early years, for both Cheney and Rumsfeld, was their attempt to mount a palace coup that if entirely successful, would have given them effective control of the US government. It happened in late October 1975. After becoming president following Nixon's resignation, Gerald Ford—a longtime Michigan congressman—had picked

Donald Rumsfeld, who'd been his Illinois colleague in the House of Representatives, to be his chief of staff. Rumsfeld brought Cheney along as his assistant.

Technically speaking, the presidential chief of staff is supposed to be a facilitator, not a decision-maker. Rumsfeld and Cheney supposedly were there to make the machinery of the presidency run smoothly for Ford, not to implement their own agenda. But both then and later, that wasn't how they operated. Once in the White House, Rumsfeld and Cheney started plotting to bring down the mightiest mandarins of the administration—notably Secretary of State Henry Kissinger, Secretary of Defense James Schlesinger, and Vice President Nelson Rockefeller. They prepared the way by infiltrating, and then occupying entirely the mind and calculations of President Ford. Then they struck. In the so-called Halloween Massacre of 1975, President Ford, in the manner of a complaisant emperor, did the bidding of the two viziers, Rumsfeld and Cheney. Henry Kissinger—hitherto considered to be invincibly clever—was outwitted and demoted. Nelson Rockefeller—whose very name was synonymous with power in America—was told to start looking for another job. Secretary of Defense Schlesinger was simply ordered to clear out his desk at the Pentagon, and be gone. Some of the mightiest men in America had been laid low by Rumsfeld, whose sole prior governmental experience had been as a suburban congressman, and by Cheney, who had no real government experience of any kind, other than manipulating the Selective Service Administration in order to avoid military service. Even for the age of LSD, this was a hallucinogenic outcome.

Their next step was to reward themselves. Rumsfeld named himself secretary of defense, at forty-five the youngest ever. Cheney became chief of staff in the White House—at age 31, virtually the acting president. Then they set out to implement their hidden agenda. This was to sweep away détente with the Soviet Union and to get rid of those shameful arms-limitation treaties that wimps like Kissinger had negotiated with the Communists, but their plotting and recklessness led to defeat. In part because of several astonishing foreign policy gaffes that might not have occurred had his chief of staff made sure the president was adequately briefed, Ford was defeated in the 1976 presidential election. While Ford became an affable has-been, Rumsfeld was cast into the political darkness. He would not get another Cabinet post for twenty-four years—when George W. Bush, as though plucking Rumsfeld from a time capsule, reinserted him into the same office, secretary of defense, he had vacated nearly a quarter of a century earlier.

And Cheney? For the first but not the last time, disaster for his boss (Gerald Ford) and mentor (Rumsfeld) was Dick Cheney's ticket to new success. Many Washington staffers dream of leaving Washington and going out to some place like Wyoming and getting elected to Congress—so that they can come back to Washington and resume playing the power game there as elected, not appointed, officials. Very few ever succeed. The talents of the adept Washington courtier are very different from the skills of a successful political candidate. But following Ford's defeat in 1976 and Rumsfeld's banishment, Cheney did just that. In 1978, he was elected to Congress from Wyoming. He then used the House of Representatives, as he'd earlier used OEO and the White House, to further his career as one of Washington's consummate insiders. On the surface, he was only one of 535 members of Congress. Below the surface, Cheney became a key player to whom top-ranking Republicans turned when the going got rough.

His next big opportunity came in 1989, soon after the first George Bush succeeded Ronald Reagan. Bush had picked John Tower, a former senator from Texas, to be his Secretary of Defense, on the supposition that the Senate would not reject a nominee who had been one of its own. But when Tower's reputed problems with women and the bottle derailed his candidacy, Bush tossed Cheney into the breach. The Wyoming congressman wowed his Senate inquisitors with the same mastery of detail and unthreatening persona that, in 2000, he would show in the vice presidential debates.

Cheney was confirmed as secretary of defense unanimously. The fact he had no military experience of any kind apparently did not disqualify him, in the eyes of one single senator, from taking charge of the most powerful military forces in the world. The US military is one of America's most racially complex institutions, but Cheney's record on race didn't seem to bother the senators any more than Rehnquist's had, even though Cheney, like Rehnquist, was on record as opposing equal rights for black Americans. In Congress, he had been one of the very few representatives from outside the Deep South who opposed legislation protecting equal voting rights. It gives an idea of Cheney's private usefulness to the mighty over the decades that, as secretary of defense, he did so well in a public post for which, if his résumé was to be trusted, he was entirely unqualified. During Cheney's tenure as Secretary of Defense, the US fought and won its two biggest military actions since the Vietnam war—Panama and Kuwait—with stunning speed and almost no casualties. It was also under Cheney that Gen. Colin Powell became the first nonwhite Chairman of the Joint Chiefs of Staff. The stunning military successes of the first Bush administration, however, didn't save Cheney's latest boss, like his earlier one, from political defeat. In the 1990 presidential election, President George H.W. Bush went down to defeat, just as President Gerald Ford had earlier. Cheney was a master at winning the confidence of presidents but his gift evidently did not prevent them from turning into losers.

President Bush's defeat for reelection in 1992 opened new doors for Cheney, this time in Texas. Having overseen trillions of dollars in military spending as secretary of defense, Cheney now went on to win billions of dollars in contracts for the Dallas-based Halliburton Company. He also made himself a millionaire many times over in his position as president and CEO of the Texas company whose profits came, in large part, from rebuilding things, at US taxpayers' expense, that US forces had destroyed. By the time George W. Bush picked Cheney for vice president, it fairly could be said of him that, whenever and wherever the United States made war, and for whatever reason, Dick Cheney was sure to be the winner, both coming and going. Had George W. Bush reappointed him secretary of defense, the choice would have seemed logical—though it would have raised an obvious conflict-of-interest question. Cheney was a figure sure to profit from war, any war. But Cheney for vice president?

With this first of his truly big strange "presidential" decisions, George W. Bush tipped the hand of his ideological agenda. The label Bush had chosen for himself was "compassionate conservative," but Cheney's voting record in Congress forecast the relentlessly extremist positions the George W. Bush presidency would take on a whole slew of issues, both at home and abroad. Cheney, while in Congress, hadn't just opposed equal voting rights for blacks. He'd opposed measures to protect the lives of American policemen, notably the ban on "cop killer" bullets. He never stopped pushing for more billions for weapons spending at the Department of Defense, but he opposed school books—and school lunches—for America's children. Cheney voted against establishing the US Department of Education, while also trying to take food and medicine away from old folks and preschool tots. Cheney even opposed Head Start, a program that, with its emphasis in getting underprivileged children ready to compete with kids from wealthier families, fit right in with standard Republican rhetoric about individual competition on a level playing field.

In Congress, Dick Cheney had stood resolutely opposed to government meddling in all aspects of the individual citizen's private life except where the sexual organs of women were concerned. In that realm, he supported legislation making it a crime for a woman to have an abortion even when her doctor certified that was medically necessary to save her from dying. In the realm of foreign relations, Dick Cheney allied himself with the apartheid right wing in South Africa; he opposed releasing Nelson Mandela from prison even when white South Africans favored it.

The other top player in the George W. Bush administration would be Cheney's old pal and mentor, Donald Rumsfeld. Over the decades, their careers had run in tandem. In or out of office, one of the many traits the two shared was a disinclination, after their initial ventures into electoral politics, to win power through the democratic process. After being appointed secretary of defense, Cheney didn't go back to Wyoming and never sought elective office again. After only three terms in Congress, Rumsfeld had also quit electoral politics for good. Like Cheney, Rumsfeld organized his career around the acquisition of unelected power, and money. Both were highly successful in both endeavors, though Rumsfeld, unlike Cheney, was never offered what, in fact as opposed to form, is America's ultimate appointed office, the vice presidency.

Back in the 1970s, when Rumsfeld had been a Republican wonder boy, it had seemed that he, not Cheney, was the one more likely to get the call to national office. But in 1980, Ronald Reagan chose the elder George Bush to be his vice president. Rumsfeld, who had hoped to be nominated himself, didn't even get a Cabinet post. What made the snub all the more bitter was that Rumsfeld despised the older Bush. Even though the elder Bush, unlike Rumsfeld, had seen combat in World War II, Rumsfeld, who'd gone to Princeton, considered the elder Bush a Yalie wimp. Under the photo-opportunity smiles, the ill will was reciprocated. Rumsfeld got no job in the first Bush administration, which lasted from 1989 to 1993.

Republican insiders initially supposed that George W. Bush would do Rumsfeld no favors either, but after getting himself nominated for vice president, Cheney became a one-man search committee for all sorts of powerful positions in the incoming Administration. With George W. Bush's decision, at Cheney's behest, to bring Rumsfeld back into the center of power, the Rumsfeld-Cheney team (now transmuted into the Cheney-Rumsfeld team) once again grasped the immense powers that had come so tantalizingly close following their 1975 Halloween Massacre.

In the interval the world had changed but the Cheney-Rumsfeld agenda had not. As events showed, Rumsfeld's open contempt for the "old Europe" during the buildup to the Iraq invasion was not a random outburst. Like Rumsfeld, Cheney—as well as George W. Bush himself—despised the traditional, pro-UN, NATO-centered, multilateral approach that the elder

Bush and his secretary of state, James Baker, had taken with US foreign policy. Rumsfeld, Cheney, and George W. Bush, as the world would learn, had quite a different idea of how, and for what purposes, American power should be used.

By Inauguration Day a Bush-Cheney-Rumsfeld axis had emerged, dedicated to using the military power of the United States to pursue a radical agenda. Its intermediate aim was to destabilize, indeed destroy, the current world order, based as it was on close coordination with our allies in the pursuit of such lofty goals as human rights and environmental protection. Its long-range objective was to impose a new order on the world in which the US could do whatever it wanted, whenever and wherever it wanted—our allies, along with our American values, be damned.

This agenda, while not entirely hidden, had been artfully camouflaged by the Bush anti-elitist campaign persona. In order to see what was actually afoot, however, you only had to look into the eyes of the two men at George W. Bush's side, whose world view and policies, more than any others, he adopted as his own.

Cheney and Rumsfeld both had started out, four decades earlier, as bright boys from the Midwest, but their version of the American success story, by then, had turned them into twin personifications of a dark and antidemocratic agenda. The policies the Bush administration pursued would also be far removed from the kind of American electoral politics where, as a public servant, you were expected to produce results that made a positive difference in people's lives. As always with Bush and his crowd there was something laughable, as well as lamentable, about their shamelessness. The best example was Rumsfeld: Having left office, five presidents earlier, as America's youngest secretary of defense, he now resumed office as the oldest secretary of defense and, like a resuscitated velociraptor, began stomping across NATO and the UN as though the world were Jurassic Park.

It was all as clear as Cheney's voting record, if you bothered to look. Starting way back—under Nixon, working together at OEO—the Cheney-Rumsfeld team had forged an approach to government that now became the George W. Bush paradigm. Closing preschool and senior centers, while sending American teenagers off to die in foreign wars: That was how Rumsfeld and Cheney had started under Nixon, and that was how it would be once again under George W. Bush—government of the few, by the few, for the few. There would be welfare—corporate welfare. There would be compassion—for Enron and Arthur Andersen executives. When it came to social programs, the George W. Bush administration would apply a means test: the greater your means the bigger the tax break you got.

The only long-term beneficiaries of Rumsfeld's and Cheney's labors at the Office of Economic Opportunity were themselves. Once back in power, they would continue to use the federal government to give themselves and their friends a head start. Between 1969, when Richard Nixon provided them both with entry into the world of unelected power, and 2001, when George W. Bush made them the two most powerful men in his administration, these two sons of the American heartland had become consummate practitioners of what George W. Bush told America he was running against: insider politics. In that sense, as in many others, the George W. Bush presidency was a lie from day one.

VI
Capos

CHENEY AND RUMSFELD WERE capos of the ideological clique that, right from the start, gave the George W. Bush presidency its peculiarly nasty taste. Sharing a chip-on-the-shoulder attitude toward the outside world, including America's allies, as well as a sneering contempt for human rights and international law, these ideological apparatchiks were embedded by the score in key appointive posts. It didn't take them long to turn the United States from the most respected into the most resented nation on earth. The first casualty of this unprovoked war on the world as it is was trust in America.

The Bush spinners call all this breaking and trashing "conservatism." It's actually a petulant crusade to destroy time-tested policies, as well as decades-old strategic relationships, that anyone who truly valued America's security would strive to conserve. This isn't "standing up for America," as George W. Bush claims at his fundraisers. It's giving the world the finger.

With George W. Bush in the White House, there was no situation too big or too small to turn into a global wedge issue. Millions of illiterate, malnourished women in Africa would get AIDS. They would pass the virus on to unwanted children born of avoidable pregnancies, because the Bush administration snatched health care funds away from village clinics that had provided information on abortion. Playing politics with AIDS in Africa made for terrific soundbites about family values. It also produced, during a stopover in Nigeria, one of the classic George W. Bush laugh-or-cry moments.

To a vast assembly of Africans—mostly young and poor, many of them too poor even to afford condoms—George W. Bush pledged the following: "We will support abstinence-based education for young people in schools and churches and community centers." This was his born-again riff on what practically every American bigot thinks at one time or another, though very few say it out loud: Forget family-planning clinics, IUDs, birth-control pills, or condoms. If we can only teach these people to control their sex urges, they won't need our charity.

International agreements that had staved off nuclear holocaust were also trashed. For more than fifty years, American statesmen had labored to construct a system that would limit testing and deployment of the most terrifying of all weapons of mass destruction—nuclear warheads fired at long range in ballistic missiles. Wrecking this system became George W. Bush's strategic goal. First step: turning the United States into the first nation in history to repudiate a nuclear-arms limitation treaty, opening the way to multitrillion dollar development of the unworkable "Star Wars" missile defense systems.

Land mines? Let little children play hopscotch on 'em! War crimes? Let mass murderers go free! The ozone layer? Keep those chemicals belching into the stratosphere; that'll show outer space who's in charge down here. Bush, Cheney, and Rumsfeld provided the vision. But when it came to the lower levels of government, where things actually get done and undone, the totemic figure in all this destructiveness and disruptiveness was a bland-looking, middle-aged "defense intellectual" with a reassuringly deep voice and honest-looking eyes named Paul Wolfowitz. Until George W. Bush made Wolfowitz's dangerous ideas US strategic doctrine, Wolfowitz—like Rumsfeld—had been out of power a long time, operating on the far fringes of the intellectually respectable in the think tanks of Washington, D.C.

Wolfowitz had been a longtime protégé of Dick Cheney, just as Cheney had started out as Rumsfeld's protégé. All three had become fixated on the idea of invading and occupying Iraq long before George W. Bush decided to use 9/11 as the pretext for an attack. Wolfowitz's official title in George W. Bush's administration was Deputy Secretary of Defense, but WARNING TO THE WORLD should have been stenciled on the door of his Pentagon office. He personified the deep need of the Bush crowd, above all of George W. Bush himself, to start a war. Like Bush, Wolfowitz was a chip-on-the-shoulder Ivy Leaguer (not some Sunbelt cowboy), in his case from Cornell. In addition, Wolfowitz had that tell-tale qualification shared by so many of George W. Bush's most trusted pro-war appointees—avoidance of service in the US military. Like Dick Cheney and almost all of the George W. Bush war hawks, he had been a persistent and successful Vietnam war draft-dodger.

Once in the saddle, George W. Bush would rough-ride across the globe like a tourist atop one of those coin-operated broncos in a Texas theme park. Then, in Iraq, he would embark on the most juvenile and unjustified overseas US military adventure since the 1970 Cambodia invasion. Wolfowitz, backed by Rumsfeld and encouraged by Cheney, came up with the strategic gobbledygook used to rationalize Bush's recklessness.

In the Bush-generated crises to come, Wolfowitz would be to the doctrine of "pre-emption" what Ptolemy had been to the idea that the sun revolved around the earth: chief theoretician of a system that defied reality. Secretary of State Colin Powell would play the Galileo figure. He knew how the world really moved, but when called before the Oval Office curia, Powell—the only one of them with any firsthand knowledge of war, and much else—would mumble acquiescently, letting Cardinal Cheney, Archbishop Rumsfeld, and Monsignor Wolfowitz have their way. Did Powell imagine that, in the end, reason and reality would prevail, once George W. Bush thought things over? If so, that was his illusion.

Power to shape the strategic thinking of a president of the United States had been a long time coming for Paul Wolfowitz. As early as 1992, he had urged that the United States adopt as strategic doctrine the notion that world law and world order counted for nothing when the United States wished to violate the one and overturn the other. This made him quite a thinker so far as the ultraradical neocon pamphleteers were concerned. According to the media propagandist William Kristol, Wolfowitz was "ahead of his time," "prophetic," and "vindicated by history" for having been among the first to propose a unilateral US invasion of Iraq.

George W. Bush's father knew better. When Wolfowitz's boss and mentor during that first Bush administration, then–secretary of defense Dick Cheney, presented Wolfowitz's policy proposals to him for approval, Bush the elder rejected this first draft of what later would become the blueprint for his son's "for-us-or-against-us" foreign policy. Then, tellingly, he ordered Cheney, not Wolfowitz, to rewrite it. Cheney retailored the words to fit the prevailing expediency. A less offensive approach to military policy, for the time being, remained in force, but Cheney never would have slipped Wolfowitz's document onto the president's desk if Wolfowitz's vision hadn't reflected his own views, as would become clear eight years later, when he became vice president.

Whatever his limitations, the elder Bush, a combat veteran of World War II, had grasped that Wolfowitz's strategic nostrums, which he and his staff churned out so copiously at US government expense, weren't just dumb; they were recipes for disaster—a threat in themselves to America's security. It is a measure of the difference between father and son that George W. Bush adopted as his own the same proposals his father had recognized as dangerous and foolish.

In the interval between the two Bush administrations, Wolfowitz remained a little-noticed figure outside ultraradical circles. Then George W. Bush rebestowed presidential favor upon him. Like the resuscitated Rumsfeld, he acquired cult status in Washington. The proposals that had been rejected earlier received the scrutiny normally reserved for Dead Sea Scrolls. The *Ur*-document in the Wolfowitz dossier, however, is his official Defense Department *curriculum vitae*. It's the résumé of a life as dangerously divorced from the world's realities as the Bush foreign policy has turned out to be.

When Wolfowitz graduated from Cornell with a degree in mathematics in 1965, the United States was already deeply divided by the Vietnam war. Among strategic thinkers the great controversy was whether to escalate in Vietnam. Wolfowitz played no part in the cut and thrust of that debate. Instead, at a time when other young Americans were either fighting the Vietnam war or protesting it, Wolfowitz—like Cheney—began learning how to use the internal levers of government to realize his own agenda, in this case how to evade involvement in the traumas of Vietnam entirely.

Wolfowitz not only dodged the draft; he got the federal government to pay him for doing it. Right out of college, he collected his first government paycheck, along with his first deferment. "A year as a Management Intern at the Bureau of the Budget (1966–67)" is how the future presidential adviser on strategic warfare describes his first work experience in a career that would never involve meeting a payroll, turning a profit, or producing something of actual use to the American public. One thing Wolfowitz could have learned at the Bureau of the Budget, though he evidently did not, is how an unnecessary war can bust a nation's finances.

Graduate studies could not be hurried during those war years, which included the Tet Offensive and the Kent State killings, as well as Nixon's Vietnamizaton program. Following his government internship, Wolfowitz spent the subsequent five years holed up in select ivory towers, including Yale and the University of Chicago, where work on a PhD thesis helped keep his draft deferment in order for half a decade.

Besides avoiding military service, Chicago allowed Wolfowitz to immerse himself in the quasi-superman, negative-Platonic theories of the neoconservative guru, Leo Strauss, who supervised his doctoral thesis. The sad history of nineteenth- and twentieth-century political philosophy can be read, in part, as the story of a series of gypsy-moth German philosophers who, having failed either to halt or to explain the triumph of intellectual barbarism in Germany itself, then went on to addle impressionable grad students from Chicago to kingdom come. Think of Strauss as an emigre Midwestern anti-Marx, and Wolfowitz, the son of a mathematics professor in upstate New York, as the anticommunist suburban equivalent of all those callow grad students who, back in the sixties, thought Che and Marcuse were so neat, and you get the idea. As Strauss saw it, America's love of freedom and its protests against an unjust war were signs that America, the nation which had defeated Hitler and saved him and so many others from persecution and death in their own homelands, was turning into another Weimar Republic. It's an interesting prefiguration: Wolfowitz soaking up Strauss' notion that America is decadent, while the professor authorizes his draft deferment.

After passing his twenty-sixth birthday, it was time for Paul Wolfowitz to get back on the federal payroll: "Four years (1973–77) in the Arms Control and Disarmament Agency, working on the Strategic Arms Limitation Talks and a number of nuclear nonproliferation issues" is the way his résumé describes it. In Washington, Wolfowitz met other young ideologues who also had decided that the thoughts of (philosophy department) chairman Leo Strauss provided a key to the global use of American power. These "defense intellectuals" included Richard Perle, whose prescription for the Middle East was, always and inevitably, to place US might entirely and unquestioningly at the service of whatever Israel, at any one moment, happened to think it wanted to do. Another figure in this circle was Elliott Abrams, whose idea of the proper exercise of US power was inciting terrorism (the neocons called it "Low Intensity Warfare") against Third World nations of whose governmental philosophy Leo Strauss would have disapproved. Abrams later would be indicted (though have his conviction reversed on appeal) as a result of his involvement in the Reagan scandal with the Contra insurgents in Central America.

For the next quarter-century Leo Strauss was to this clique of busy Washington neocons what Ayn Rand was to the *Fountainhead* nuts. There was always, also, the whiff of Tolkein and his hobbits about them, as well as *Superman* (Nietzche, but also the comic book). Though these guys imagined themselves to be deep thinkers, they were actually steeped in the modern cultural trivializations of Plato and Homer—Leo Strauss, not *The Republic, Lord of the Rings*, not the Trojan wars. Decades later, the Iraq war would be launched by a bunch of post-docs who, all too clearly, never had bothered to read *The Iliad*, and understand what it reveals about war, and what war does to human beings, during all that time they were avoiding their military service. The diplomatic analyst William Pfaff later described the Wolfowitz crowd in the following terms: "They have a political philosophy, and the arrogance and intolerance of their actions reflect their conviction that they possess a realism and truth others lack." Their future obsession with taking out Saddam Hussein would be their kitschy, post-modern trivialization of Kierkegaard's *Purity of Heart Is to Will One Thing*.

While preparing for the day when George W. Bush would give him the actual power to enforce his ideological notions, Wolfowitz passed the time writing policy proposals. In the Washington world of staff-generated policy papers—the kind of documents that mean nothing unless and until someone with real power picks them up and takes them seriously—one talent all successful strategic scriptwriters must have is a knack for making sure events like presidential elections don't disrupt the steady output of their position papers. This was a skill Wolfowitz displayed very early on. As far as most Americans were concerned, Jimmy Carter's election to the presidency in 1976 marked a big change—away from the Nixon-Kissinger conception of US power, to one based on human rights. But under Carter, as later under Reagan, Wolfowitz's career marched on regardless of how Americans voted or what happened around the world. So did his proposals. Whoever was President, Wolfowitz's approach to power remained simplistically arithmetical: The more weapons America had, and the more it used them, the better (whether or not there was any strategic or moral justification). It is this inflexible approach to America's "national security," unchanging over the decades and impervious to geopolitical reality, which, like some harmless hamster in a sci-fi film, would grow into an earth-threatening monster once bombarded by the radioactive attention of George W. Bush.

It was under the peaceable Jimmy Carter, however, that Wolfowitz got the breakthrough job that would lead to all that. While still in his early thirties, he was named deputy secretary of defense for regional programs. The recent US defeat in Indochina had started out as a regional problem. Then, through more than a decade of body counts, the Johnson and Nixon administrations had escalated it into a global humiliation for the United States. Following that self-inflicted catastrophe, the United States certainly needed new approaches to regional problems. Nowhere was the old domino-theory approach more outdated than in the vast Indian Ocean region, stretching from southeast Asia through the Indian subcontinent and Iran to the Arab world and Israel. Here the traditional US approach, emphasizing military "solutions" to economic and social problems, combined with political support for local dictators, was more than wrong. It was meaningless.

Change was in the air after the Indochina defeat. A new kind of strategic understanding, not just new kinds of weapons systems, would be needed if the United States was to avoid further disasters. All this was as lost on Wolfowitz as it was on Rumsfeld and Cheney and, later, George W. Bush. Wolfowitz described his actions back then to forge a new American regional approach, following the military disaster in Vietnam, as helping to "create the force that later became the United States Central Command and initiated the Maritime Pre-positioning Ships, the backbone of the initial US deployment twelve years later in Operation Desert Shield."

This technically proficient military-mechanical exercise did foreshadow the unbounded faith America's strategic planners would place in techno-wars over the next quarter-century. It did nothing to separate US regional interests from the fate of the Shah of Iran. He, like various other US-supported despots, remained "a pillar of stability" in the US strategic approach—until in 1979 his own people overthrew him. Entirely unforeseen by America's national security mandarins, the fall of the Shah led, among other things, to the ayatollahs' seizure of power in Iran, Saddam Hussein's invasion of Iran, and the Iran/*contra* scandals, to say nothing of the two Iraq wars the United States would later fight.

Billions spent on weapons hadn't made the Shah's regime viable, let alone a pillar of stability. Wolfowitz's warships positioned in the Indian Ocean would not stop the rise of Islamic fundamentalism, either. They couldn't even stop demonstrators from taking over the US embassy in Tehran and keeping the American staff there prisoners for more than a year. The revolutionaries of Iran—like Osama bin Laden twenty years later—were simply undeterred by the Wolfowitz-Rumsfeld-Cheney and (eventually) the George W. Bush strategy of "projecting" America's billion-dollar weapons systems into the Indian Ocean. Then as later, Wolfowitz along with the rest of them hadn't a clue as to how US military force really connected—

and even more important, failed to connect—with the real world. As often happens in Washington, Wolfowitz's detachment from reality turned out to be an enormous career advantage. It freed him up to generate just the kind of "strategic" fantasy nonsense that Rumsfeld, Cheney, and George W. Bush love to find in their In boxes.

For most Americans, the shift from the approach to the world Jimmy Carter embodied to the one personified by Ronald Reagan was another big change. For Paul Wolfowitz it meant changing his commute. In spite of his complete lack of diplomatic experience, he was shifted from the Department of Defense to the Department of State, where he was made head of the policy planning staff. This always is a frustrating post since US foreign policy never gets planned, at least not in the State Department, but it served as a stepping stone to Wolfowitz's biggest preferment yet, assistant secretary of state for East Asian and Pacific affairs.

This appointment was a bizarre illustration of how Washington actually works. It wasn't just that Wolfowitz had completely absented himself from the war in Vietnam and now was being put in charge of America's relations with the whole of the Pacific Rim, including Indochina. He had no academic, or diplomatic, or personal experience of any part of the Far East; he didn't even know it as a tourist. More than that, Wolfowitz had never represented the United States abroad in any capacity. He didn't know what it was like to fight or make peace in an Asian country, or for that matter run the branch office of a US business. Yet now, in Wolfowitz's own words, he "was in charge of US relations with more than twenty countries," including China and Japan, in the post–Vietnam war era.

During Ronald Reagan's second term, Wolfowitz finally got

some limousine-level experience of the world beyond America's shores. He was named ambassador to Indonesia. This remains the only government post George W. Bush's chief strategic theoretician ever has ever held that has involved him performing some actual service for the taxpayers and citizens of the United States. Being ambassador to a vast, fascinating land like Indonesia was a form of exile from what, for Wolfowitz, really mattered: generating war plans in Washington. He was ambassador in Jakarta during 1986, 1987, 1988, and 1989. The principal triumph he lists as resulting from his ambassadorship there is that "during his tenure, Embassy Jakarta was cited as one of the four best-managed embassies inspected in 1988."

Wolfowitz's workday changed dramatically when Dick Cheney became Bush the elder's secretary of defense in 1989, and called Wolfowitz back to the Pentagon to be his under secretary of defense. In the Washington mandarinate, being an assistant secretary is nice. Being named under secretary is almost Heaven. The Pentagon prose sings as Wolfowitz describes what happened once his Indonesia exile ended: "From 1989 to 1993, Dr. Wolfowitz served as Under Secretary of Defense for Policy in charge of the 700-person defense policy team that was responsible to Secretary Dick Cheney for matters concerning strategy, plans, and policy. During this period Secretary Wolfowitz and his staff had major responsibilities for the reshaping of strategy and force posture at the end of the Cold War."

The key phrase to grasp there is "the end of the Cold War," which posed a bigger threat to the Pentagon's purse and power than the schemers in the Kremlin ever had. At Cheney's behest, Wolfowitz and his policy spinners spent millions of man-hours conjuring up ways to increase US military spending even though, with the collapse of the Soviet Union, the Communist menace had vaporized without the United States having to fire a shot. The best boondoggle of them all—Star Wars—had been invented by wily old Ronald Reagan, all by himself. But lock 700 "defense intellectuals" in their offices at the Pentagon. Then inform them that unless and until they dream up enough spurious new threats to America's security, along with the new multibillion-dollar weapon systems necessary to counter them to ensure that US military spending cannot possibly be reduced, they won't get their next promotion. Before you know it, you'll have a "defense" budget guaranteed to ensure that not one red cent of the post–Cold War "peace dividend" ever gets back to the people of America. That's the nerdy work Wolfowitz and his minions were busily doing when, on August 2, 1990, Saddam Hussein invaded Kuwait. This event caught Wolfowitz, Cheney, and the rest of them as totally unaware as the attacks of September 11, 2001 later would.

The American turnaround after the Kuwait invasion was magnificent. Not since World War II had America's military might been so perfectly wedded to a legitimate military purpose. The liberation of Kuwait in February 1991, kick-started what, back then, even Republicans proudly called the New World Order. As well as a military victory, the Kuwait war was a historic diplomatic triumph for the United States. Both the elder Bush and his secretary of state, James Baker, had seen to that. They understood that, in order to succeed, any new, post–Cold War international order would have to be based on right as well as might, and they had organized the United Nations–sanctioned, US-led effort to reverse Saddam's aggression on that basis. That was why George H.W. Bush in 1991, unlike George W. Bush in 2003, was able to assemble a genuine coalition of the willing. Nations ranging from Argentina to

Syria, and from France to Turkey enthusiastically helped fight, and also to pay for that first Iraq war because it was fought for reasons they understood, to defend principles they shared—and because then, unlike later, the United States didn't act like a bully. A decade later, the same countries would keep their wallets closed and sit on their hands. There was an additional reason US efforts were so successful in 1991. Back then, the United States treated other countries with respect.

The swift totality of that first Iraq victory was stunning, but nothing impressed the world more than the principled approach the United States took once Saddam was defeated. US forces could have surged on to Baghdad. Instead, the first President Bush won the world's admiration with his decision not to transform the United Nations–authorized liberation of Kuwait into an American conquest of Iraq. It was a painful as well as principled decision to stop the war before Saddam Hussein was toppled, but Bush the elder understood that upholding the rule of law among nations was more important than settling scores with an unsavory dictator. Unlike George W. Bush later, he also understood that a unilateral, unauthorized US assault on Iraq, followed by a US military occupation of the country, would undermine American security by turning most of the Arab and Muslim world against the United States.

Wolfowitz and his 700 paper-pushers played no role in the stunning Kuwait victory. While they'd been churning up strategic "doctrine," the actual war was planned, run, and won by military professionals like Colin Powell. That didn't stop Wolfowitz from deciding that he should be the one to ordain what US national security policy should be in light of that decisive victory. More than a year after Operation Desert Storm had already demonstrated the best way for the United States to fight, and win wars in the post–Cold War era, Wolfowitz weighed in with a radically different counterproposal. It was the same blueprint for disaster that eleven years later would play itself out under George W. Bush.

Wolfowitz's war plan bore an innocuous-sounding label. He called his prescription for destroying the postwar international security system "Defense Planning Guidance." Even had its contents not been pernicious, its existence would have been redundant. In the form of Operation Desert Storm, Powell and the others had already created and successfully tested the paradigm of successful US action that, following the 9/11 attacks ten years later, would serve the United States as well in Afghanistan as it had in Kuwait. The key to both the 1991 Kuwait triumph and the 2002 success in Afghanistan was not America's overwhelming technological superiority in modern warfare. The key to success was that America's overwhelming superiority was used legitimately, in pursuit of a worthwhile objective, supported by the overwhelming majority of the nations of the earth.

"Defense Planning Guidance" took the form of a forty-six-page pamphlet that repudiated both the proven military-diplomatic success of the Desert Storm model of warfare and the democratic ideals and strategic conceptions—from the Four Freedoms to containment—which had, through all the follies and dangers, managed to save America and the world from utter disaster during the first half-century of the nuclear age. The Kuwait victory had been a victory for the internationalists and multilateralists within the Republican Party—for all those wimps, ranging from Kissinger to Powell, that Rumsfeld and Cheney had first tried to purge from power during their 1975 Holloween Massacre. "Defense Planning Guidance" was the opening gambit in a campaign which would only achieve success in 2001, when George W. Bush, deftly guided by Dick Cheney, brought Donald Rumsfeld back from the political wilderness, and Rumsfeld, in turn, put Wolfowitz in charge of putting an intellectual gloss on their nutty policy of ceaseless provocation all over the world.

By the time "Defense Planning Guidance" appeared in 1992, the world in which Paul Wolfowitz and the rest of us live had changed enormously. Many strategic theories had been tested by events, and proven wrong. The Vietnam war, for example, had been lost. Yet even after the United States was defeated, the dominoes had not fallen. It was Communism that fell after America lost the war it supposedly had been necessary to fight in order to halt Communism's otherwise inexorable advance. In the course of Wolfowitz's own unelected rise to a degree of power few elected public officials ever achieve in a democracy, a multitude of other gigantic, unforeseeable events had reduced to rubble the strategic conceptions that had guided—and all too often, misguided—American policy-makers for decades.

What was the result of these changes? Somehow, the United States not only had survived the "Communist threat" and all the other supposed menaces. It had remained the most powerful nation on earth. There were great lessons to be learned from these unforeseen turns of events. As Under Secretary of Defense for Policy, Wolfowitz was in charge of trying to think through what the nagging discrepancy between America's strategic preconceptions and what actually happened in the world meant when it came to the United States spending trillions of dollars on weapons. Instead he ginned up a proposal for US military-industrial domination of the world.

Later, the damage-control folks in the George W. Bush administration tried to make it seem like Wolfowitz had only been kicking around some ideas. But "Defense Planning Guidance," as its title states, is a set of explicit instructions, from Wolfowitz to his staff, providing guidance as to how they should plan policy following the great changes that marked the beginning of the post–Cold War era. By then, many believed a new era of global relations, transcending the old nationalist and ideological rivalries, was at hand, in which no one nation would try to dominate the others. They believed it was America's responsibility as the world's most powerful nation, as well as in America's own national security interest, to nurture the emergence of this new era of globalization. In this new era, it was hoped, something other, and better, than nation-state arrogance would determine the world's response to problems ranging from political terrorism to the emergence of new, global health threats. Furthermore, for billions of ordinary people around the world—and billions had watched the Gulf War on TV—the recent victory over Saddam in Kuwait had provided the model for maintaining global law and order in the new era.

In "Defense Planning Guidance," Wolfowitz threw out that whole successful approach, with its emphasis on multilateralism and the rule of law. He propounded an opposite, dark paradigm—of a world in which only one nation, the United States, would dominate the world the way the Soviet Union once had dominated eastern Europe. All these years later, "Defense Planning Guidance" still makes chilling reading. It combines the objectives of the Brezhnev Doctrine with the rhetoric of Imperial Japan's Greater East Asia Co-Prosperity Sphere. It's hard to believe, reading it, that such conceptions could emanate from an American mind at all. The first President Bush was right to slap down Cheney, when he brought him Wolfowitz's proposal.

"Defense Planning Guidance" would have been an alarming document if it had been discovered in the KGB archives. Coming from an American, it was shocking.

Americans grow up believing it's their destiny to save everyone else from the bully on the block. The strategic objective Wolfowitz put forth in "Defense Planning Guidance" was to turn America into the global bully. The first step to permanent global domination, according to Wolfowitz, was to make sure no one got in America's way, ever. Over the next decade, America's most dangerous enemies would turn out to be infiltrating viruses (as AIDS had already shown), and groups of fanatics acting independent of any national authority (as 9/11 would show). Yet Wolfowitz was fixated on fighting a new Cold War against a new Soviet Union. Only this time the war wouldn't be cold, and America wouldn't settle for containment.

"Our first objective is to prevent the re-emergence of a new rival," Wolfowitz announced. (Throughout "Defense Planning Guidance," he writes "is," not "should be.") "This is," he continued, "a dominant consideration underlying the new regional defense strategy and requires that we endeavor to prevent any hostile power from dominating a region whose resources would, under consolidated control, be sufficient to generate global power." Here as throughout "Defense Planning Guidance," people don't count. Like George W. Bush later, he equates domination of "resources," notably oil, with "power," and the potential loss of control over those resources as defeat. People don't count, nor does rightful ownership of the resources the United States might decide to control. Also absent is the idea that the United States might eliminate "threats" to its national security by modifying its own behavior—for example, by consuming less imported oil—rather than by dominating others or resorting to military force. This approach, too, would become the George W. Bush approach. Not once during the invasion of Iraq, for example, would Americans be asked to support the war effort by driving fewer SUVs. George W. Bush's Iraq war would be a struggle in which Americans would be expected to sacrifice their lives, but not turn down their air-conditioners, give up their tax cuts, or buy less gas.

The overall US goal, Wolfowitz emphasizes in "Defense Planning Guidance," is not merely to retain control over oil supplies. Nor is the strategic objective to deter aggression, or even to contain it, as had been US strategy under every US president, Republican or Democrat, since the end of World War II. The goal, instead, is to impose a "new order" that will make it impossible for any country other than the United States "to generate global power" under any circumstances, for any reason.

Later, George W. Bush's petulance, as well as the arrogance he and those around him displayed, mystified many. Secretary of Defense Rumsfeld's outbursts against the "old Europe" especially startled people. Why did they get so ticked off simply because members of the United Nations Security Council, including America's allies on the council, disagreed with them? One reason Bush and those around him treated America's allies so contemptuously was that, by then, the ideas expressed in "Defense Planning Guidance" had been an ingrained part of their shared world view for years. As Wolfowitz himself had put it, "even aspiring to a larger regional or global role" on the part of "potential competitors," including America's allies, was not to be tolerated.

Combine this intolerant world view with George W. Bush's for-us-or-against-us approach and you have what, ten years after Wolfowitz wrote "Defense Policy Guidance," has become a self-fulfilling prophesy. By the time Bush invaded Iraq, it wasn't just the Russians and the Chinese, and all those Africans and Asians, and, as usual, the French who were "against us." Even Canada had turned into a "competitor."

Having defined the US objective as eliminating even the possibility of others aspiring to provide an alternative to American leadership, or even supplementing it on a regional basis, Wolfowitz then proposed that the United States do away with the entire post–World War II system of collective security, epitomized by US cooperation with NATO and the United Nations. In his own words: "First the US must show the leadership necessary to establish and protect a new order that holds the promise of convincing potential competitors that they need not aspire to a greater role or pursue a more aggressive posture to protect their legitimate interests."

And then? "Second, in the non-defense areas," Wolfowitz continued, "we must account sufficiently for the interests of the advanced industrial nations to discourage them from challenging our leadership or seeking to overturn the established political and economic order." After pausing to consider what that last sentence actually means, it's hard, even now, to think of a statement by a US official more profoundly contemptuous—and ignorant—of the human and cultural, as well as military and strategic, realities of Europe, and of the rest of the world. Here we have, in words, what the Bush Doctrine became in deeds ten years later. While the United States decides what to do, where to do it, when to do it, and who will do it, the United States nonetheless will be magnanimous enough to "account sufficiently for the interests of the advanced industrial nations to discourage them from challenging our leadership."

It was one thing to propound universal US hegemony, as

"Defense Planning Guidance" did in 1992. But how to achieve it? This was the question raised beginning in January 2001 when George W. Bush actually tried to put into practice Wolfowitz's megalomaniacal approach to world politics. As America's allies, among others, would try fruitlessly to make George W. Bush understand, it would be no cakewalk imposing US control even on one medium-sized Middle Eastern country, like Iraq. How, then, to achieve the global domination of which Cheney, Rumsfeld, and the other ultraradicals dreamed? And even if such dominance could be achieved, what would be the benefit for the people of America?

These were the practical questions "Defense Planning Guidance" raised but never answered. Fortunately, for the time being the United States had no serious global rivals—which was why George W. Bush, once he got into office, would have to create one, in the form of the "axis of evil." Russia was only a shambling giant after the collapse of the Soviet Union. Those uppity Europeans might in due course become the world's second democratic superpower, but that was unlikely to happen soon. On the other hand, it seemed not only likely but inevitable that—at the opposite end of Eurasia, facing America across the Pacific Ocean—China would become a "new rival," and not a friendly one, if the United States insisted on treating China's rise to great-power status as a "threat."

And that's exactly what any such development was, from the strategic perspective ordained in "Defense Planning Guidance"—a threat. It didn't matter if a modernized, prosperous China (or India, or Indonesia, for that matter) was friendly or not. Its mere emergence as a great power was a "threat" that the United States must prevent from arising. Indeed George W. Bush would start out labeling China as a "strategic competitor in the Pacific basin."

Soon, however, even he had to recognize that cooperating with China was vital to US security in many matters, including dealings with North Korea.

That pointed to one fundamental problem with such a domineering approach. In the real world, as opposed to the world of radical neocon polemics, what is true for ordinary people is also true for nations. We may feel threatened when the neighbors get a bigger car, or install a bigger swimming pool, but if we don't want garbage dumped on our front lawn, it's better not to treat the neighbors with contempt, let alone announce to them that you, and you alone, are going decide from now on what goes on in the neighborhood. The same holds true at the level of global politics. Even countries as powerful as the United States normally have no choice but to treat other countries, including rival countries, as partners. The business of the world, including the business of pursuing US foreign policy goals, requires a cooperative approach. But suppose the United States chose to act abnormally? Suppose it actually decided to apply Wolfowitz's global version of the Brezhnev Doctrine to China? What could the United States actually do to stop China and its billion-plus people from rivaling and, indeed, someday outstripping the United States—the way, a century earlier, the United States had surpassed the British—to become the single most powerful nation in the world? What options would it have?

Even to mention the kinds of "options" that might actually result in the United States maintaining permanent superiority over China reveals the suicidal nuttiness of the "Defense Planning Guidance" approach. The United States, for instance, could bomb the Chinese back into the Stone Age, as had actually been proposed during the more hysterical phases of the Cold War. Nuclear attack on China's industrial heartland would indeed interrupt its emergence as a "potential rival"—though that was an option few American strategic thinkers still considered advisable, now that China's own nuclear missiles might reach Washington before US missiles reintroduced neolithic culture to the land where more advanced forms of human civilization had flourished for so long.

Another possible way, in Wolfowitz's words, "to prevent the reemergence of a new rival" would be for the United States to encourage radical Maoists to reassert control in China. Unleashing another Cultural Revolution would quite probably retard China's capacity "to generate global power." It would also panic global finance markets, and destroy the vibrant Pacific Rim economy on which the US economy counts for future growth. What about less drastic forms of economic warfare? Reinstating the US trade embargo would slow down China's military as well as its economic development. But it would also destroy the World Trade Organization, and unleash a worldwide depression. It also would mean no more cheap, high-quality videogames and PCs down at the suburban malls, where Republican appeal to the swing vote is essential for keeping George W. Bush, as well as Paul Wolfowitz, on the federal payroll.

Yet Wolfowitz not only proposed preventing China's emergence as "another rival" but proposed precluding such an eventuality, or even the possibility of it ever arising, in "Western Europe, East Asia, the territory of the former Soviet Union, and Southwest Asia" as well. But how to lobotomize the rest of the world? Strategically speaking, that more or less was the grand global policy "Defense Planning Guidance" ordained.

"Finally," Wolfowitz wrote, "we must maintain the mechanisms for deterring potential competitors from even aspiring to a larger regional or global role." Even aspiring? US domination of the world, as propounded here, was not merely to be over the world and each region in it. It was to be a dominion over the world's aspirations as well. And what on earth did he mean by "mechanisms"?

These are difficult questions. They are dangerous questions. Both before and after he mounted his mechanical bronco, these are the kinds of questions George W. Bush never bothered to ask.

MOTHER OF ALL WEDGE ISSUES

☆ ☆ ☆

VII

Usurping 9/11

PEOPLE WILL TALK ABOUT that September morning as long as leaves turn gold in Central Park. Did the sky only seem so blue just before the first plane hit? Did the air truly seem to promise all that is wonderful about summer, and all that is perfect about autumn, before the debris spewed so high and thick it made lower Manhattan look like an erupting volcano? People who had looked at the rivers surrounding Manhattan every day of their lives now for the first time realized they were made of water. As the Twin Towers collapsed, they wondered: Can I make it if I swim?

Every human good and every human evil was on display that day because good and evil surround us all the time, like nitrogen in the air. The richness, the sadness, the sweetness of life, and its fragility and bitterness: They are always there, around us and inside us, but until some great event shakes us by the shoulders, they are like starlight in daytime. We cannot see them. Then some great eclipse occurs, like the events of September 11, 2001, and we are astounded.

Bravery, solidarity, and calmness were the great civic virtues people displayed that day in New York, at the Pentagon, and in the skies over Pennsylvania. Nothing can ever change the nobility ordinary people showed on 9/11. But the future actions of George W. Bush would dishonor the magnificence of their response. As he had before, as he would later, when presented with a great unearned opportunity to do good, George W. Bush capriciously made things worse. He did this so thoroughly and skillfully, it is impossible, now, to envisage any clear, honorable means by which the ill he has done can be reversed easily, or at all. Before 9/11, George W. Bush had ruined his presidency once. After September 11 he dishonored the presidency of the United States for a second time, this time on a worldwide scale.

Almost everybody wanted to know two things about 9/11: How did it happen? How can we make sure it won't happen again? You have to say "almost everybody" because from the beginning George W. Bush had a reverse agenda. His goal was to block any meaningful inquiry into this latest stupendous failure of US intelligence. He had good reason for wanting a cover-up. Any honest inquiry into the failure of the CIA and the FBI to provide forewarning of the Al Qaeda attacks was sure to lead directly and inevitably to a consideration of George W. Bush's own incompetence and dishonesty. So he engaged in a vast diversionary exercise to prevent people from understanding what actually happened that morning of September 11, 2001, and why. This is the fundamental reason why his ensuing "war on terror" was so wildly off-target. How can you fight something you refuse to understand?

Iraq would become the most spectacular of George W. Bush's diversionary exercises. Meanwhile, at home, dispassionate inquiry into the greatest failure of US intelligence since Pearl Harbor was stymied at every turn. WHITE HOUSE DENIES FUNDING TO COMMISSION, BUSH'S ROADBLOCKS

THWART 9/11 COMMISSION, ANGERS VICTIMS' FAMILIES, the headlines read, both in the immediate aftermath of the tragedies—and then month and month after month.

The attacks of September 11 revealed the moral depravity of the Osama bin Laden–playboy school of Islamic fanaticism. Its political bankruptcy was revealed as well. Here was an act of mass murder as darkly exquisite as a Rimbaud poem, but to what result were these nightmare resonances unleashed? Would people in Iraq or Afghanistan become better Muslims as a result of Al Qaeda's perfect act of nihilism? Would the humiliation of Arabs end in Iraq or the Occupied Territories? Would America—under George W. Bush of all people—suddenly become empathetic as a result of being smashed in the face? Or, thanks to Al Qaeda, would Americans become even more oblivious to their complicity in the injustices afflicting Osama bin Laden's part of the world?

The aftermath of September 11 revealed George W. Bush's moral vacuity and the depravity of his world view. In response to such an event, what kind of leader—what kind of American—would allocate more for Halliburton-style boondoggles in Iraq than for homeland security? George W. Bush's inadequacy was more fundamentally the product of a philosophy of government that always puts the American people last. Even had he been a less slipshod chief executive, George W. Bush's approach to government guaranteed that on the morning of September 11, as well as afterwards, he would be found wanting when it came to ensuring the performance of those humdrum yet essential tasks that are most important to the American people. Keeping track of visa violators, screening passengers as they board airplanes, making sure that interstate travel is safe: These civic duties are the responsibility of the executive branch of the federal government, headed by George W. Bush.

None of those things were done. If any of them had been done, thousands of people might not have been killed that day. This wasn't a matter of trillion-dollar "Star Wars"–style weapons systems. You didn't need the approval of the UN Security Council. Government-mandated locks on the doors to the pilots' cabins could have protected America and its people, just as the previous November simple safeguards on voting machines could have protected their right to choose the president.

The possibly preventable attacks of September 11 demonstrated what already was evident to those who look honestly at the way the United States is governed. America's governmental system, which never works very well, worked even worse with George W. Bush in charge. Blaming the horrible things that happened to Americans on Osama bin Laden (or later, Saddam Hussein) was a not a sufficient explanation, let alone justification, for gross and negligent unpreparedness on the part of the US government. The US Constitution charges the president—not foreign terrorists and tyrants—with defending the United States. Had the US government not been so grossly inept when it came to performing the simplest functions of government, 9/11 might have been averted in spite of the undeniable fact that there are indeed bad people around the world who wish America harm. A systemic crisis in the nuts-and-bolts operations of the US government explains why more than 3,000 people were burned, crushed, and suffocated to death. As Commander in Chief, Bush bears responsibility for this monumental failure of government to get the big things, the medium-sized things, or even the little things right.

Big failure: Had the National Security Agency's multi-billion-dollar secret snooping devices had any actual relevance to national security, the United States would have had some forewarning of the 9/11 attacks. But here, as later in Afghanistan and Iraq, US "intelligence" hadn't a clue. Medium-sized failure: Had the US Immigration and Naturalization Service been doing its job, making sure only people entitled to valid visas got into the United States, and then left before their visas expired, the key plotters of the Al Qaeda attacks would not even have been in the United States on September 11. Instead, the INS—having ignored the presence of the hijackers in the United States while they were alive and plotting their attack—then went on to grant some of them visas after they had killed more than 3,000 people and were themselves dead. Little failures: Had the most rudimentary administrative procedures been in place to regulate mundane operations ranging from admissions standards at private flight schools to accurate identity checks for driver's licenses, the attacks might have been thwarted. The events of September 11 stirred the deepest emotions. They always will. But once the crying is done, how not to laugh at a federal government that, under George W. Bush's leadership, confers posthumous permission to reside in the United States on mass murderers?

It's not as though George W. Bush had no warning in advance. There were a number of attempts to warn the administration of the danger. All were spurned. One important warning came from former Senators Gary Hart, a Democrat, and Warren Rudman, a Republican. Hart and Rudman were co-chairmen of an official task force called the United States Commission on National Security. The commission was established by act of Congress specifically to analyze unconventional threats to America's safety. This was no ploy to embarrass a Republican president. Among the commission's members was Newt Gingrich, the former Republican Speaker of the House of

Representatives. As early as September 1999, two years before the attacks, the Commission on National Security issued the first of a series of prescient warnings. Unless there were major changes in the way the United States defended itself, it warned, "Americans will likely die on American soil, possibly in large numbers" as the result of the federal government's unpreparedness to deal with terrorism. Then, at the end of January 2001, just as George W. Bush was taking office, Hart and Rudman issued a detailed, 150-page set of proposals for making America safer. Their report was called *Road Map for National Security: Imperative for Change*. In it they wrote: "We need orders-of-magnitude improvements in planning, coordination, and exercise." Among their many useful and prescient suggestions was a proposal to create a new National Homeland Security Agency to coordinate efforts to protect America from Al Qaeda–style attacks—a proposal George W. Bush would continue to oppose even after September 11.

Less than a week before the September 11 attacks, Hart met with George W. Bush's National Security Adviser, Condoleezza Rice. He urged her to start focusing on what, only days later, would be proven to be the greatest security threat to the United States since World War II. One of Hart's concerns was the total lack of preparedness for acts involving "a weapon of mass destruction in a high-rise building." As usual, Rice was heedless as well as clueless. The national security adviser did nothing, either then or after the attacks, to act on Hart's warning. Hart's attempt to communicate with Rice was a preview of later futile attempts by people like Hans Blix, the chief United Nations weapons inspector for Iraq, to put Rice in touch with reality. The vain hope was that she somehow might, then, bring a ray of reality into George W. Bush's view of the world. But Rice herself is one of the symptoms of George W. Bush's strategic autism: Why else choose a person of such mediocrity to be your national security adviser, if your goal isn't to isolate yourself from useful information and honest thinking?

Hart met Rice in the White House on Thursday, September 6. The following Tuesday the twin towers would be collapsing. The Pentagon itself would be ablaze. As Harold Evans, former editor of the London *Sunday Times*, has observed, the White House deliberately stymied efforts to alert Americans to the danger that, in the end, would burst upon the country so unexpectedly. In early May 2001, Congress had actually planned hearings aimed at publicizing the Hart-Rudman proposals. The exact date scheduled was May 6, but the White House scuttled the effort the day before by announcing it would not even be considering the proposals.

The Commission on National Security had conducted its inquiries with admirable objectivity, in a completely bipartisan way. It had been established, with both Democratic and Republican support, specifically to advise the White House and educate the nation on new kinds of threats to America's safety. Both liberals like Hart and right-wingers like Gingrich supported the commission's proposals, yet the George W. Bush administration was refusing even to consider them. "It did not want Congress out front on the issue," noted Evans. "On May 5, the administration announced that, rather than adopting Hart-Rudman, it was forming its own committee headed by Vice President Dick Cheney, who was expected to report in October."

The White House delaying tactics worked. "States, terrorists, and other disaffected groups will acquire weapons of mass destruction, and some will use them. Americans will likely die on American soil, possibly in large numbers," Hart and the others had warned. But, just as Bush and Cheney wished, Americans remained oblivious to the potential threat until the morning of September 11, after which Cheney quickly filled the new hole the administration had dug for itself with his own bland, authoritative persona. "The administration actually slowed down response to Hart-Rudman when momentum was building in the spring," former Speaker Newt Gingrich told Evans. After September 11, there was no longer any need for the administration to steal Hart's thunder. Osama bin Laden had seen to that, though Cheney's "October report" was eventually issued—in October 2003, not October 2001.

More than three years earlier, in their detailed 150-page report, Hart and the others had made specific suggestions on how to prevent attacks like 9/11 from happening. Cheney's *Comprehensive Strategy to Combat Terrorism* took the form of a pep talk to the Wakonda Club in Des Moines, Iowa. In his speech, Cheney reiterated the falsehoods the administration had used to rationalize the attack on Iraq, including the allegation that Saddam had functioning weapons of mass destruction, not a trace of which had been found by the UN. Cheney seemed moved to pity more than anger by unpatriotic suggestions that the failure to find any evidence supporting the administration's allegations somehow demonstrated that Bush and he hadn't been justified in going to war.

"One of the debates you've seen in recent days," Cheney told his audience, "is this question of, well, maybe Saddam didn't really have any WMDs [weapons of mass destruction]. And there are people out there peddling that notion—those who are trying to undermine our attack, the decision the President made. But I have never believed that for a minute. I think the record is overwhelming that he had, in fact, had major investments in weapons of mass destruction." Amidst all the applause and convoluted rationalizations, a revealing one-liner escaped Cheney's lips. "What we learned on 9/11 was that we are vulnerable," Cheney said, as though that had not been evident before then.

There was another reason, in addition to the political adeptness of the Bush-Cheney administration, that former Senator Hart's extraordinarily valuable warning was ignored. Hart was the prototype victim of what Bill Clinton later called the "politics of personal destruction." Hart had been a serious contender for president and a national force in American politics until massive media coverage of his sexual misadventures provided a rehearsal for the later Monica Lewinsky affair. Long after the telephoto lenses refocused on others, an odor of sexual ridiculousness lingered around Senator Hart—and in the world of early-twenty-first-century Washington politics, the fact that a man had once been involved in a sex scandal disqualifies him from being taken seriously even when he utters a warning that could save thousands of lives.

There were many other warnings, some of them made directly to Vice President Cheney and to George W. Bush himself, before September 11. Even had there been no warning, the warning signs still would have been there. It didn't require Congressional hearings to alert Bush, Cheney, Rice, and Rumsfeld to the fact that Osama bin Laden had been one of America's top celebrity-enemies for years. The earlier twin bombings of the US embassies in Kenya and Tanzania had demonstrated Al Qaeda's penchant for synchronized attacks on pairs of US landmarks. Islamic terrorists had already attacked the World Trade Center once. An attempt to finish the job, combined with assaults on other iconic landmarks in the United States, should hardly have been beyond the realm of imagination in the White

House, the CIA, and the FBI. Then, in late February 2001, an even bigger hint of things to come flickered across America's TV screens. In Afghanistan, the Taliban dynamited the two Bamiyan Buddhas.

Juxtapose before-and-after images of the twin towers and the two Buddhas. The visual similarity between the two sets of doomed, giant, perpendicular monuments is striking. Together they amounted, in the perverted Al Qaeda–Taliban form of Islam, to monstrous and blasphemous symbols of idolatry on the one hand and usury on the other, which must be destroyed. Well before the 9/11 attacks, it was evident that Afghanistan was a source of weird emanations. What might happen next? Prior to 9/11, these were questions of utterly no interest to George W. Bush and his capos. They not only ignored such questions; they worked actively to stop them being asked.

Could things have turned out differently had someone else been president? Everyone is a prophet after the fact. Every mistake is avoidable once the disaster has occurred, but still it seems extraordinary that all across 2001, as the terrorist timebomb ticked away, George W. Bush's entire "security" establishment worked to stifle awareness of such a threat. Instead they remained obsessively focused on state-to-state confrontations with Saddam Hussein–like villains.

As a result of their carelessness, tens of thousands would die, both in the United States and in the Middle East—first, those whose lives were lost on September 11, then all those others who would perish later in George W. Bush's wildly misnamed "war on terror." Surely he could have done something? At least he could have done nothing. Looking back, we are left with the definite possibility that even had the administration itself done absolutely nothing, the attacks of September 11 still might conceivably have been thwarted. That is what the fate of the plane that went down over Pennsylvania on September 11 demonstrates. It didn't take long for the passengers on that flight to understand what needed to be done to defend their country. They didn't need "Star Wars" or a presidential pep talk. All they needed in order show real heroism—in order to really defend America—was the vaguest awareness of the true nature of the threat.

What if Americans, on the morning of September 11, had been just a little more alert at the car rental agencies, at the airport check-in desks, in the passenger cabins? One of the main reasons America was so unready on September 11 was that the George W. Bush administration hadn't done "nothing" prior to the attacks. It had worked aggressively to stifle public awareness of the terrorist threat that actually existed. What if George W. Bush, starting in January 2001, had heeded the warnings of the Commission on National Security? What if in his inaugural address he had called attention to the fact that unless the United States changed its idea of "national security," Americans truly would die "on American soil, possibly in large numbers"? One easily can imagine President Al Gore holding up the Hart-Rudman report at his press conferences while Governor George W. Bush and the Republicans snickered. But asking "what if" in this instance is like wondering why, if Middle East oil seems to be at the heart of so many problems, does George W. Bush never, ever, ask Americans to consume less gas?

The sight of the two towers of the World Trade Center smoking like overheated hard drives, then collapsing, will always be shocking. In fact US policy had facilitated the attacks. The terrorists who planned and executed them, for example, were not the agents of some "rogue state." Most of them were citizens of America's, and the Bush family's, great friend Saudi

Arabia—so, even as they plotted to murder thousands of people in America, the Saudi agents of Al Qaeda got special treatment in America. The US Immigration and Naturalization Service, as September 11 demonstrated, is as woefully pathetic at regulating foreign visits to the United States as the CIA and FBI are at counterterrorism. But that was not the essential reason why the terrorists who killed more than 3,000 people that day were free to rent cars, buy airplane tickets, and hijack airplanes without hindrance from the federal government. They were free to roam America as they pleased because Saudis—including terrorist Saudis—got the same kind of privileged treatment in George W. Bush's and Dick Cheney's America that Texas Republicans and Halliburton executives were accustomed to getting when they traveled over there.

It was in keeping with the ethos of unmerited reciprocity running through George W. Bush's whole life that even on September 11, concern for his Saudi friends and associates, including members of the bin Laden family, was high on his hidden agenda—"hidden" being exactly the right word here. As the attacks occurred, the Bush administration secretly took special care to ensure that citizens of Saudi Arabia, including relatives of Osama bin Laden, were not inconvenienced by the attacks their countrymen had just launched on Washington and New York. As hundreds of thousands of US citizens remained marooned at distant airports across the United States—and in Canada, which had generously (and bravely) thrown open its airspace to US planes—members of the bin Laden family, along with other well-connected Saudis, were granted a special exemption denied to Americans. A Saudis-only White House–approved secret airlift began.

From Washington to Boston their secret plane flew across the otherwise empty skies of America. Where in Boston, hours earlier, Saudis had hijacked the planes flown into the World Trade Center and the Pentagon, now other Saudis—unidentified men along with their uninspected documents and unopened baggage, but also Saudi rich kids who were being snatched out of their prep schools in the Boston area—boarded the plane. As it had been on the morning of September 11, so it was in the afternoon: No US official bothered to learn who they really were or what they were doing.

No American taxpayer could fly in or out of New York after the attacks. Kennedy, Newark, and LaGuardia airports were all closed to travel for Americans, but in zoomed the Saudis-only jet, to pick up members of the bin Laden family resident in SoHo and along Park Avenue in Manhattan. To Houston and LA—ten American cities in all—the plane carrying the Saudis wafted its way. Meanwhile, by the millions, Americans sat stranded on the ground, forbidden to travel on orders of the federal government. Only citizens of Saudi Arabia were permitted to travel in US airspace on September 11, 2001. By the end of the day, the White House–authorized secret flight had airlifted more than 140 Saudi citizens out of the United States, safely beyond the reach of American investigators.

Who boarded that plane? Why was it necessary for them to leave the United States so quickly? Can we know for sure that people implicated in the 9/11 attacks did not leave the United States on that plane? No passenger list was ever made available, but it is inconceivable that there were not on that plane people whose testimony could have provided information about how and why the 9/11 attacks occurred. Permitting the Saudi evacuation was the presidential version of tampering with evidence—but, of course, that was the kind of information George W. Bush wanted stifled from the start.

The very existence of the flight was something George W. Bush and those around him tried to keep secret. Then, when denial was no longer an option, a George W. Bush spokesman, as usual, passed the buck. The FBI had cleared the passenger list, the White House claimed, to which Special Agent John Iannarelli, the FBI's spokesman on counterterrorism, responded: "I can say unequivocally that the FBI had no role in facilitating these flights one way or another." Dale Watson, the FBI's former head of counterterrorism, explicitly confirmed that the Saudis permitted to fly out of the United States that day "were not subject to serious interviews or interrogations."

Incompetence followed by cover-up: That has always been the George W. Bush pattern—his truly passionate zeal for protecting the rich and defending the privileged propelling both the miscalculations and the lies.

The empathy he showed on September 11 for Osama bin Laden's family was the revelation of George W. Bush's visceral priorities—the priorities that would drive his whole presidency. The secret flight, White House sources eventually claimed, had been approved for humanitarian reasons. "High officials" in the White House, they said, had been concerned that members of the bin Laden family might be subjected to ill treatment. The extremely few attacks on Arabs and Arab-looking people following the 9/11 attacks was one of the most remarkable features of the admirable conduct of the American people on and after September 11. Concern that something unpleasant might befall bin Laden's relatives was of course understandable—but did Osama bin Laden's kith and kin really merit a level of presidential solicitude that families of his American victims were denied? No planes were sent out to crisscross the United States that afternoon, bringing relatives of those killed and missing at the World Trade Center to New York. Hundreds of policemen and firemen died that day. Their widows and orphans got no special treatment, not even a free bus ride to Ground Zero.

Thanks to George W. Bush's solicitude, the events of September 11 acquired symmetry. That morning, Saudis had taken to the air to attack the Pentagon and the World Trade Center. That afternoon, Saudis took to the air over America for a second time. The most traumatic day in America since the Kennedy assassination had begun with Saudis abusing their privileged position in America by committing mass murder. It ended with Saudis abusing their privileged position to avoid even being questioned about the crimes that had been committed. September 11 supposedly was the day "everything changed," but in the case of George W. Bush, nothing changed. Nothing ever would. A ferocious commitment to unearned privilege was knitted tightly into everything George W. Bush did before and after 9/11. On that memorable day, about the only thing George W. Bush did not do for his privileged Saudi friends was award them bonus frequent-flier miles.

Following the September 11 attacks, George W. Bush did not come immediately to New York to visit Ground Zero—though Ronald Reagan or Bill Clinton might have appeared on the scene the same day. Bush's absence at Ground Zero on September 12 was widely noticed. By September 13 it was starting to become a major news event. What could be more important than a presidential visit to Ground Zero? Yet by September 13, George W. Bush still had not made the short trip from Washington to New York. Instead he remained in Washington, among other things, in order to welcome Prince Bandar bin

Sultan, the Saudi ambassador to the United States, to the White House; he actually conferred with Prince Bandar, a member of the Saudi royal family, before he met Mayor Rudolph Giuliani and other New York officials. The ruins of the World Trade Center smoked, and the victims and their families went without the consolation of a presidential visit until September 14.

Preferential treatment for Saudis—including Saudis suspected of supporting terrorist activities—continued long after that. After 9/11 citizens of many Arab countries living in the United States were summarily ordered to present themselves for interrogation by the FBI. Saudis were explicitly exempted from this requirement. Meanwhile many Iraqis—most of them, ironically enough, fierce opponents of Saddam Hussein—along with other Arabs living in the United States, were rounded up. Some were held secretly, without right to bail, habeus corpus or defense attorneys. This was a violation of their human and legal rights, as well a diversionary waste of US government manpower and resources. It also was an early manifestation of the nutty logic propelling George W. Bush's decision to invade Iraq: The September 11 attacks had been plotted by Saudis. They'd been carried out by Saudis. Solution? Exempt Saudis from interrogation!

On the morning of September 11, 2001, all America's weapons systems, at a stroke, were shown to be a high-tech, multitrillion-dollar Maginot Line. The spies in the sky, the MIRVs in nuclear-powered submarines, the hydrogen bombs in their silos had provided no protection for America. The only people who did anything to defend America that day were unarmed civilians—the passengers aboard United Airlines flight 93 who, at the cost of their own lives, prevented the hijackers from hitting their fourth target. Meanwhile America's Commander in Chief, along with his vice president, national security adviser, and secretary of defense watched history happening on TV.

And then? As they had with the Hart-Rudman warning earlier, Bush and his capos began to figure the angles, to calculate the spin. They treated 9/11 as an event to be exploited politically, to be turned to their ideological purposes. Between September 2001 and March 2003 when he invaded Iraq, George W. Bush did what his administration earlier had done with *Road Map for National Security: Imperative for Change.* He tore up the road map; he ignored the imperative for change. The trajectory from 9/11 to Bombs Over Baghdad would be the predictable one: Whatever happens, keep pursuing our hidden agenda. Usurp every issue, turn every legitimate concern about the safety and prosperity of the American people to our purposes. And what are those purposes? Privilege and war, war and privilege, as George W. Bush's response to every issue invariably would show. As the ensuing distant-dictators diversion would demonstrate, the only thing 9/11 truly changed, for him, was that his agenda grew one item longer. To tax cuts and "Star Wars" an Iraq invasion was now definitely added.

VIII
The Anthrax Addendum

It is an honor, as President John Quincy Adams once remarked, for a citizen to serve as selectman of his own town, let alone as president of the United States. George W. Bush is both symptom and protagonist of an ongoing degradation of American public service—a dishonoring of honor in which millions of dollars are expended, and almost any political tactic is employed, in order to get installed in public office. Yet, once the prize is gained, what's the power for—to interfere with stem cell research? To block efforts to cope with global climate change? To make sure that cheap small arms—the real weapons of mass destruction—keep pouring into the poorest nations on earth, as well as into America's own slums and ghettos? To redistribute wealth upward, while using patriotism to divert attention from a policy of injustice?

For George W. Bush and his ilk, the US Constitution has no Preamble. They don't want a "more perfect union." Their goal is not to "establish justice, insure domestic tranquility," let alone "promote the general welfare." As he showed before and after 9/11 it is not on George W. Bush's agenda to "provide for the common defense." His agenda is to secure "the blessings of liberty to ourselves"—but only provided the words "blessings," "liberty," and especially, "ourselves," are given very privileged definitions. Ideologically committed to the boundless use of US government power to such overseas activities as creating a new political and social order in Iraq, George W. Bush remains committed to a "damned if" approach when it comes to promoting the general welfare of the American people—as in, "Damned if I'll help any poor kids." "Damned if I'll help any old folks."

There were many other things the US government under George W. Bush's leadership wasn't doing that morning of 9/11 when it wasn't protecting America from terrorist attack. It wasn't protecting the ozone layer or America's forests. It wasn't devising a fiscal system that, following the latest Wall Street bust, would balance out local and state revenues in the lean years to come. It wasn't preventing giant corporations—many of them contributors to Bush's own political treasury—from finding ways, far too many of them legal, to avoid paying any federal taxes at all. George W. Bush, however, cannot be accused of idleness during the time between his January inauguration and the morning of September 11, 2001. Without waiting for a great crisis to crash upon the scene, he had unleashed the petulant, nonstop outburst of offensive behavior that eventually would be gussied up by Condoleezza Rice, and then officially titled "The National Security Strategy of the United States of America." What more properly might be called the "Bush Middle-Finger Foreign Policy" had as its ideological foundation a meld of arrogance and ignorance, but what from the first gave it its uniquely nasty flavor was George W. Bush himself. Although from a very great distance, George W. Bush looked like an acceptable representative of the American nation, as he drew closer, the smirk about the mouth, the hostile glint in the eyes, became apparent. These, combined with the rippling ire of his response to even the most well-reasoned unwillingness to line up behind him and America 100 percent, no questions asked, angered and frightened people. It made them sense they were in the presence of an America that, until now, they had believed was part of dark, bygone history.

Later, one of George W. Bush's biggest boasts was that his rude behavior was somehow part of the "war on terrorism," a response to 9/11. In truth, his approach to America's "national security" had centered on insulting allies, embittering adversaries, and turning friends into foes from the day he took office. Even among our mildest, most faithful allies, George W. Bush provoked unprecedented reactions of hostility and resentment.

This Bush knack for making it absolutely clear to people that he has no respect for them was not limited to foreigners. Some members of his own Republican Party recognized early on there was something aberrant about Bush and his presidency. Among them was a member of the US Senate named James Jeffords who represents Vermont. On May 26, 2001, he called a press conference. Bush had been in the White House just over four months. That short time had been sufficient for Jeffords to measure the man and gauge the new climate of intolerance George W. Bush had brought with him to Washington.

In the past, Jeffords pointed out, the Republican Party had tolerated a diversity of views. "The election of President Bush changed that dramatically," he added. Jeffords went on to recall a time when the "Republican Party stood for opportunity for all, for opening the doors of public school education to every American child. Now," he added, referring to Bush and his radicals, "for some, success seems to be measured by the number of students moved out of the public schools." Senator Jeffords then made the announcement that turned this soft-spoken legislator from a very small state into Washington's biggest news story. "In order to best represent my state of Vermont, my own conscience, and principles I have stood for my whole life, I will leave the Republican Party." Jeffords was taking this courageous step because, as Jeffords himself put it, "control of the Senate will be changed by my decision." George W. Bush's "for us or against us" approach had produced its first big self-inflicted defeat: loss of the US Senate. Had he not been so intolerant of diversity, Republicans could have kept control. But Jeffords's departure gave the Democrats a one-vote majority.

In the run-up to the Iraq invasion, Bush would dwell obsessively on the existence of evil, but as the Jeffords incident was among the first to demonstrate, George W. Bush's biggest obstacle to achieving his goals would be the existence of good. On the podium at the United Nations, as well as on his fundraising-flag-waving tours, Bush talked as though if he could just rid the world of Saddam Hussein, Kim Jong Il and a few other "evil tyrants," the world would turn into all that he wanted it to be. But it was people like James Jeffords who would incur Bush's greatest ire as—at the UN, in NATO, and, sometimes, in America itself—they stood by their principles and refused to submit to his agenda.

Hans Blix, Kofi Annan, Gerhard Schröeder, Jacques Chirac, Jean Chrétien: Not just in Washington, but around the world, there was a growing honor roll of statesmen with the courage and self-confidence not to be bullied, even when the bully held the office of president of the United States. The giant among them all was Nelson Mandela, arguably the most respected man alive. In the years after 9/11, Nelson Mandela would be to the world what James Jeffords was to Washington politics. They would be joined by a host of distinguished people—along with millions of citizen-protesters.

Jeffords's decision to quit the Republican Party was the defining moment of the early George W. Bush presidency. Jeffords had been a loyal Republican member of Congress for twenty-six years; he had stuck with the Republicans even when the neocons reigned supreme. Why, after all this time, had he finally found his situation intolerable? As usual, George W. Bush passed the buck—this time to the Republicans' neocon (as in neo-Confederate) Senate leader, Trent Lott of Mississippi.

Iraq was the wedge issue that in 2003 would turn the majority of the world community against George W. Bush. In 2001, tax cuts for the rich were what finally drove Jeffords to switch sides. Bush's actions demonstrated from the beginning that people, principles, institutions, and alliances didn't matter. Nor did the consequences, so long as he got what he wanted—and George W. Bush did get his tax cut in 2001, just as later he'd get his Iraq war.

Starting in January 2001, George W. Bush launched a series of attacks on the structures of international peace. He, Cheney, and Rumsfeld crashed into the towering monuments of nuclear arms control, solidarity with our allies, and international respect for human rights, human justice, and the rule of law. Target after target was subjected to the assault—the Comprehensive Test Ban Treaty, the Kyoto Protocol to the United Nations Framework Convention on Climate Change, the International Criminal Court, the Biological Weapons Convention, the Convention on the Prohibition of the Use, Stockpiling, Production and Transfer of Anti-Personnel Mines and their Destruction, the Chemical Weapons Convention. In matter of months, George W. Bush trashed the work of decades.

What triumph of negativity awaited him next? The answer

was the Anti–Ballistic Missile, or ABM, Treaty. In the months leading up to 9/11, Bush strove hard to start a new Cold War. The centerpiece of his campaign to humiliate Russia and anger its president, Vladimir Putin, was his insistence on renouncing the ABM Treaty. Dating back to the days of Nixon and Brezhnev, the ABM agreement was one of great arms control achievements of the era of détente. That is to say, it was one of those agreements that—going way back to their 1975 Halloween Massacre under President Ford—Dick Cheney and Donald Rumsfeld had hoped to undo. They had waited more than twenty-five years for their chance. Now it came, and with George W. Bush's enthusiastic approval, they grabbed it.

Taking apart the ABM Treaty was a major escalation of what truthfully could be called George W. Bush's "war on peace." Refusing to ratify arms control treaties, walking out of negotiations aimed at defending the environment, blocking the prosecution of war criminals—like stymying agreements aimed at protecting the United States from chemical and biological attack—all manifested George W. Bush's deep need to show contempt for the world and efforts to make it peaceful. Now he prepared to go a giant step further. Not even the wicked Communists had ever renounced a nuclear-arms-control treaty. It amounted to a signal from George W. Bush that the rule of law didn't matter in international relations, as far as he was concerned. It was his way of announcing that the United States, now that he was in charge, would stop leading the struggle for an international rule of law, and become an outlaw state itself.

He could not have picked a more fitting target. The ABM Treaty was not just a solemn legal commitment, or a set of specific agreements. It was one of the cornerstones of the still very imperfect international order of peace on which every

American president, including George H. W. Bush, had labored for fifty years. The ABM Treaty was part of the fragile fabric of restraint that for all the world's dangers had saved America from nuclear holocaust for nearly two generations. Now George W. Bush proposed ripping that fabric. As usual, he seized upon a trivial pretext for doing great harm. As he explained it, the ABM Treaty had to be junked because it blocked development of the radical Republicans' favorite military-industrial extravaganza, "Star Wars."

Though research on "Star Wars" had started under Ronald Reagan, the ABM treaty never posed a problem until George W. Bush took office. Until then, the constitutional separation of powers had prevented enough money for "Star Wars" from getting into the Pentagon's budget to pay for the kinds of tests that would violate the ABM Treaty. But now the Republican radicals in Congress had voted the money, and a radical president was eager to start spending it on the multitrillion-dollar system. As 9/11 was about to show, developing "Star Wars" had about as much relevance to defending America as banging on kettledrums and firing buckshot at the moon. But "Star Wars" was what George W. Bush, Cheney, and Rumsfeld wanted. It defined their idea of power.

The repudiation of the ABM Treaty showed the Russians, the Europeans, and everyone else that control of the destructive might of the United States had fallen into the hands of people who were out of control. It showed what Kim Jong Il in North Korea, the hard-line Iranian ayatollahs, and who knows how many other tyrants and regimes all recognized immediately. With George W. Bush in the saddle, possession of nuclear weapons was a very prudent insurance policy. Nothing else seemed likely to make George W. Bush think twice, or at all, when his ire strayed in your direction. With his renunciation of the Anti–Ballistic Missile Treaty, George W. Bush spat on the grave of détente. He also waved a checkered flag at tyrants and terrorists everywhere: Let the new nuclear arms race begin!

"Star Wars"—or what the Wolfowitz types prefer to call the "Strategic Defense Initiative"—is aimed at producing an American missile able to stop an enemy missile before it reaches the United States. Hitting a bullet with a bullet—or rather, hitting dozens of bullets, along with thousands of decoys—is something no one knows how to do. It may be technologically impossible to do on a scale and with a reliability sufficient to justify the expense of trying even to produce the prototype of such a system. Could a "Star Wars"–type antimissile prevent a nuclear bomb reaching its target in the container of a ship sailing past the Statue of Liberty in New York, or in the back of some SUV with tinted windows driving past the White House in Washington? The next time you take an overnight car trip along the Interstates, notice all those RVs passing you in the darkness. Any one of them could carry a bomb big enough to kill everyone in Richmond, Virginia, or Toledo, Ohio, or downtown Washington, D.C., or wherever it is you're heading. That's the real threat we face.

In 2002, George W. Bush's Washington got a tiny foretaste of what could happen when a country has a government that is simply uninterested in developing defense systems that actually protect us. The Washington area was terrorized by two men, one of them a teenager, randomly sniping at people through a hole in the trunk of their car. Thanks to the globalization and democratization of technology—including the technology of mass destruction—it is entirely possible for two guys to do the same thing using a dirty nuclear weapon. The great revelation of 9/11 was that it doesn't take an "evil empire" or even a nasty tyrant to menace America anymore, because a great civilization's strengths are sometimes inseparable from its weaknesses. In America, anybody is free to go to any airport, to get on any airplane, and to fly anywhere he wants, and on 9/11 that's exactly what happened.

Freedom is America's glory, also its Achilles' heel. How to deal with that daunting paradox? What America needed most after 9/11 was precisely what George W. Bush is still striving to prevent: a practical understanding of how and why the attacks happened, leading to a practical understanding of how such events might be prevented or at least countered in the future. In the age of globalization, is there any way to monitor the contents of the sea-, land-, and airborne cargos flooding into the United States without disrupting America's economy? What changes in US foreign policy are most likely to discourage critics of America from turning into terrorists? At home, can we find ways to ensure respect for civil liberties while also making sure our freedoms are not abused for terrorist purposes? These are difficult questions with expensive answers—but not nearly as difficult and expensive as developing "Star Wars" or invading Iraq.

On many different levels, 9/11 gave George W. Bush the chance to reevaluate his approach to the world. Two and a half months later, at the end of December 2001—in spite of all that had happened—he went ahead and repudiated the ABM Treaty. To date, only one other statesman, Kim Jong Il of North Korea, has chosen to repudiate a nuclear-arms-control agreement. That leaves the rest of us on this planet to live with the curious coincidence that so far, only the unelected sons of former presidents of their respective countries have chosen to tear up treaties designed to prevent nuclear catastrophe.

In light of the vulnerabilities the attacks revealed, the US government might well have spent billions, if not trillions, of dollars trying to devise mechanisms capable of preventing US seaports and airports from being used for nuclear or biological attack. But it never happened; the appropriations were never even proposed. The budget for the Department of Homeland Security would be less than George W. Bush's slush fund for postinvasion Iraq because of something else 9/11 did not change. Getting government to work better had not been a priority for George W. Bush before September 11 and it did not become one afterwards. Instead of trying to find out what had gone wrong so that he could fix it, Bush fought the creation of a bipartisan panel to assemble the facts surrounding the security failure of 9/11. He is still fighting to prevent its findings from being released to the public. He also opposed the creation of the new Department of Homeland Security. Then, when it became politically inexpedient to oppose it any longer, he turned the new department into a joke by leaving out of it the two federal agencies most directly responsible for homeland security. After 9/11, as before, the FBI and the CIA would remain largely, and in the most crucial cases, entirely exempt from accountability. They would remain free to go on pursuing agendas that, like George W. Bush's own, had little, and then only coincidental, relevance to the cause of making America safe.

As always, when trying to understand why George W. Bush does something, the search for an explanation leads first into an elusive world where spin merges into ideology, thence into a darker miasma of hostilities and resentments whose origins, wherever they may lie, are certainly not to be found in the events George W. Bush uses as the pretext for his actions. In the end, we are left with fact: After September 11, as well as before, his actions continued to show that a safer America was, for George W. Bush, like a more just America, or a less polluted America, like an America that respected international law. It simply did not figure on his agenda. Nothing he did after 9/11 made America significantly safer, even when his administration advised Americans to stock up on duct tape. Most of what he did in the name of preventing "another 9/11"—combined with what he prevented others from doing—amounted in the aggregate to a policy of continuing reckless endangerment.

September 11 had unfolded with Sophoclean majesty. Then, as a kind of absurd addendum to that horror, America's vulnerability took sitcom form. Anthrax started appearing in envelopes addressed to a members of Congress, as well as ordinary citizens. The point that had already been made on September 11—that America couldn't defend itself—was now rubbed in with anthrax. It wasn't just the CIA, the FBI, and the Department of Defense that were impotent and incompetent, events now showed. The United States Postal Service, too, was powerless to protect Americans—from paying with their lives for opening their mail. Yet again, on George W. Bush's watch something happened for the first time since the British attacks during the War of 1812. America's federal legislators were forced to flee Capitol Hill—this time to avoid anthrax spores, not British musket fire.

It was as though Destiny had peered down at George W. Bush's obliviousness, and said: "Well, if jet airliners smashing into the World Trade Center can't make you think, maybe deadly white powder in little envelopes will bestir you from your arrogant complacence." But here George W. Bush's response combined incompetence with indifference. The same George W. Bush superstars of intelligence who later couldn't find Osama bin Laden likewise couldn't track down the anthrax perpetrator. An "intelligence" community with a multibillion dollar annual budget and a zero-for-zero batting average no more caused George W. Bush to rethink his priorities than the attacks of 9/11 had.

As always, Dick Cheney found even in this home-grown American terrorism the means to further his own far-flung agenda. Just as the CIA knew from the beginning that Saddam Hussein and Iraq had nothing to do with the 9/11 attacks, FBI investigators very early on came to the conclusion that the anthrax attacks had nothing to do with Osama bin Laden or Al Qaeda. Quite probably, they concluded, the anthrax perpetrator was a native-born white professional American male living on the east coast of the United States. Quite possibly he was a medical expert and an employee of the federal government. What the federal investigators did not know was how to find and apprehend this particular American, and then prove in a court of law what he had done.

As with Iraq's supposed weapons of mass destruction two years later, Cheney used the absence of any evidence that bin Laden and Al Qaeda were to blame for the anthrax attacks as proof that the United States should act on the assumption that they were. On October 12, 2001, just a month after the Al Qaeda attacks, in an appearance on PBS's *News Hour,* Cheney attempted to portray the recent anthrax attacks as part of an outside terrorist conspiracy. Cheney used the very fact that US intelligence findings failed to support his arguments to buttress a rambling series of observations that stumbled along, leading his audience with him until—presto!—the only patriotic and right-minded thing to do was to defend America by starting a war in the Middle East.

An extended quote helps reveal the fatuity of Cheney's

reasoning. "We've had this ongoing disclosure now of anthrax problems," he observed. "Are they related?" he asked rhetorically, in response to a question from Jim Lehrer as to whether the anthrax attacks were related to the 9/11 attacks or not. Cheney went on to recite the obfuscating litany that would become so familiar in the run-up to the Iraq invasion: "We know that Osama bin Laden and the Al Qaeda Organization clearly have already launched an attack that killed thousands of Americans. We know that for years he's been the source of terrorist attacks against the United States overseas, our embassies in East Africa in '98—the USS *Cole* last year, probably, in Yemen. We know that he has over the years tried to acquire weapons of mass destruction, both biological and chemical weapons. We know that he's trained people in his camps in Afghanistan, for example; we have copies of the manuals that they've actually used to train people with respect to how to deploy and use these kinds of substances. So, you start to piece it all together. Again, we have not completed the investigation and maybe it's coincidence, but I must say I'm a skeptic."

"A skeptic?" Lehrer asked, giving Cheney the opening he needed to say: "I think the only responsible thing for us to do is proceed on the basis that they could be linked"—that is, work on the assumption that the anthrax attacks were the work of Osama bin Laden, too. One of the facts Cheney did not include in his "we know" litany is that the anthrax used in the attacks was manufactured in the United States for the US military. Proposing, contrary to the evidence, that the United States "proceed on the basis" that 9/11 and the anthrax attacks were linked helped Cheney shepherd along his war plans. It also diverted attention from the real linkage: The anthrax attacks, too, flowed from a monumental foul-up of US government operations, an appalling breach of American security. Someone had been not been minding the store when that white powder was lifted from its US warehouse, just as someone had not been watching the skies on September 11. And whose job was it to guard federal warehouses, to keep our skies safe? This was a question Jim Lehrer apparently did not consider germane to the discussion.

What did George W. Bush himself make of these two great national security disasters, coming one right after the other, while he supposedly was in charge? At this point, somebody—almost anybody—other than George W. Bush might well have said to himself: Instead of plotting to invade Iraq, I might perhaps better spend my time trying to get my own government to work a little better. Instead, the anthrax failure, like all the other failures, would be obscured by the creation of new diversionary crises. But before it became part of the post-9/11 blur, the anthrax attacks showed, with the same clarity 9/11 itself had, just how incompetent the US government was to protect Americans, and how little George W. Bush cared—and, of course, yet again, how deft Dick Cheney was at moving events in the direction he wanted them to go.

George W. Bush never would make any serious, consistent, or meaningful effort to impede a recurrence of the September 2001 attacks. He never would confront the organizational crisis of American government which first made him president, and then allowed Osama bin Laden's attack to succeed. Instead, in the name of "preventing another 9/11," he would compound the catastrophe by invading Iraq, a country as uninvolved in the September 11 attacks as Al Qaeda was in the anthrax attacks. Meanwhile he would continue to cover up his own administration's failure to protect America's security. Whether the threat was external or internal—the villain some Islamic fanatic, or just some Made in America sociopath—was of no concern to George W. Bush so long as the buck never stopped with him.

IX
Sins of the Sons

EVERYONE HAD KNOWN THERE were people who hated and wanted to harm America. But until 9/11, who understood how much America was loved?

WE ARE ALL AMERICANS. That was what the French newspaper *Le Monde* proclaimed the morning after the attacks. The upwelling of sympathy, love, and support for the United States and its people was worldwide. America at heart was a good country; it did not deserve this. On that, the most implacable enemies agreed. From his office in Ramallah, on the West Bank, Yasser Arafat denounced "this heinous attack." So did Ariel Sharon. Nowhere was the spontaneous upsurge of support stronger than at the headquarters of the North Atlantic Treaty Organization in Brussels—the same NATO headquarters whose funding Donald Rumsfeld would soon threaten to cut unless they stopped the chatter about punishing war criminals.

For fifty years, NATO had existed in order to ensure that the United States would protect Europe if it were attacked. Now America had been attacked—and without having to be asked, the member nations of NATO, every one of them, pledged to treat the attack upon the United States as an attack upon themselves. It was the first time in history that this provision of the treaty was invoked. This, truly, was "collective security"—the weaker rallying to the defense of the stronger, not just the other way around.

The worldwide wave of support for America evoked by the 9/11 attacks gave George W. Bush a historic opportunity to empower America and transform himself. Teddy Roosevelt had called the presidency and its power to determine how Americans see themselves and look at the world the "bully pulpit." Washington and Lincoln had used it to enormous effect long before it got that name. Kennedy's "pay any price" inaugural address was one of the most dramatic uses of it ever. Now George W. Bush had his chance. As if driven by a continuing inner necessity, he turned an occasion for majesty into one of spite, and ever since has given the "bully" in "bully pulpit" his own gratuitously antagonistic spin, using it to make sure Americans forget the love extended to them, while keeping the hate going. He has been so adept at warping the meaning of 9/11 that now, when they look back, what do Americans remember? In George W. Bush's own words, they remember only that: "Today, our nation saw evil, the very worst of human nature."

Instead of using 9/11 as the pretext for a series of ideological and military vendettas, George W. Bush could have seized the occasion to mobilize a sympathetic world in a meaningful effort to fight terrorism and its causes. With the right leadership, America might have gone on to lead the world in a serious attempt to grapple with other great problems requiring solutions on a global scale. This was more than something nice or noble to do. It was a strategic necessity: 9/11 had revealed how reckless and foolish it was to imagine the United States could ever spurn collective security and go it alone.

After 9/11, the world was eager to respond to a new kind of American leadership. But in order to become that new kind of leader, George W. Bush would have had to reappraise his view of the world. Instead, George W. Bush's obsession with "regime change"—symptoms rather than causes—continued, even though the 9/11 attacks had demonstrated something of enormous importance. The Saddam Husseins of the world were no longer the greatest threat. Power vacuums—like the power vacuum created in Afghanistan when the place was abandoned after the fall of the Soviet-backed regime there—were even more dangerous. Dictators, after all, can be held accountable if their lands and weapons are misused. That explained, among other things, why Saddam Hussein had played no role in the 9/11 attacks. It was also why, following the attacks, dictators like Qaddafi in Libya were so eager to prove they posed no danger.

A fundamental revision of America's strategic priorities would have been necessary whatever the circumstances. There was hardly an item on George W. Bush's ideological or strategic agenda that had not been called into question by the success of the September 11 attacks. "Star Wars" was shown to be utterly irrelevant. Even so George W. Bush, in the aftermath, has kept insisting that spending go on, and up, for the useless antimissile missile. In the aftermath of 9/11, "Star Wars" should have been scrapped altogether. Instead, George W. Bush and Rumsfeld irresponsibly went ahead and deployed the missiles, which never hit their targets and sometimes fired wildly. Citing these deficiencies as the reason for even more spending on the useless system, they then went on to allocate more money for "Star Wars" than for the entire reconstruction effort in New York and Washington, and for compensation for all the victims of the attacks, combined.

More than anything else, 9/11 illustrated the perils of George W. Bush's absolute refusal to do anything serious about reducing America's dependence on imported oil. After 9/11 the addiction only got worse. The problem is not, as his critics in the 2004 political campaign contend, that George W. Bush has refused to have an energy policy. The problem is that he does have one: a policy that aims to needlessly consume as much energy as possible, regardless of the consequences—while falsely portraying advocates of rational energy use as shirkers in the "war on terrorism."

The malign effects of America's prodigal use of energy, especially of energy derived from petroleum production, are economic, environmental, social, political, and military. But as with most addictions, the consequences go deeper. US overdependence on oil affects Americans in their bodies and in some ways can be said to affect their souls. It has worked its way into the neurons and viscera of American life.

An America that depended less on cars, for example, might be a nation in which chronic obesity is less of a problem. An America less dependent on car payments might not have become a nation where personal debt overhangs the country's prosperity like an impending avalanche. A nation of people who walk more, use less air-conditioning and rub up a little more against their neighbors in shared public spaces, might also conceivably be an America where the politics of paranoia plays a smaller role. It's also conceivable that if Americans spent less of their lives sitting in isolated cubicles—some stationary, others mobile—they might be less divorced from the realities of the world, and not so apathetic about misuses of power by their own government.

But as George W. Bush proclaimed after 9/11, the American Way of Life is "nonnegotiable." For him forests are for snowmobiling, not thoughtful walks in the snow. What the Conestoga wagon once was to America, the SUV is to George W. Bush's oil-addicted idea of the American Way of Life. Enclosed in a climate-controlled, tinted-windowed, surround-sound gas-guzzler, the driver of the SUV is a little like George W. Bush aboard Air Force One: free to imagine himself master of the universe. Who cares that the SUV is only a station wagon pretending to be a tough guy, that the strategic objective is the mall, not Baghdad? As for those news reports that some of that gas money you pay at the pump goes to people who kill Americans, no problem there, either. Grab the remote. Press "Mute." By the way, that great 4x4 traction means you don't have to shovel the driveway.

Before 9/11 the SUV was already the symptom vehicle of America's energy addiction. After the invasion of Iraq, it proved—like America's weapons systems—not to be sufficiently expensive to acquire and run. Something even larger, something that consumed even more money and energy, was needed now that George W. Bush's widening wars and deepening deficits were providing the template for Americans and their approach to life.

As in Iraq, so on our Interstates: Defense Department spending came to the rescue. The even bigger and more cumbersome vehicle Americans needed at home turned out to be the Hummer. Adapted by General Motors, this was a civilianized version of the same monster-on-wheels Humvee military vehicle that was constantly rolling over, sliding into culverts, and also killing Americans in Iraq by flipping off bridges into rivers. During the Thanksgiving–Christmas holiday of 2003, the Associated Press ran two stories with the following headlines:

> 6 US SOLDIERS HAVE DIED OVER WEEKEND
> GM UNVEILS MIDSIZE HUMMER CONCEPT

In Iraq, according to the first report, the Humvee was turning into a death trap for GIs. Its soft skin made it vulnerable to rocket and rifle attack. When it stalled in traffic, Iraqis were able hop aboard and slit the throats of soldiers. Americans in Iraq were also getting killed just the way tens of thousands get killed back home: by slamming gargantuan vehicles into each other.

Half the US war fatalities that Thanksgiving weekend were traffic-related. According to the AP report, "Two soldiers from the 1st Armored Division were killed and another was injured when an M-1 Abrams tank crashed into their Humvee west of Baghdad Saturday night. And a soldier drowned," the report continued, "when his vehicle fell into a canal while he was pursuing a suspicious vehicle near Balad. The soldier was with the 4th Infantry Division." No names of the dead were given; there was no way of knowing their hometowns. The wire services had stopped providing that kind of information around the same time the Bush-Cheney media manipulation folks started forbidding the press to take photographs of the flag-draped coffins of dead GIs being offloaded from military planes when their bodies got home to America.

The story about the "Midsize Hummer Concept" reported a development related to those weekend deaths in Iraq (though the relationship wasn't reported, and few casual readers would have noticed it). "With a mix of muscle and sizzle," the report noted, "the Hummer has become America's new status ride, attracting celebrities and athletes who aren't bothered by its steep sticker price and gas mileage that barely rises above single digits."

That had been true for some time. The new development was that GM was thinking about diversifying its consumer model of the military vehicle originally developed at US taxpayers' expense for occupying countries like Iraq. This led to the possibility of an exiting new George W. Bush–style trickledown benefit for the American middle class. The problem for the kinds of American taxpayers whose votes George W. Bush needed in the 2004 election wasn't just the mileage the Hummer got. It was the sticker price, which started at $100,000.

The "midsize concept vehicle," in contrast, promised more affordable "muscle and sizzle." Though "built on a modified GM midsize truck platform," snazz had not been sacrificed to some liberal concept of frugality. The prototype, according to AP, was "powered by a 350-horsepower, five-cylinder turbocharged engine," and featured "a power-operated folding canvas sunroof and drop-down rear window to offer open-air driving." In order to bolster the illusion that driving around in this still-enormous vehicle with the power-operated sunroof open was actually a form of exercise, "designers from sports apparel giant Nike Inc. collaborated on several aspects of the vehicle, including its tires and seats."

The Iraq invasion is the prime example of how Bush defended America abroad. The midsized Hummer perfectly illustrated how the George W. Bush consumer chain was supposed to operate, right here at home. Step One: Invading foreign countries with bad roads requires the Defense Department to develop Hummer-like vehicles for our troops to use. Step

Two: Giant corporations like General Motors ("What's good for GM is good for America") translate that military equipment into consumer items for civilians to buy. Step Three: American taxpayers get to pay for these gargantuan, polluting, dangerous behemoths all over again, but this time they get to keep them in their garages.

There remains the subliminal concern (spread by the liberal think tanks and news networks) that driving to the corner Seven-Eleven in gigantic converted trucks is unhealthful for the people who buy them, and that it pollutes America too. Step Four: Healthy cross-branding with sports marketers like Nike takes care of that. Suppose this dangerous elitist toy actually gets produced? Wouldn't even a midsize Hummer break the budget of most middle-class Americans?

This is where George W. Bush's "compassionate conservatism" enters the big picture. He'll give you a tax break for buying a Hummer. In fact George W. Bush already has done his part by exempting the Hummer from taxes imposed on more affordable cars that consume less gas more efficiently. Like his financial rewards ("vouchers") for families who take their kids out of public schools, like his zero-tolerance policy toward inheritance taxes for the sons of wealthy, famous fathers, and like his legislation forbidding federal health care agencies from bargaining for lower prices with the giant pharmaceutical corporations, it's part of George W. Bush's economic stimulus plan to help the average, hard-working people of America by getting government off their backs. In fact the more expensive your vehicle, and the more gas it consumes, the bigger the tax break you get. But wait, things get even better. Since 9/11, George W. Bush has actually increased the tax exemption you get for buying such wasteful vehicles, and with your support he will make even more tax breaks for people who pay almost no taxes anyway part of his 2004 election campaign.

How did the Hummer tax break slip through? This tax break for road hogs was sold to Congress as part of George W. Bush's compassionate commitment to encouraging the survival of our endangered American family farms. The spin was that tax exemptions for small trucks, such as the kind used to haul around farm equipment, would encourage free enterprise in our rural communities. Things did not turn out that way. The reason, according to a Taxpayers for Common Sense white paper titled "A Hummer Of A Tax Break," is that "The tax code defines industrial vehicles by weight instead of function."

If the SUV you buy weighs more than 6,000 pounds, you're entitled to a George W. Bush tax break, even if your use of it is entirely recreational. It's not just Hummers. "Currently," the white paper notes, "there are 38 different luxury passenger SUVs, vans and trucks including the Lincoln Navigator, Cadillac Escalade, and the new Hummer H2, which weigh more than 6,000 pounds and therefore qualify for tax breaks."

"Hummer sales," note the authors of the white paper, Aileen Roder and Lucas Moinester, "have been skyrocketing since last year's deduction increase." Such vehicles waste energy and degrade our highway infrastructure at home. "There is also the argument," they diffidently observe, "that in these times of uncertainty in the Middle East, it does not make sense to encourage the purchase of fuel-inefficient vehicles, enhancing our dependence on oil producing nations."

George W. Bush—the Commander in Chief who gives tax breaks for Hummers in wartime—is himself a manifestation of what happens when oil addles a culture the way alcohol saturates the brain. It's a two-way street: oil consumption and oil production, and the deformities they produce at both ends. Osama bin Laden also is a product of the extractive world of global oil. So it has come to pass that in the first decade of the third millennium, some of the most dramatic events in current world history can be read, if only in comic-book form, as a grudge match between two overprivileged, out-of-control children of the Age of Energy Addiction.

Oil brings wealth; it seldom seems to teach its beneficiaries the value of work or the importance of tolerance. It does seem to provoke a need for grandiose gestures. When wealth and power come like gifts from God, they also foster the delusion among some people that their prejudices, their hatreds—and their crimes—have divine sanction. Perhaps because there is no legitimate, explicable reason for why these privileged few should be the beneficiaries of such good fortune, it also seems to excite a need to prove things to people, to show off.

You see this in Saudis like Osama bin Laden; you see it in Americans like George W. Bush. Of course, when one feels entitled to everything, including a world that corresponds to your doctrinal or ideological requirements, and anything is missing from that perfect picture, the response is more likely to be outrage than stoical acceptance. In extreme cases, the need for a reality warp arises. So Osama bin Laden decides the way to deal with the corruption of Islam in Saudi Arabia is to blow up skyscrapers in New York. George W. Bush decides the way to deal with a failure of airport security in Boston is to invade Iraq.

One way of understanding George W. Bush's behavior in the White House is to look at it as a TV series. The series might be called *The W Files*. In every episode, some apparently stable and explicable situation—the proceedings of the Electoral College; the verification procedures of international arms inspectors—

turns out to have a *Twilight Zone* quality that allows it to be transformed in such a way that reality is adjusted to conform to the requirements of George W. Bush.

At the opening of the 9/11 episode in the series, events demonstrate that George W. Bush's intolerant, profligate, and divisive approach to the world is wrong and dangerous. The challenge for the scriptwriters—the Wolfowitzes, the Cheneys, with spell-checking by Condoleezza Rice—is, by the end of the episode, to transform a refutation of George W. Bush's strategic and ideological fantasies into a vindication of what he's been telling us all along.

This is what happened, in essence, on America's TV screens between September 2001 and March 2003, when George W. Bush invaded Iraq. But this weird counterfactual transformation would never be a complete success. This was because 9/11 presented George W. Bush with a far more difficult—and very different—reality challenge than the results of the voting in Florida had. In that case it was only democracy in America that had to be transmuted for his convenience. It would be a much larger and harder task transforming the reality that Saddam Hussein had nothing to do with the 9/11 attacks into the justification for attacking him. Another inconvenient reality was that invading Iraq would not fight terrorism, but encourage terrorism, so that had to be fixed too. Finally there was the reality that the United States was going to invade Iraq not because of what Saddam Hussein had done, but because of who George W. Bush was. Dramatic plot twists—confrontations at the UN, for example; the sudden discovery of an axis of evil—would be required.

There was, however, an additional problem that putting Nike logos on Hummer tires could not solve. The reality-manipulation techniques of the White House, the Republican Party and the neocon apparatchiks, which worked so brilliantly on Americans, weren't nearly as effective outside the United States. In fact they often failed entirely. The problem was that foreigners showed a perverse insistence on clinging to reality even when important Americans like Rumsfeld, Cheney, Rice—even George W. Bush himself—took the trouble to fly all the way over there and tell them what to think. Faced with this obstinate insistence on putting reality instead of America first, George W. Bush in the end would simply have to go ahead and invade Iraq, as he had wanted to do all along anyway, all by himself.

Even getting to that unilateralist happy ending of the episode, however, would not be easy. For a year and a half, George W. Bush was unable to invade Iraq because, after 9/11, something very disconcerting happened. He and his capos not only lost control of events, they lost their ability to make global events seem to justify their military and ideological requirements. More than that, as the tidal wave of love, support, and cooperation engulfed Americans after 9/11, George W. Bush and his crowd were forced to modify their behavior. For a brief period, they were obliged to act in a responsible, reasonable way—to consult with allies, to take a bipartisan approach in Congress, to embrace multilateralism.

It was tough. With even those Paris-intellectual editors of *Le Monde* proclaiming "We Are All Americans," who was there to despise any more in Europe? The ex-Soviets were useless. After 9/11, Bush not only went ahead and renounced the Anti–Ballistic Missile (ABM) Treaty, he and Rumsfeld projected US military power deep into the underbelly of the former Soviet Union. Just like the French and Germans, the neocommissars of Kazakhstan, Uzbekistan, and the other former soviet republics of Central Asia threw open their arms, and air bases, to the Americans. And what was Putin's reaction? A big Russian bear hug for George W. Bush: Welcome to the War on Terrorism! Want to help us out in Chechnya too?

Overnight the biggest of all the "stans"—Pakistan—flipped to the American side. Pakistan had been the Taliban's longtime supporter. This was a legacy of the fact that the Taliban and Osama bin Laden himself were former allies of the United States. Osama had started out fighting his jihad with American weapons supplied through Pakistan. He had started out fighting Satan as an ally of the CIA in the US-supported insurgency against the Soviet-installed regime in Afghanistan. After America's attention wandered elsewhere, Osama bin Laden continued to use the Pakistan connection. He could not have operated out of Afghanistan the way he did before 9/11 without Pakistani complaisance, at least. Yet now Pakistan's dictator, Gen. Pervez Musharraf, who had seized power in a military coup less than two years earlier, announced that he too was a friend of freedom. Normally anything Pakistan does, India opposes. But even the Indians were absolutely delighted to see Rumsfeld getting off the plane in New Delhi, his briefcase bulging with proposals for military cooperation.

Would no one give George W. Bush the chance to be irate? Certainly not the Chinese. He had spent his first six months in the White House playing video war games with the Chinese, among other things. Now all that talk about treating China as a "potential strategic rival" was forgotten as the cries of "We Love America!" resounded from the Forbidden City to the Halls of Moctezuma, in every language from Tagalog to Basque. Even Fidel Castro offered to throw open Cuban airspace to US military overflights, the better to help George W. Bush scour the earth for terrorists (and to prove he wasn't harboring any himself).

Soon Castro himself—thanks to US use of its base at Guantánamo Bay to hold prisoners in metal cages without trial or legal representation—would become George W. Bush's de facto ally in the "war on terrorism."

There was simply no way to use 9/11 as a wedge issue, and—judging by his facial grimaces and the whine in his voice—having to cope with that fact was disconcerting for George W. Bush. He couldn't fully express his natural meanspiritedness until the run-up to Iraq war. Only when he at last had the faithless allies on the Security Council to accuse of supporting terrorism, and millions of antiwar demonstrators to compare to focus groups, did he seem, once again, to be his normal self.

The idea that a person's psychological idiosyncrasies can explain his impact on history is as widespread now as belief in phrenology was in the nineteenth century. By the time he made his "dead or alive" comment, speculation was bubbling about the nature of George W. Bush's psyche. Since then it has only increased.

When someone seems constantly to be acting for reasons other than those he claims, people begin to wonder. When those actions include such things as invading Afghanistan and then invading Iraq, and the person involved is both the son of a president of the United States, and an occupant of that office himself, you start getting a variant of the Kennedy assassination speculation syndrome. Something so immense as killing Kennedy could not have happened just because a little misfit named Lee Harvey Oswald shot him with a rifle, people tell themselves. People naturally need to believe that big events with far-reaching results have big, convoluted explanations, so the conspiracy theorists start to spin their tales. Or at least the amateur psychohistorians do.

Let's assume George W. Bush actually does have what, in the current idiom, are called "issues" with his father. So did Hamlet, Oedipus, and many other sons of famous, powerful fathers, even before Doctors Ruth and Phil came on the scene. Does that really explain why Alexander the Great conquered the world? It would appear that, in some way, George W. Bush's behavior actually does have something to do with his relationship with his distinguished father. Both the broad similarities in their lives and the sharp divergences are too striking to ignore. From prep school to the White House, George W. Bush's résumé is almost a photocopy of his father's. But where the older Bush strove for consensus; George W. Bush loves to divide. The first Bush president played by the rules; his son scorns the rulebook. In 1991, the elder Bush stopped at Kuwait. His son has gone all the way.

The bottom line of the elder Bush's résumé? After all the high-mindedness, the first Bush gets defeated for re-election in 1992, which brings us to George W. Bush in 2004. Whether it's a matter of intergenerational rivalry—or only a divergence of political tactics—you can be sure George W. Bush's eye never strays far from his father's defeat, and the question of what he can do to avoid the same political fate.

Then there are the non-Freudian explanations for George W. Bush's behavior. Take a look at the following list of traits, provided by an Iowa health care professional:

Exaggerated self-importance and pomposity
Grandiose behavior
A rigid, judgmental outlook
Impatience
Childish behavior

Irresponsible behavior
Irrational rationalization
Projection
Overreaction

Most people who are not partisan supporters of George W. Bush would agree he manifests those characteristics more than most people—certainly more than has been considered up until now appropriate for someone holding the office of president of the United States.

As is very well-known, George W. Bush had a drinking problem until, at 40, he stopped drinking entirely. The spokesmen and spinners don't use the words "alcoholic" and "alcoholism" when describing this key event of his life, but according to Professor Katherine van Wormer, co-author of *Addiction Treatment: A Strengths Perspective*, George W. Bush has the profile of a "dry drunk." "Dry drunk," she explains, "is a slang term used by members and supporters of Alcoholics Anonymous and substance abuse counselors to describe the recovering alcoholic who is no longer drinking, one who is dry, but whose thinking is clouded. Such an individual is said to be dry but not truly sober. Such an individual tends to go to extremes."

Such explanations are like saying that Ronald Reagan authorized the disastrous and illegal arms-for-hostages trade with the Iranians because he may have had incipient Alzheimer's. They may possibly explain why Reagan acted in certain ways. They may even explain why George W. Bush—now "drunk on power"—starts wars the way some drunks pick fights in bars. They do not, however, explain why millions of other Americans think invading Muslim countries is such a nifty idea—why millions of Americans not only support

George W. Bush's vindictive, zero-sum view of the world, but say they'd do the same thing if they had the chance.

Whatever his personal condition, George W. Bush taps into a powerful American syndrome of self-indulgent chauvinistic behavior that involves, on a national level, the "dry drunk" characteristics just listed. "Impatience" is practically a synonym for "American" in many parts of the world. "Projection" (worldwide communist conspiracy; axis of evil) and "irrational rationalization" (the domino theory, nonexistent Iraqi uranium purchases in Africa) are longtime characteristics of US foreign policy.

"Overreaction" and "childish behavior," as any French cinephile will tell you, are as American as Jerry Lewis. George W. Bush's opponents and detractors have always underestimated him because they have associated his most disagreeable characteristics with those of the misbehaving son of the famous father. But as the popularity of his "for-us-or-against-us" approach shows, these same negative qualities are also inherent to a widespread view of America as destiny's heir, a nation entitled to whatever it wants, wherever it wants, no matter what others say because, well, that's just how things are.

George W. Bush is very American in that way, but in his elitist sense of entitlement he's quite "un-American," and in fact bears a striking resemblance to Osama bin Laden. The two have other traits in common—most notably, their tendency to express their displeasure at the complexities of world through spectacular acts of violence. George W. Bush and Osama bin Laden also share the ability to use others for the grunt work, while making sure the final outcome accurately reflects their own need for apocalyptic scenarios. Osama bin Laden's Dick Cheney is said to be the Egyptian Ayman al-Zawahiri, who has provided him with both the organizational and ideological framework for his campaign of destruction.

George W. Bush is as uninterested in remedying the injustices of America as he is passionate, for the moment, about turning Iraq into a democratic paradise. Similarly, Osama bin Laden's free-enterprise war on the American Satan has been accompanied by zero attempts to make things better in his own homeland. Then there's the parallel of the acquired persona: Osama bin Laden's flowing beard and ascetic robes are as far removed from his air-conditioned origins in the Saudi elite as George W. Bush's "mad cowboy" persona is from his prep school dorm.

What links the two, most of all, is their shared contempt for the diversity of the world and its people. On September 11, 2001, it is true, Americans discovered firsthand what harm hateful men can do to the world, but the darkness in Osama bin Laden's soul was not the only revelation. Over and over, George W. Bush continues to show us that in his bully pulpit, hate and violence take pride of place, along with privilege.

September 11 was Osama bin Laden's defining moment, but Afghanistan was not George W. Bush's. How could it be, after the Texas Rangers came up dry? For some months US forces searched Afghanistan for Osama bin Laden. They then abandoned the chase while, of course, never admitting it. George W. Bush's attention had long since wandered.

What happens when the bounty hunter's trail grows cold, and the polls start slipping? You start a new episode; you ride off in pursuit of a new villain.

X

Forgetting Osama

NOTHING BETTER ILLUSTRATES THE delusional quality of the radical neocon approach to defending America than Wolfowitz's rejection, in the "Defense Policy Guidance," of the proven diplomatic-military success of the Desert Storm model of warfare that liberated Kuwait.

In the shocked aftermath of 9/11, he went to an even more radical extreme. Even as the ruins of the World Trade Center reeked smoke and death, Wolfowitz did everything he could to prevent the US strike into Afghanistan. It was as though, in the stunned aftermath of the Al Qaeda attacks, he had suffered some momentary fit of ideology-epilepsy, and started writhing around like a peacenik. Again and again, he opposed taking retaliatory military action against Osama bin Laden. Had Wolfowitz's views prevailed, the mastermind of 9/11 would have kept his Afghanistan safe haven. The Taliban would have remained in power. Afghanistan would have remained a staging area for murderous attacks on Americans.

Scene: Camp David, the weekend retreat in the Maryland mountains where presidents love to go when it's time to do historical heavy lifting. Participants: George W. Bush and his most trusted advisers, plus Secretary of State Colin Powell. Time: September 15 and 16, 2001. Purpose: historic and strategic, to decide the nature of America's response to the attacks suffered only four days earlier. This conclave, every participant at Camp David knows, is one for the history books. Think of President James Madison after the British burned the White House. Imagine President Franklin Roosevelt in the fateful hours after the attack on Pearl Harbor. This conclave, too, will be remembered as long as the American flag flies.

Interior shot: A room with an immense stone fireplace whose flames cast deep shadows. Fill the room with famous faces and tension you can cut with a knife. Now focus on the faces—first a group shot, then focus on each face one by one. Now, give us one deep close-up. Frame just his eyes and eyebrows as this trusted presidential counselor says, in that tone of voice which (in docudramas) brings the room, and all in it, to the precipice of history: "Mr. President." All fall silent. The president nods gravely in his direction. Every eye is upon this eminent presidential counselor, as he says: "Whatever we do, President Roosevelt, let's not declare war on Japan." He continues: "We might not be able to win. Besides, Japan is too far away."

Or, if you prefer, dress Paul Wolfowitz in breeches and frock coat. Some of those present are looking at him through Ben Franklin–style spectacles as he says, following the burning of Washington in the War of 1812: "Whatever we do, President Madison, let's not be unpleasant to the British." It's hard to imagine some other adviser not being fired on the spot. But on September 15, 2001, George W. Bush did not even reprimand Wolfowitz. He merely deputized a senior gofer, Andrew Card, to shut Wolfowitz up when his opposition to taking the war on terrorism to Osama and the Taliban in Afghanistan grew too repetitive.

It's unusual for an ideologue to use the arguments of an appeaser to oppose the legitimate defense of the United States, but that is the tactic Wolfowitz used to try to get George W. Bush not to invade Afghanistan. "At Camp David the weekend after the September 11 attacks, Deputy Secretary of Defense Paul Wolfowitz argued on three separate occasions that the United States should immediately target Iraq instead of the more difficult Afghanistan," Franklin Foer and Spencer Ackerman later wrote in *The New Republic*.

"Attacking Afghanistan would be uncertain," Wolfowitz argued, according to accounts of the meeting Bob Woodward uses in his book, *Bush at War*. In the large meeting, with all the principal presidential advisers listening, he fretted "about 100,000 American troops bogged down in mountain fighting in Afghanistan." As soon as he got the chance to have a private word with George W. Bush, Wolfowitz "expanded on his arguments about how war against Iraq might be easier than against Afghanistan." It was an attempt, on Wolfowitz's part, with Rumsfeld's backing, to go behind the backs of the Joint Chiefs of Staff who, from a professional military point of view, considered an attack on Iraq inappropriate as well as impractical.

When George W. Bush asked Wolfowitz why "he didn't present more of this at the meeting," Wolfowitz replied, "It is not my place to contradict the chairman of the Joint Chiefs unless the secretary of defense says to," giving us a glimpse of a master bureaucratic maneuverer at work. While saying it isn't his place to do it, that is exactly what Wolfowitz is doing—contradicting the chairman of the Joint Chiefs, and doing it behind his back, with the chairman's commander in chief.

And, of course, Wolfowitz never would have done such a thing without Rumsfeld's backing.

Rumsfeld also wanted to attack Iraq immediately, and not attack Afghanistan, even though Wolfowitz himself, in front of all the others, stated that there was only "a 10 to 50 percent chance Saddam was involved in the September 11 terrorist attacks." No one at the meeting, including George W. Bush, disagreed with that assessment. Colin Powell, objecting to Wolfowitz's proposal to attack Iraq, used the lack of proof as his principal argument for refocusing US military retaliation on Afghanistan. "If you get something pinning September 11 on Iraq, great—let's put it out and kick the mat at the right time," Powell argued. "But let's get Afghanistan now."

This is a bizarre and revelatory spectacle for several important reasons. First: A mere four days after terrorists from an Afghanistan-based terrorist organization have killed 3,000 people on American soil, the US secretary of state has to argue hard to fight down a proposal from the department of defense that the United States not retaliate against that country at all, but instead embark on a unrelated military adventure. Second: As both Wolfowitz's and Powell's comments make clear beyond doubt, George W. Bush and his inner circle from the beginning understood there was no evidence giving them any justified reason for believing Saddam Hussein was involved in the attacks. No such evidence would ever be found, as George W. Bush himself would publicly concede on at least two occasions. This puts the falsity of their future claims that attacking Iraq was somehow a response to the September 11 attacks in even clearer perspective. Lacking evidence from the beginning, in the end they all simply lied.

Also on full display in the Camp David meetings, quite

simply, is the profound and pathetic lack of good judgment that would characterize the whole Iraq fiasco. While completely misjudging the dangers of the Afghanistan invasion, Wolfowitz—whose views in the end would become the military policy of the United States—also gets Iraq entirely wrong "It was doable," he argued, in favor of attacking Iraq, and leaving Osama and the Taliban unscathed.

Wolfowitz was not acting alone. He was acting with Rumsfeld's approval, and as his stalking horse. "Is this the time to attack Iraq?" Rumsfeld asked, reopening the subject when the meeting reconvened, apparently in hopes Wolfowitz had been able to sell George W. Bush on the idea during the break.

Wolfowitz argued Afghanistan was too difficult to attack. Rumsfeld implied Afghanistan wasn't worth attacking at all; he professed himself "deeply worried about the availability of good targets in Afghanistan." Even after Powell intervened, successfully refocusing George W. Bush and his advisers on the necessity of the United States taking some retaliatory action against those who had attacked it, Wolfowitz would not desist. It was at that point, according to Woodward's account, when George W. Bush ordered Wolfowitz silenced.

While the test of a true conservative is that reality always and invariably takes precedence over theory, nothing can deflect an off-the-wall, out-of-control neocon ultraradical ideologue from compulsively acting out his doctrinal fantasies—not even when it means letting the killers of Americans go unpunished. Even as serious people who were seriously committed to defending America (such as Secretary of State Colin Powell and his staff) tried to take real action to pursue and punish the terrorists, as well as prevent future attacks, the neocon claque, starting with

Wolfowitz and including Cheney and Rumsfeld, took up the cry "Invade Iraq!"

At this point George W. Bush must be given his due. Unlike his deputy secretary of defense, he on this one occasion showed himself, if only temporarily, capable of grasping the idea that the use of US military power, as the name "Department of Defense" implies, should have some relationship to the defense of the United States. At Camp David George W. Bush demonstrated appreciation for an even subtler nuance of strategic thinking. He grasped that if US military power failed to protect America (as it had failed to protect it on 9/11), then it was best used in retaliation against the attackers, and rejected Wolfowitz's advice. In his capacity as Commander in Chief, he directed the US military to retaliate against those who had actually attacked the United States, not some bystander.

The lapse was brief. "Saddam. We're taking him out," George W. Bush started telling visitors, soon after the Osama-hunting in Afghanistan failed to produce instant gratification. If Secretary of State Powell or any other members of the administration's token sanity brigade imagined the rebuff to Wolfowitz at Camp David was anything but temporary, they had misjudged the character of their Commander in Chief. George W. Bush wasn't against invading Iraq. He just wanted to invade Afghanistan first. For once, even Paul Wolfowitz had thought too small. He had allowed his vision of US supremacy over the world, in every region of the world, to become befuddled by either/or choices. He had momentarily forgotten, perhaps under the pressure of 9/11-induced stress, that with George W. Bush in the saddle, choices no longer were necessary.

America would invade Afghanistan. Then it would invade Iraq, and why ever stop there? With George W. Bush in the

White House, the unimaginable became unthinkable, and the unthinkable was what he did. American troops had never invaded a central Asian country, though now they would. Until now, the United States seizing control of an Arab country had been unimaginable. If Baghdad was possible, why not the moon? The road to the stars would run through Baghdad, Tehran, Damascus, even Pyongyang, and anywhere else he wanted if George W. Bush had his way. As Afghanistan showed, who was to stop him?

Logistically and tactically, the Afghanistan riposte to the Al Qaeda attacks was a most remarkable feat. As long as human beings consider killing each other an acceptable method for dealing with their political, philosophical, and religious disputes, the 2001 US strike into Afghanistan will be admired as a triumph of cooperative destructive behavior.

On September 11, 2001, no place on earth had seemed more remote from the site of the World Trade Center—and safer from US retaliation—than the Al Qaeda bases and training camps in Taliban-controlled Afghanistan. Yet before September was out, US advance teams were on the ground in Afghanistan. Then on Sunday, October 7, only three and a half weeks after the 9/11 attacks, the United States launched a devastatingly successful air and ground offensive that would take American forces, for the first time in history, deep into territory where the armies of Alexander the Great—and, more recently, Soviet occupation forces—had fought and lost. Within days, the Taliban were losing towns and cities in every region. Within weeks, they had abandoned their last urban stronghold, the city of Jalalabad in the south of the country. By November 11, the United States had avenged the attacks of September 11 almost unimaginably.

Seemingly from out of nowhere, the Tomahawk cruise missiles, B-52 Stratofortress and F-16 fighter jets had hit the Taliban and Al Qaeda literally where they lived. Honorable diplomacy, not techno-war magic, explained why the United States had been able to retaliate so effectively and swiftly, and also why it faced so little resistance. France, Canada, Germany, Russia, Bahrain, Jordan, Turkey, Pakistan, and many other countries that would later oppose the Iraq invasion, were among those who provided crucial diplomatic, logistical, and military support. Though the Taliban denounced the attack on them as "an attack on Islam," even Iran cooperated, agreeing to open its borders to facilitate an orderly departure of refugees. The US victory was so quick and total, however, that it produced the opposite problem. Hundreds of thousands of Afghans joyously returning to their homeland now that the Taliban had been deposed. The Afghanistan foray demonstrated that when it comes to military conquest, US armed forces at the beginning of the third millennium are as invincible as the Roman legions were at the beginning of the first. It also raised a familiar question for George W. Bush. What to do with the victory once it has come to you?

Presidents Clinton, Bush, Reagan, Carter, Ford, Nixon, Johnson, Kennedy, Eisenhower, Truman, and Roosevelt all would have treated the Afghanistan success as another step toward the construction of a rational world order, but their goals were not the goals of George W. Bush and his advisers.

In 1992, following victory in the first Gulf War, President George H.W. Bush had rejected the radical strategy plan that Wolfowitz and Cheney sent him. This time things would be different. Following the success in Afghanistan, Wolfowitz—with Rumsfeld's and Cheney's backing—once again proposed to disregard that proven multilateral approach, and replace it with a militaristic, ethnocentric American unilateralism. It was the latest case of the neocons getting it wrong. They urged that the US treat the whole world the way it did the Taliban, starting with Saddam Hussein.

Their aim was not to fight terrorism or defend America. It was to teach the world a lesson. The lesson would be Iraq. Instead of rejecting the proposal, George W. Bush would turn it into the central event of his presidency. "Taking out" Saddam would become to George W. Bush's crusade to remake the world in his own image what destroying the World Trade Center had been to Osama bin Laden's own jihad. There would be a deeper symmetry. The thousands of people killed on 9/11 were innocent. So, on this one particular occasion, was Saddam Hussein.

When the time comes, Saddam Hussein's attorneys will no doubt try to subpoena George W. Bush as a defense witness. On two separate occasions—once before, and once after the war—he has vouchsafed that Saddam Hussein was not involved in the terrorist attacks of September 11. The first time was on January 31, 2003. A British television journalist, Adam Boulton, in the course of a White House press conference, put to George W. Bush the question that, hitherto, no American reporter had evidently had the presence of mind to ask: "Do you believe that there is a link between Saddam Hussein, a direct link, and the men who attacked on September the 11th?"

"I can't make that claim," George W. Bush replied.

When asked a similar question on September 18, 2003, this time by American members of the White House press corps, George W. Bush responded: "We have no evidence that Saddam Hussein was involved with the September 11 attacks." By then US forces in Iraq had been searching six months for evidence of Saddam consorting with Al Qaeda, and come up with nothing. Nor had they found any evidence that Saddam Hussein had weapons of mass destruction.

Following Saddam's expulsion from Kuwait in 1991, most of the world had moved on to other business. Yitzhak Rabin and Yasser Arafat shared a Nobel Peace Prize. So did F.W. de Klerk and Nelson Mandela. As the globalization of commerce, technology, and culture widened and deepened, the world seemed headed toward a new era in which nations no longer acted like street gangs, and officials of powerful nations no longer operated on the assumption that their cultural values must prevail over all others. Saddam Hussein's Iraq remained a manageable problem, an annoying but successful example of containment.

Everywhere apparatchiks seemed on the retreat, but in Washington they still found sanctuary. Their lairs were tax-exempt organizations with names like the American Enterprise Institute and the Project for a New American Century. Now that the "Sino-Soviet bloc" was no longer there, new threats were needed to justify new proposals for more military spending. This meant a continuing demand in the tax-exempt sector for Paul Wolfowitz's creative talents.

Few in Washington, in or out of office, had his gift for strategic fantasizing. Back in 1992, for example, he had looked at the shambling but remarkable success of democratic India, and perceived the threat of "Indian hegemonic aspiration." Even that early, a democratic consumer-society revolution was sweeping East Asia. All the way from Thailand to South Korea the dictators were falling. Soon life in Indonesia and China as well would be astonishingly transformed by the growth of free markets, personal (if not always political) freedom, and access to technology and the truth. This did not stop Wolfowitz from conjuring up just the kind of "threat" Cheney, Rumsfeld, and George W. Bush loved to confront. In this case it was an Asia "with fundamental values, governance and policies decidedly at variance with our own."

It is one thing to conjure up a threatening world. What to do when the world fails to comply? A constant preoccupation of Wolfowitz and his ideological co-illusionists was the specter of a newly aggressive Russia, should democracy fail there. But democracy did not fail in Russia. Was there no place left that fitted into the apocalyptic vision of evil that Cheney, Wolfowitz, and the others needed to justify their dark visions and deficit spending? Actually there were several, the world being a place of great diversity, but the sadistic hellhole that most neatly filled their requirements continued to be Saddam Hussein's Iraq, even after his resounding defeat.

Year after year, the neocons' Saddam obsession intensified. Was this a case of group neurosis or psychosis? The neurotic retains some appreciation that his fantasies arise from within himself. Psychotics become so utterly detached from reality they come to assume the whole world will finally understand, if they can only get the right person to listen!

Their response to events of September 11, 2001, would show just how isolated from reality this crowd was, but as early as 1998, Wolfowitz, Rumsfeld, Richard Perle, and a number of other like-minded agitators did something that in and of itself signaled a generalized cognitive instability in their ranks. These Republican ultraradicals got together and wrote a letter to President Bill Clinton, pleading with him to adopt their strategic hallucination as his own, although a Democratic president was hardly likely to adopt a policy approach that a Republican president had already rejected. Their letter was symptomatic in other ways, notably in its wild-eyed grandiosity. Rumsfeld, Wolfowitz, and the others impetuously urged Clinton not merely to reverse US policy totally, but to do it dramatically and without warning—without consulting either Congress or America's allies. Specifically, they proposed that he use his annual State of the Union address to suddenly announce that the United States was unilaterally rejecting the multilateral, United Nations–sanctioned policy of containing Saddam, and instead, making "the removal of Saddam Hussein's regime from power" America's new policy. To put it another way, they were proposing that the United States unilaterally reject all the international agreements that had ended the first Gulf War in 1991, and resume the march on Baghdad that the first President Bush had ordered halted after the liberation of Kuwait. Why? If he did not immediately do as Wolfowitz, Rumsfeld, Cheney, and the others demanded, terrible unspecified things would happen.

The key paragraphs of the 1998 letter follow. They outline the exact same policy that many of the same signers of the letter, having been empowered by George W. Bush, would adopt in 2001. That is to say, they demonstrate that the terrorist attacks of September 11 later would be used as a pretext for implementing a plan—some would go so far as to say a plot—that was hatched years earlier. As this 1998 letter shows, the proposed invasion of Iraq was from the outset like "Star Wars"—a nonnegotiable doctrinal demand, not a rational response to the security needs of the American people.

"Dear Mr. President," the letter began: "We are writing you because we are convinced that current American policy toward Iraq is not succeeding, and that we may soon face a threat in the Middle East more serious than any we have known since the end of the Cold War. In your upcoming State of the Union

Address, you have an opportunity to chart a clear and determined course for meeting this threat. We urge you to seize that opportunity, and to enunciate a new strategy that would secure the interests of the US and our friends and allies around the world. That strategy should aim, above all, at the removal of Saddam Hussein's regime from power." Why undertake such a melodramatic reversal of policy in such a theatrical way? "Mr. President," the letter continued, "the security of the world in the first part of the 21st century will be determined largely by how we handle this threat." End of explanation, though as in the future Wolfowitz, Rumsfeld, Perle, and the others argued that the United States must act unilaterally not only because Saddam was evil, but because our allies were worthless. In their exact words: "Given the magnitude of the threat, the current policy, which depends for its success upon the steadfastness of our coalition partners and upon the cooperation of Saddam Hussein, is dangerously inadequate."

From there, they plunged straight into the "for-us-or-against-us" syllogism that would become the centerpiece of George W. Bush's conduct of US foreign policy later. "The only acceptable strategy," they announced, "is one that eliminates the possibility that Iraq will be able to use or threaten to use weapons of mass destruction. In the near term, this means a willingness to undertake military action as diplomacy is clearly failing. In the long term, it means removing Saddam Hussein and his regime from power. That now needs to become the aim of American foreign policy."

On one level, the image of these neocon ultras urging Clinton to embrace their paranoid misinterpretation of events in the Middle East seems simply daffy—a little like a crowd of protesters thrusting an antiwar petition on George W. Bush, and expecting him to sign it. But it's also sort of creepy—the "policy guidance" equivalent of being accosted by a neighbor who normally glares at you. Only today he doesn't just glare. He grabs you by the shirt collar and—eyes dilated, face red—shouts that unless you do what he wants, and do it right now, a great unnamed cataclysm will occur. (In fact, catastrophe did lie ahead, though, as 9/11 showed, Saddam Hussein wasn't the source.)

Here, as in the later arguments heard in Congress and at the United Nations for actually launching the Iraq war, the key verbs are "convinced" and "must," used to connect bald assertions like "dangerously inadequate" and "only acceptable strategy." These guys are convinced. Therefore the United States must "enunciate a new strategy." And this must done immediately, in the most dramatic way, which is exactly how George W. Bush and his capos actually would proceed, five years later, as they steamrollered America into the conquest and occupation of an entire foreign nation.

President Clinton ignored the "Get Saddam" letter for the same reason George W. Bush's father had rejected "Defense Guidance Policy" earlier. It was hysterical baloney. Yet the "Get Saddam" letter is nonetheless enormously revealing. For one thing, there is the recklessness. Here, as later, a president of the United States was being told he had no choice but to embark on a series of highly disruptive and dangerous actions solely because a crowd of Washington apparatchiks from the Maryland and Virginia suburbs, whose chief intellectual activity is pounding out pro-war op-ed pieces, said so.

There was also the gratuitous disregard for fact. Here, as in the later debates over the invasion of Iraq, no actual evidence was provided to support any of the letter's contentions, including the key assertion that "current American policy toward Iraq is not succeeding." Your neighborhood bowling team could have come up with a better-sourced strategic prospectus using the local high school library. Yet somehow Wolfowitz and his buddies imagined themselves entitled to dictate US foreign policy. Once installed in the White House, that's exactly what George W. Bush, the supposed outsider and champion of ordinary common sense, would give these "Inside the Beltway" critters free rein to do.

The "Get Saddam" letter shows us what the neocon fantasy was in 1998. Since then, the exact same fantasy has been acted out on our TV screens, though with real American and Iraqi blood. But what was the reality? From February 1992, when he was defeated in Kuwait, until he was captured near Tikrit in December 2003, Saddam Hussein never stopped playing his mouse-and-cat game (and what a scruffy rodent he proved to be, when finally rooted out from his hole). In 1998, he expelled the UN inspectors; the immediate challenge the international community faced was to force him to take them back. There never was any evidence, however, that Saddam Hussein, after 1992, posed a danger to his neighbors or to the United States. Of course that was no reason for complacency. The essence of successful containment is constant vigilance, as well as an ability to be patient. What is necessary for success in such situations, most of all, is the capacity to understand that the long-term frustrations of peace are usually preferable to the instant gratifications of launching a war.

The allegations contained in the "Get Saddam" letter were unfounded at the time, but it would take their 2003 invasion to prove how totally wrong its authors were when they asserted that Iraq posed an apocalyptic danger. As US troops scoured Iraq, searching for weapons of mass destruction, what they actually discovered was how successful the policy of containment had been. All the dreadful weapons the Neocons had predicted Saddam might use against US forces were nowhere to be found—because, thanks to the UN trade embargo and the other sanctions for which George W. Bush and his advisers had such contempt, Saddam had not been able to develop such an arsenal.

The real problem—before and after the invasion—was not what Saddam was capable of doing, but what the US government was capable of understanding. Billions had been spent on "intelligence" that wasn't worth a dime. Yet instead of rejoicing at the happy discovery that the danger had been grossly overexaggerated, officials of the George W. Bush administration continue to claim that Saddam posed a great danger.

Obtaining reliable information without having to invade Iraq would have involved doing things that would never be priorities for George W. Bush. For instance, reaching the point where the US government was capable of actually assessing, when Saddam Hussein posed a threat, and then evaluating the importance of that threat, would have required, just for starters, finding a way to convert the CIA and its sister agencies into effective intelligence-gathering organizations.

In the unlikely event that were ever accomplished, the next challenge would have been to build up a corps of competent Iraq analysts with the necessary skills to assess the information that was gathered, starting with the bare minimum skill of fluency in the Arabic language. None of those changes in the way the United States gets and evaluates "intelligence" would have meant anything, however, unless its use of intelligence had been depoliticized—and in the case of George W. Bush, de-ideologized.

Americans today are dying in a open-ended war because

George W. Bush invaded Iraq not on the basis of bad or mediocre intelligence, but on the basis of no intelligence whatsoever. Intelligence did not matter because George W. Bush, Cheney, Rumsfeld, and the others had no interest in understanding the actual situation. All they needed were phantom missile sites in the Iraqi desert and imaginary attempts to purchase uranium in Africa. What they wanted the "intelligence community" to produce were ever more exotic pretexts to go ahead and do what they were already absolutely determined to do, and had been determined to do for many years, regardless of the consequences for the American people.

What if George W. Bush, having learned that Iraq did not in fact pose a great threat, had called off his invasion? Saddam no doubt would have gone on playing his game as long as he stayed in power. Dealing with him would have continued to require a combination of patience, pressure, and close cooperation with our allies, and with the United Nations inspectors. Keeping the successful containment of Saddam's Iraq going, in sum, would have required all those qualities that George W. Bush and those whose advice he follows not only lack but despise.

Let us assume something even more hypothetical—that the fears of the authors of the "Get Saddam" letter had turned out to have some basis in fact. Let's further suppose that the defeated, encircled Iraqi dictator had actually been trying to get weapons of mass destruction, just as they alleged. That development would have been of serious concern to the United States. But would it truly have posed "a threat in the Middle East more serious than any we have known since the end of the Cold War"? Would "the security of the world in the first part of the 21st century" truly have been "determined largely by how we handle this threat"?

Most revealing of all are the threats the authors of the "Get Saddam" letter never mentioned. By the time their letter was written, the dreams of peace in the Middle East created by the 1993 Israeli-Palestinian Oslo Accords, and Yasser Arafat's and Yitzhak Rabin's handshake on the White House lawn, were turning into a nightmare. Prime Minister Rabin had been assassinated by an Israeli terrorist, just as earlier President Anwar Sadat had been assassinated by an Egyptian terrorist in retaliation for his courageous attempt to make peace. Radical extremism in all camps was the great emerging threat. As the authors of the "Get Saddam" letter themselves demonstrate, that threat wasn't limited to the Middle East.

Meanwhile, as America's addiction to imported oil only kept growing, Saudi Arabia was already showing signs of the kind of instability that gave the arguments of terrorists like Osama bin Laden greater and greater appeal. On the other hand, the Islamic Revolution in Iran was starting to show signs of democratic evolution. Turkey, more than 99 percent Muslim, remained a stable democracy. Egypt—the region's single most important nation—remained a strong US ally. It would stay so until George W. Bush outraged President Hosni Mubarak with his contemptuous behavior.

In their 1998 letter urging regime change in Baghdad, however, George W. Bush's future advisers took no more account of this complicated tapestry than George W. Bush himself does today. They expressed no concern that the continuing Israeli occupation of the West Bank and Gaza would provoke a new intifada, or that Pakistan would get nuclear weapons. The danger of another Middle East war wasn't even mentioned. In fact, the only war mentioned specifically was "the Cold War." Nearly a decade after the fall of the Berlin Wall, the end of the

Cold War had left Wolfowitz, Rumsfeld, and their pals disoriented and adrift. Desperate to find a new enemy, they picked an old stock villain out of central casting, Saddam Hussein!

Islamic fundamentalism has been a stupendous force in the Middle East since the outbreak of the revolt against the Shah of Iran in 1978, yet the most astonishing feature of the 1988 letter—indeed the whole canon of neocon radical policy proposals—is the utter obliviousness to the real threat of Islamic terrorism, even when George W. Bush finally got into the White House. This absolute refusal to face up to the living, breathing threat that was actually haunting the Middle East, and which really was menacing America, reached its surreal apotheosis in Wolfowitz's post-9/11 behavior at Camp David. Even within that closed circle, it's hard to see Wolfowitz as anything but aberrant in terms of the way more or less normal people react to life-threatening events, such as Osama bin Laden's Al Qaeda attacks on America.

As events tragically have shown, the neocons are so obsessed with pursuing their private ideological agenda that they are simply incapable of anticipating the real danger. The lack of evidence and absence of logic, as well as the shrillness, in the "Get Saddam" letter have proven to be prophetic. George W. Bush's Iraq war would be an ideological act, undertaken (among other reasons) in the attempt to prove that the doctrinal assertions of the authors of the "Get Saddam" letter were right. In the annual State of the Union address of 2002, George W. Bush transformed the ideologues' 1998 ultimatum into his own.

Do what we tell you, the signers of the "Get Saddam" letter had informed Bill Clinton, and "We stand ready to offer our full support in this difficult but necessary endeavor." And if he didn't? Republican radicals already were getting ready to plunge the government of the world's most powerful nation into crisis—and they were prepared to use Bill Clinton's sexual gropings in the Oval Office washroom to do it. If, indeed, Saddam Hussein at that time truly was plotting to unleash "a threat in the Middle East more serious than any we have known since the end of the Cold War," impeaching the president of the United States because he had encouraged Monica Lewinsky to stimulate his penis during office hours was an odd way of protecting America's national security.

A final prophetic detail of the "Get Saddam" letter needs to be noted. This is its date—January 26, 1998. President Clinton's State of the Union address was scheduled for the very next day, January 27, so here we see adumbrated another feature of the George W. Bush presidency. This is the headline-grabbing political ultimatum delivered in the guise of some absolute moral choice that must be made right now, between good and evil, but it's actually just a cheap trick. George W. Bush would use the same tactic to belittle the United Nations and split NATO, but the truth is that respectable "defense intellectuals" don't present American presidents with either/or choices and twenty-four-hour deadlines. Citizens seriously concerned for the security of their homeland don't either.

George W. Bush and those he empowered have never cared very much about fighting either terrorism or its causes. The US invasion of Afghanistan was initially code-named Operation Infinite Justice, and was presented to the American public as a law-enforcement operation. Osama bin Laden was America's most wanted outlaw. George W. Bush sent our forces over there to capture him "dead or alive," but reality turned out to be "against us," yet again.

Whatever else it was, the invasion of Afghanistan had been a triumphant display of US military logistics. It extended the NATO model of collective security into one of the most remote places on earth. It had produced the happy though ancillary effect (like the Iraq invasion later) of overthrowing a repulsive regime. Furthermore, according to all prevailing legal and moral standards, the Afghanistan invasion—like the liberation of Kuwait eleven years earlier—was a significant advance for world law and order.

A fabulous feat of American technology was accompanied by a failure of US "intelligence" in both senses of the word. Earlier, neither the CIA nor the air traffic controllers had seen 9/11 coming. Now all those US troops in Afghanistan turned out to be like the security guards at Boston Logan on the morning of September 11. While they frisked grandmothers, Osama bin Laden got away. As thousands of people would discover in the terrified final moments of their lives over the next couple of years, invading Afghanistan neither deterred nor defeated terrorism. It simply displaced it. This the Australians and Indonesians would learn in Bali; the British and Turks would learn in Istanbul; and Spaniards, Italians, Romanians, and many others would discover in Iraq, after they had signed up for guard duty in George W. Bush's "coalition of the willing."

Afghanistan simply did not turn out as it should have—which of course could be said of George W. Bush's whole presidency. This failure to apprehend bin Laden—like Cheney's fake Wyoming residency earlier—nonetheless gave George W. Bush a much-needed opportunity to think again. Instead, he chose not to think at all. Asked about the failure to find and capture Osama bin Laden, he made his famous "dead or alive" remark, manifesting another George W. Bush pattern: When the time comes to pass the buck, last month's great crusade is demoted to the back burner with a smirk and a few snide remarks.

Had the United States followed up on its intervention in Afghanistan with a serious and successful effort to construct a viable civil society there, it would have had an enormous impact on the Muslim world. Instead George W. Bush bugged off to Iraq. Nor did he resume efforts to make peace between the Israelis and the Palestinians. Instead he stood aloof from that deepening threat to peace month after month, while the entire framework for peace there collapsed. George W. Bush's refusal to become engaged in the Israeli-Palestinian peace process was to that conflict what his renunciation of the ABM Treaty was to nuclear proliferation. As most dispassionate people with experience of the Middle East agree, doing "nothing" has been an irresponsible crime of omission that will shadow the lives of Palestinians, Israelis, and Americans for years, if not generations, to come.

Today, Afghanistan is becoming a power vacuum once again. We know it is once again exporting opium; time will tell what other poisons will eventually reach America, thanks to George W. Bush's Afghanistan disconnection. Of course trying to turn an actual base for terrorism into a functioning peaceful society would have involved enormous expenditures—but probably not as enormous as the ones in Iraq.

The Afghanistan thrust, which seemed so decisive at the time, quickly turned into a military example of what happens when a diversionary tactic no longer serves George W. Bush's immediate purposes. A multinational force, manned by those same NATO allies he later derided for failing to support him in Iraq, occupied Kabul, turning the capital city into a photo opportunity for visiting journalists, and the latest hardship post for packs of politicians and bureaucrats. Down in the south of the country, the Americans established a big base, and settled into that habitual activity of armed forces in a conquered country: guard duty. There were some other outposts of civil administration and military power, but on the whole Afghanistan was like a giant leopard's skin which, instead of spots, has freckles scattered here and there.

The posse out sent out to get Osama bin Laden came back with a spacey-looking American kid from northern California named John Walker Lindh. As a result, George W. Bush's "war on terrorism" produced the first of its redefinitions of American liberty. Was it a crime for a US citizen to wear a scruffy beard and hang out with some Taliban radicals if—subsequent to that US citizen arriving in Afghanistan—the United States decides to attack the Taliban? In the eyes of George W. Bush and his attorney general, John Ashcroft, it was. An American judge and jury never got the chance to decide. Lindh's parents, as is the custom with affluent Americans, hired attorneys who negotiated a plea bargain for their kid. It turned into a celebrity news event.

"A very un-American confession from the so-called American Taliban John Walker Lindh," is the way anchorperson Kimberly McBroom headlined it. "After a surprise deal with prosecutors, John Walker Lindh's attorney announced the change in plea this morning in Alexandria. The news even caught the judge by surprise. Lindh is pleading guilty to two charges. The plea agreement will keep him from getting a life prison term."

From Kimberly it was over to Teri in front of the courthouse: "After arriving in court, twenty-one-year-old John Walker Lindh shocked the court by changing his plea to guilty on two charges," she said into the camera. "The first, willfully and unlawfully supplying services to the Taliban and then carrying explosives during the commission of a felony. In exchange, all other charges against Lindh will be dropped."

"Carrying explosives during the commission of a felony"? This apparently meant that at some point after the US invasion, Lindh admitted to moving a box of ammunition. Why the Taliban attempting to defend themselves from US attack in Afghanistan (if indeed that was what had happened while Lindh was "carrying explosives") should constitute a felony under US law was never explained.

Meanwhile, down in Guantánamo Bay, Cuba, there is no telling how long a variety of others prisoners taken in Afghanistan—among them citizens of allied countries, including Tony Blair's United Kingdom—could be held without trial. Like Muammar Qaddafi later, Fidel Castro was turning into a model of dictatorial cooperation when it came to George W. Bush's "war on terrorism." The aging guerrilla war icon did not so much wave his cigar as protest at this use of "revolutionary" Cuba's sacred soil. The US cargo planes full of prisoners flew halfway around the world to the one spot under George W. Bush's control where he didn't have to respect anybody's laws—including, for the time being, the laws of the United States.

When US military operations fail to achieve their objectives, they tend to get transformed into generalized crusades for freedom. This happened in Afghanistan, where Operation Infinite Justice was rechristened Operation Enduring Freedom. Meanwhile, months, and then years passed, in the empty fastness of Afghanistan, with no sign of Osama and, from the White House, scarcely any further mention of his name. Would Osama bin Laden someday slip into the net, the same way Saddam Hussein eventually did? Every platoon, night-vision sniper scope and billion dollars expended on the war on Iraq is a diversion from the real war on terrorism, including the successful pursuit and apprehension of terrorist leaders. American intelligence remained so defective that, on those occasions when US forces still did go out Osama-hunting, all they unfortunately seemed to do was kill lots of little Afghan children.

In any event, bringing Osama bin Laden to justice ceased being a priority for George W. Bush within months of the arrival of US forces in Afghanistan at the end of 2001. It was demoted, instead, to a potential news option for the 2004 election year.

XI

Mother Of All Wedge Issues

DECADES BEFORE THE INVASION of Iraq, Barry Goldwater had enjoyed telling his Republican acolytes the story of the man who was asked why he'd sat on the cactus. "Because it seemed like such a good idea at the time," was the answer. It was the same with George W. Bush and invading Iraq. From his peculiar vantage point, what wasn't there to love about "taking out" Saddam?

Temperamentally, the adventure was enormously appealing. Label it "regime change." Call it the "war on terrorism," as it was renamed after 9/11. Whatever you call it, George W. Bush's mania for transforming the complexities of global politics into single-issue wedge politics merged perfectly with his consuming need to "take out" Saddam. It wasn't just that he liked going after bad guys or that invading Iraq provided the perfect chance to transform an enormously complicated situation into a shootout. There were the ancillary satisfactions. As he never stops showing, George W. Bush delights in abusing America's truest friends. Invading Iraq gave him a new and welcome chance to really stick it to all those "allies."

Ticking off the Germans, the French, the Canadians and the

others was only part of a much bigger payoff. From September 2001 onward, George W. Bush had found himself struggling in a viscous treacle of international good will and multilateral cooperation. Invading Iraq provided a welcome escape from the constraints of the Kuwait-Afghanistan multilateral approach to international security. It also provided the opportunity for a satisfying resumption, and escalation, of the George W. Bush Middle-Finger Foreign Policy.

In the upwelling of pro-American sentiment after the 9/11 attacks, the world had half-forgotten that George W. Bush had already used issues like global warming and genocide to polarize the international community. Invading Iraq gave him the wedge he needed to divide the world even more deeply, while striking new blows at international peacekeeping organizations. Whatever the consequences for the Middle East, invading Iraq would transform the United Nations and NATO from consensus assemblies of free partners into confrontation pits of ill feeling where, exactly as George W. Bush wanted, the only question was whether you were on his side or not.

Invading Iraq was to global politics what capital punishment and abortion were to domestic American politics: a perfect wedge issue. The key concept to grasp here is that in wedge issue politics the enemies you make are as important as your friends, sometimes even more important. Make everyone your friend, and they'll all ask you for your support. Make the right enemies, and it's you who'll get the votes. The money will pour in too, if you make the right people mad at you.

Wedge-issue politics provides the inner consistency as well as the logic propelling everything George W. Bush does. It also explains why his actions seem paradoxical, as well as gratuitously hurtful, to so many people. They don't understand that creating divisions is not some "mistake," some lamentable side-effect, for example, of his decision to invade Iraq. Getting people upset and angry is the essence of every George W. Bush victory plan. As the divisions within America grew in the months leading up to the invasion of Iraq, George W. Bush's fellow Texan, Senator Kay Bailey Hutchison, was asked for her definition of a liberal. A liberal, she replied, was someone who took into account what Europeans wanted when deciding what was right for America. As his behavior has shown again and again, George W. Bush didn't decide to invade Iraq in spite of the fact that the US invasion would divide the world. He was all the more enthusiastic about the war because invading Iraq would drive a hurtful wedge between him and all those fancy foreign "friends."

When it comes to US domestic affairs, invading Iraq has provided an even more perfect fusion of ideological need and political expediency. For one thing, when you get people to focus their frustrations, anger, and resentment on all those dictators, Europeans, and liberals, they are less likely to take a hard, clear look at what you've been doing to them.

George W. Bush has turned more people against America than its enemies ever have. The anger and disapproval he generates have traversed cultures and continents to become a worldwide phenomenon according to studies undertaken by the Global Attitudes Project of the Pew Research Center. In Indonesia, the world's most populous Muslim country, the proportion of those having a favorable opinion of the United States has dropped from 61 percent to 15 percent of the population. In Germany, Europe's most productive nation, the proportion of those having a favorable opinion of the United States has fallen from 78 percent to 45 percent.

To what purpose? The more he has polarized the world against America, the stronger his political position has grown inside the United States. George W. Bush's critics know that Iraq is an unjustified misadventure that will cause America and the world problems for decades to come. He and his election strategists know that Iraq is the domestic political wedge issue that has allowed George W. Bush to transform himself from an accidental President into the defining figure in America today.

True, millions of Americans detest what he has done and are ashamed of the disrepute he has brought upon their country. But for at least as many Americans—perhaps a third of the voting public—the only complaint is that George W. Bush doesn't invade a few more countries, and why not nuke the Champs-Elysée too?

As for George W. Bush's opponents, they face the unenviable task of trying to get the middle third of Americans to understand some rather complicated issues and events, in order to show them just how malign George W. Bush's presidency has turned out to be. He, in contrast, presents voters with a classic wedge-issue choice. If you love America, vote for me. And if you don't love America? Vote for one of those Europe-loving liberals who, when it came time to choose between good and evil, sided with Saddam Hussein. George W. Bush knows that—unless too many Americans get killed in Iraq, or the economy goes too far down the tubes—waving the flag wins most elections, especially when your opponent's catchiest soundbite is: "Hey there. Now just wait a minute. It's not that I'm against defending America, but things are just more complicated than that—" (Power surges on TV remote controls all over the country, as American voters, what few voters are left, switch channels.)

According to a variety of accounts, the decision to invade Iraq was taken more than a year before it actually happened. The fact that, having decided to take out Saddam, George W. Bush waited a year to do it provides the most convincing evidence that Saddam Hussein's supposed trove of weapons of mass destruction, even in George W. Bush's eyes, never posed the kind of threat he later pretended justified the attack. The big decision having been made, its implementation, as always in the George W. Bush White House, awaited the desired conjunction of opportunity and expediency.

The domestic political need to invade Iraq may have arisen sooner than George W. Bush's political handlers, including Karl Rove, anticipated. Within six months of the Afghanistan foray, the attention of the American media and public had wobbled back to where it was six months after George W. Bush became president—that is, uncomfortably close to an accurate reading of his and his administration's venality and incompetence.

THE RAP ON BUSH AND CHENEY ran a typical headline in *Time* magazine, in July 2002. The polls showed slippage. The 2002 midterm elections were on the way. The pundits—just as they had before 9/11—were, once again, applying the f-word (failure) to George W. Bush. The Democrats, having already gotten back the Senate thanks to Bush's knack for offending people, were planning to keep it in the November elections. They dreamed of taking the House of Representatives too. Summer 2002 was one of those down times that often turn out to presage another George W. Bush diversionary extravaganza.

In this spin-cycle age of repetitive video images and constant recycling of the truth, we seem to live in an eternal present. Thanks to George W. Bush's adroitness, "Saddam" and "Iraq," by election time in November 2002, had replaced "Osama" and "Afghanistan" as buzzwords of the eternal present: constantly on

TV, the computer screen, on the car radio. But even though it quickly came to seem so, that had not previously been the case. Until the run-up to the 2002 midterm elections in the United States, "Saddam" had not had much major play in the American consciousness since 1998 when he had expelled UN inspectors. Iraq had not dominated the world's attention since 1991.

It's forgotten now, but from September 2001 until September 2002, "Osama" and "Afghanistan" were the inescapable pair of buzzwords. Then, suddenly, at the end of August and the beginning of September 2002, as Americans headed back to work from their summer holidays, "Osama" and "Afghanistan" vanished. It was like that moment, in George Orwell's *1984*, when the Ministry of Truth changes enemies. "Saddam" and "Iraq" were suddenly the new words in George W. Bush's spin cycle. It wasn't just in America. All over the world, in airports and offices, in front of television sets and in cafés, people were turning to each other, and asking: "What's all this about Saddam and Iraq? I thought it was Osama and Afghanistan." Summer's end traditionally is the time of year when, in America, new car models are introduced, the World Series shapes up, kids start college, and election campaigns go into high gear. It is also the time when new product lines and major advertising campaigns are launched. Starting in September 2002, the George W. Bush administration went into overdrive campaigning for its new product: "the removal of Saddam Hussein's regime from power." The campaign would succeed to a large extent in the United States, but the rest of the world never would buy the line that Saddam was the new, bigger, eviler enemy of freedom.

It's clear now that the full-scale campaign to shift America's attention from the failure to get Osama in Afghanistan to the upcoming triumph over terrorism in Iraq was concocted long in advance. As early as January 2002, while the trauma of 9/11 was still uppermost in people's minds, George W. Bush had started to prepare the way for demoting Osama from America's enemy in chief. When he delivered the annual State of the Union address that month, it was as though, five years after the post office had delivered it, the man in the White House had finally read, and embraced in their entirety, the proposals of the "Get Saddam" letter. George W. Bush even extended the agenda of regime change to include North Korea and Iran.

That night of January 29, 2002, most viewers expected George W. Bush to talk about the war on terror in Afghanistan. How soon would it be before Osama was captured? Would he announce new measures to protect the country from another 9/11? Instead, George W. Bush made a series of assertions that at first seemed simply odd.

"North Korea is a regime arming with missiles and weapons of mass destruction, while starving its citizens," he announced. This, while basically true, was hardly a revelation. "Iran aggressively pursues these weapons and exports terror, while an unelected few repress the Iranian people's hope for freedom," he added, venturing out into no-man's land. Then he plunged straight into neocon agitprop: "Iraq continues to flaunt its hostility toward America and to support terror. The Iraqi regime has plotted to develop anthrax, and nerve gas, and nuclear weapons for over a decade."

It was a deft diversionary touch, linking Saddam to anthrax, even though George W. Bush well knew Saddam had nothing to do with the anthrax attacks in America, just as he had nothing to do with the 9/11 attacks. But why were Iran, Iraq, and North Korea being lumped together? Iran and Iraq were implacable enemies. They had had fought an eight-year war that cost hundreds of thousands of lives. North Korea's Kim Jong Il was perhaps the world's single most reclusive ruler.

George W. Bush had decided to drive a wedge into the world, with the ayatollahs of Iran, Kim Jong Il, and Saddam Hussein on one side—and himself on the other.

"States like these, and their terrorist allies," he announced, "constitute an axis of evil, arming to threaten the peace of the world. By seeking weapons of mass destruction, these regimes pose a grave and growing danger." From here he deftly somersaulted from unproven accusation into hypothetical paranoia: "They could provide these arms to terrorists, giving them the means to match their hatred. They could attack our allies or attempt to blackmail the United States. In any of these cases, the price of indifference would be catastrophic."

What was the alternative to catastrophic indifference? "Star Wars" for starters, or as George W. Bush put it: "We will develop and deploy effective missile defenses to protect America and our allies from sudden attack (Applause.)" Unilateral unprovoked attack by the United States upon countries of its private selection was, in George W. Bush's judgment, another way to defend America. Or as his speech writers phrased it: "I will not wait on events, while dangers gather. I will not stand by, as peril draws closer and closer. The United States of America will not permit the world's most dangerous regimes to threaten us with the world's most destructive weapons. (Applause.)"

The words show how fully determined George W. Bush had become, only four months after the September 11 attacks, to turn the "war on terror" away from fighting terror toward his own purposes. The applause lines, taken from the official transcript of his address, show how spinelessly the politicians went along.

What initially seemed simply an eccentric digression from what truly concerned people in January 2002 (the real war on terror) can be seen, now, as the first public outline of a plan for a premeditated attack on Iraq—apparently to be followed by "regime change" in North Korea and Iran as well. Two other lines, little noticed at the time, are worth recalling. "Many nations are acting forcefully," George W. Bush said. "(Applause.) But some governments will be timid in the face of terror. And make no mistake about it: If they do not act, America will. (Applause.)" Translation: If other countries don't do what I tell them, they can be invaded too.

He also made it clear that good behavior offered no protection from American attack. As he put it, just before launching into his axis of evil riff: "Some of these regimes have been pretty quiet since September the 11th. But we know their true nature." Translation: Once the United States decided to "take out" one foreign regime or another, it didn't matter whether it continued to "flaunt its hostility" or stayed "pretty quiet." Once you're on George W. Bush's hit list, that's it.

Even this early, there was also a perceptible change in the spin. Not once in his "axis of evil" speech of January 2002—delivered less than four months after the 9/11 attacks—did George W. Bush so much as mention the name of Osama bin Laden. He also never mentioned that, even as he spoke, he and his Administration were still attempting to block the creation of the Department of Homeland Security.

Six months later, in a graduation speech at West Point, George W. Bush edged up further on his pre-decided purpose, once again in the guise of talking about terrorism. "Our security will require all Americans to be forward-looking and resolute, to be ready for pre-emptive action when necessary to defend our liberty and to defend our lives," he told the cadets. "Pre-emptive action" is neocon code for unprovoked attack. It was as though, in a speech to a Boy Scout jamboree, George W. Bush slipped in the mention that from now on, there would be a merit badge for mugging.

Did he, Cheney, and the others imagine that they eventually could slip an invasion of Iraq into world events the same way they slipped neocon code words into speeches about terrorism? If so, it was one of their countless miscalculations.

By summer 2002, the possibility that the George W. Bush administration was actually going to use the war on terrorism as the pretext for a unilateral, unprovoked attack on North Korea, Iran, or Iraq was starting to alarm the kind of people who keep track of such things. Perhaps because they understood the code language and internal doctrinal disputes better than outsiders, Republicans were some of first to take the danger seriously. These included Republicans who had been very highly placed in the first Bush administration, notably former Secretary of State James Baker, and the elder Bush's National Security Adviser, Brent Scowcroft. Alarmed by the growing danger, Scowcroft went public after the West Point speech about "pre-emptive action." He argued that instead of plotting unilateral military attacks, the United States should work with its allies to get UN inspectors back into Iraq.

In response, Cheney tipped the administration's hand big-time. A "return of inspectors would provide no assurance what-soever of compliance with UN resolutions," Cheney retorted. The administration's goal, it was now clear, was not to find out what Saddam was actually doing. It was to prevent a resumption of UN inspections that, if accurately conducted, would have shown that Saddam Hussein and Iraq did not pose the threat Bush, Cheney and the others claimed justified the invasion. Saddam would actually allow the UN inspectors to return in an attempt to fend off the US attack, but that was the inspectors' last visit to the land of the putative lakes of death serum. Once US forces were in control in Baghdad, the United Nations inspectors would be permanently barred from Iraq, on George W. Bush's orders.

That a Republican with Scowcroft's credentials should speak out so strongly and so early against the Iraq invasion was an important event in US elite policy discussion circles. It also provides conclusive evidence, if any further evidence is needed, of just how anticonservative—how totally radical—the George W. Bush administration actually is. The disregard for former Secretary of State Baker's opinions was a particularly telling sign of George W. Bush's disdain for experience and practical wisdom, even when it came to making the most important decisions of war and peace. Baker had enormous prestige throughout the Middle East and around the world as a result of his masterful handling of the diplomacy of the first Gulf War. He was also the Republican's generalissimo in Florida after the 2000 election. It was Baker who had masterminded the political maneuvering, including the appeal to the Supreme Court, that saved Florida's electoral votes for the Republicans and put George W. Bush in the White House. As much as any living American statesmen, James Baker knew when to hold them and when to fold them, but when it came to his opinions on foreign policy, George W. Bush didn't give a damn. What President George H.W. Bush thought of the bizarre renunciation of traditional

American principles being engineered by his son is beyond the realm of speculation.

Transforming Saddam and Iraq from peripheral concerns into the defining wedge issue of the 2002 election year had produced its first notable result—dissension among Republicans. In the world of wedge-issue politics, that's a good sign! If an issue can split your own people like that, just think what it's going to do to all those Democrats and foreigners. That October, with the midterm elections just a few weeks away, the nation watched as, on Capitol Hill, the Republicans stood strong and proud for freedom, war, and George W. Bush—while the Democrats tore at each other's entrails as they agonized over whether to oppose George W. Bush's war, or support it halfheartedly. In the world of wedge issues, it came down to this, folks. There are some Americans, called Republicans, who know what to do when this nation of ours is threatened by evil. And then there are some other people—they call themselves Democrats—who, when faced with evil, can't seem to make up their minds.

On September 11, 2002, George W. Bush flew to New York to mark the first anniversary of the Al Qaeda attacks. The next day he gave the key political speech of the midterm electoral campaign. Whenever George W. Bush campaigns, the backdrops are very carefully chosen. This time it wasn't an aircraft carrier or even Ground Zero that was chosen as the stage set for George W. Bush's most important partisan address of the 2002 election campaign. It was the podium of the General Assembly of the United Nations.

As always on such occasions, the ostensible audience—the people actually there in front of George W. Bush—were just extras in the production. The target audience wasn't the assembly of ambassadors and world leaders who had come to the United Nations to hear him speak. George W. Bush's audience that day was the America beyond the cameras. Looking through the teleprompter into American living rooms that day, he delivered the series of soundbites that, more than any other, would win the Republicans the upcoming midterm elections: "All the world now faces a test, and the United Nations a difficult and defining moment. Will the United Nations serve the purpose of its founding, or will it be irrelevant?"

Even in the most manipulative politics, what a politician says is not always necessarily the exact opposite of the truth, but in this case it was. "The conduct of the Iraqi regime is a threat to the authority of the United Nations, and a threat to peace," Bush announced, when it was actually his own conduct that was "a threat to the authority of the United Nations, and a threat to peace." On this occasion, too, he did not even mention Osama bin Laden.

Come Election Night that November, there was plenty to celebrate in the White House. Many Americans voted Republican in the 2002 congressional elections because they truly believed what George W. Bush told them—and don't you have to support the president when war threatens? Many others voted Republican because they liked seeing him stick it to all those fancy-pants New York foreigners up there at the UN. Thanks to his adroit creation and exploitation of the Saddam wedge issue, this time George W. Bush actually won an election, though narrowly.

As a result of Bush's success in transforming the campaign from a referendum on his failures ("Osama" and "Afghanistan") into a test of support for a new war against terrorism ("Saddam" and "Iraq"), the Republicans held on to the House of Representatives. They also won just enough Senate seats to put them back in control there too. Actually they hadn't "won" the Senate. They did hold their opponents (including Jeffords) to a 50-50 split. This allowed the ubiquitous, omni-influential Dick Cheney to tip things in the direction he wanted. As Vice President, he was entitled in his capacity as titular president of the Senate to cast the tiebreaking vote when the senators themselves were evenly split. This restored Republican control of all three branches of government: the White House, both houses of Congress, and of course the Supreme Court.

Like all his victories, this latest one gave George W. Bush yet another chance to think, and rethink. Here, once again, the pattern held. He would plunge on to Baghdad! So great was his bipolar obsession with winning the midterm elections and taking out Saddam that he never really seemed to have noticed how truly offensive his behavior was to civilized people around the world. Even more than his "dead-or-alive," "for-us-or-against-us" and "bring 'em on" lines, his "relevance" taunt at the United Nations convinced people everywhere that when it came to gratuitous arrogance, deliberate offensiveness, and culpable ignorance, he was unexcelled.

Did no one in the US government recognize that George W. Bush was turning the world against America? Some did. One was a mid-level State Department functionary named John Brady Kiesling. At the time of his resignation in February 2003, he was serving as head of the political section of the US embassy in Athens, Greece. In a letter to Secretary of State Powell, Kiesling explained why, having worked as a US foreign service officer for twenty years, he was now resigning. "I believed I was upholding the interests of the American people and the world," he wrote. "I believe it no longer."

Even if it were not so eloquently expressed, Kiesling's lament at how totally the conduct of US foreign policy had become corrupted would deserve to be quoted in extenso: "The policies we are now asked to advance are incompatible not only with American values but also with American interests," he wrote. "Our fervent pursuit of war with Iraq is driving us to squander the international legitimacy that has been America's most potent weapon of both offense and defense since the days of Woodrow Wilson. We have begun to dismantle the largest and most effective web of international relationships the world has ever known.

"Our current course will bring instability and danger, not security," he predicted, and then he put the current corruption of policy in perspective: "The sacrifice of global interests to domestic politics and to bureaucratic self-interest is nothing new, and it is certainly not a uniquely American problem. Still, we have not seen such systematic distortion of intelligence, such systematic manipulation of American opinion, since the war in Vietnam. The September 11 tragedy left us stronger than before, rallying around us a vast international coalition to cooperate for the first time in a systematic way against the threat of terrorism. But rather than take credit for those successes and build on them, this Administration has chosen to make terrorism a domestic political tool, enlisting a scattered and largely defeated Al Qaeda as its bureaucratic ally."

In this US diplomat's analysis, Americans were also the victims. "We spread disproportionate terror and confusion in the public mind, arbitrarily linking the unrelated problems of terrorism and Iraq. The result, and perhaps the motive, is to justify a vast misallocation of shrinking public wealth to the military and to weaken the safeguards that protect American citizens from the heavy hand of government. September 11 did not do as much damage to the fabric of American society as we seem determined to do to ourselves," he concluded.

It is illuminating to notice the different receptions Kiesling's resignation letter and Wolfowitz's "Get Saddam" letter got in Washington. One became an American blueprint for aggression. The other suffered the fate most memos from mid-level bureaucrats do. Powell never bothered to answer—and if he had, what could he have said? He already knew what Kiesling knew, and more, already.

"What they are introducing is chaos in international affairs," Nelson Mandela observed, summing up Kiesling's letter in a sentence. As a result, George W. Bush, not the United Nations, soon would face a test, self-inflicted, of his own relevance. It would be a defining moment.

ROADMAPS TO NOWHERE

☆ ☆ ☆

XII
Cakewalk to Babylon

IRAQ IS A COUNTRY that knows how to deal with its conquerors. The Greeks, the Romans, the Mongols, the Ottomans—to say nothing of the British—all had come and, in turn, been conquered. Now these innocuous Americans who could not make the electricity work, or the water flow, or command respect, or instill fear, were encamped, for their moment, between the Tigris and the Euphrates.

For 5,000 years the two great rivers had been dissolving conquest into mud—mud to make the bricks for the Iraqis' own palaces and temples. Now George W. Bush joined Alexander the Great and Genghis Khan on the list of Iraq's conquerors, in his case as an example of history repeating itself as farce.

Arrogance, political opportunism, plus geopolitical autism led America into a moment of biblical pathos as Eddie Murphy might have enacted it on the old, original *Saturday Night Live.* George W. Bush, who describes himself as a born-again Christian, could recite the question Christ asks in the Gospel according to Matthew: "For what is a man profited if he shall gain the whole world but lose his own soul?" The answer: "A bottomless pest hole, baby. Didn't you know those white guys was leading you on when they sold you all that cakewalk [bleep]? You ought to be listening to the Brother. Colin know whereof he speak. That Iraq is a vermin pit!"

POWELL WARNED BUSH LAST YEAR OF BLOODY WAR, ran one of the he-told-you-so headlines, but George W. Bush hadn't been listening to the only member of his Cabinet who was an experienced soldier. He'd been taking his advice from the guys who'd developed their military expertise finessing their draft-boards. As a result, Iraqi museums were now being looted. In the south of the country, a twelve-year-old girl attacked American troops with an assault rifle. While Saddam and his sons withdrew millions from the central bank, American bombs fell where they weren't.

US media reports of the chaos reflected how detached from reality American perceptions had become. The cognitive capacities of most of the American press, it turned out, had been embedded in the cakewalk illusion. HUSSEIN'S BAGHDAD FALLS, exulted the *Washington Post.* US FORCES MOVE TRIUMPHANTLY THROUGH CAPITAL STREETS, CHEERED BY CROWDS JUBILANT AT END OF REPRESSIVE REGIME, the headline added. As the "cakewalk" turned into a stumble, the US media provided wall-to-wall, 24/7 coverage of the vacillating state of America's psychopolitical condition. But to understand what was happening, you had to tune in to the BBC, Deutsche Welle, or one of the Canadian networks. China's CCTV provided more comprehensive and evenhanded reporting of the Iraq crisis than most of the American networks did.

Al-Jazeera, the first independent Arabic all-news network, of course, was the channel to watch if you really wanted a look at Iraq unfiltered by American preconceptions. During the first Gulf War, Ted Turner's CNN had allowed Americans to bypass the

Pentagon-manufactured version of events. Now, a decade later, Al Jazeera was showing how freedom—in this case, freedom of information—truly was revolutionizing life in the Arab world, though not in the way George W. Bush intended.

For the first time, Arabs were able to watch history unfold as it actually happened to them. The view they got of Iraq's latest foreign invader, George W. Bush, was as unsparing as the coverage Al-Jazeera provided of the failure of the latest Arab tyrant, Saddam Hussein, to repulse him. As US troops entered Baghdad, Al-Jazeera won a double badge of honor. One of the regime's last acts was to order Al-Jazeera expelled; one of the US occupation forces' first acts was to kill several of Al-Jazeera's correspondents. Even before the American occupation of Iraq began, the United States had lost the information war—not to the terrorists, but to the Arab world's first truly independent television news organization. If Western-style democracy ever does take root in the Middle East, it will be because the free flow of information in Arabic, not a US invasion, paved the way.

While the rest of the world perceived the George W. Bush invasion as a mad folly, journalists immured in the ethnocentrism of American discourse found it reasonable. Not just the rabid ranters on your AM dial, but such controversialists as Christopher Hitchens concluded that George W. Bush's plan to defeat terrorism and install democracy by starting a new war in the Middle East was one helluva good idea. It provides an interesting measure of the quality of a nation's public discourse when supposedly astute professionals like Thomas Friedman of the *New York Times* can look at George W. Bush's Iraq invasion folly and decide: Duh . . . looks good to me! "I was fifty-one percent for the war, and forty-nine percent against it, so I thought, why not?" Friedman later confided to a TV audience, unconsciously imitating Alfred E. Newman of *Mad* magazine fame.

Reality had become a dispensable accessory to the practice of journalism in the United States. Successful journalists—especially those who wanted to get on the talk shows—adapted themselves to the new exigencies of soundbite reporting and reality TV. Meanwhile, those who persisted in working on the anachronistic assumption that it was the duty of journalism to communicate objective truth were banished to the cybernetic gulag, that is to say, to public broadcasting and bookstores.

Commentators like Bill Moyers and programs like *Frontline* did provide astute reporting that conveyed the tragic quality, as well as the absurdity, of the vendetta George W. Bush had unleashed—but nobody except old people and liberals watched PBS. From Paris, the American foreign policy analyst William Pfaff wrote column after column accurately describing how George W. Bush's policies were destabilizing the Middle East and South Asia, but what were his demographics? Another knowledgeable commentator, especially when it came to the Cheney-Rumsfeld power plays, was John Newhouse, but his idea of a soundbite was a couplet from Yeats:

We had fed the heart on fantasies,
The heart's grown brutal from the fare.

Did he seriously expect people to think through that one? Michael Moore and Al Franken understand that to get criticism taken seriously in George W. Bush's America, you have to act like a clown.

Journalism had become technology's tool long before the George W. Bush media manipulators took command of our television sets, of course. There is just so much more of it now. In the nineteenth century the invention of the telegraph changed the speed with which war, politics, and public opinion interacted; it also fundamentally changed the nature of their relationship. By 1898, reality had already become dispensable. When ace war correspondent Frederic Remington got to Cuba, and found there was no war there, his boss, William Randolph Hearst, cabled back: "You furnish me the pictures, and I'll furnish you the war." This was the entertainment-news philosophy in a nutshell, and TV hadn't even been invented yet.

In the 1930s, radio changed everything again. Great events now had human—and inhuman—voices. Hitler's ranting, Roosevelt's fireside chats, and the King of England's abdication speech about "the woman I love" were all radio events. Radio was history now. It was also power. What made this new technology dangerous as well as liberating was that some people could use it so much more effectively than others—and this effectiveness had no inherent relationship to right and wrong. Churchill, Hitler, and Roosevelt were all masters—as was the young Orson Welles who, using radio, convinced millions of Americans that Martians had landed in New Jersey.

TV is to radio as radio was to Morse code. Starting in 1960, when television cost Richard Nixon the presidency, everything in America started revolving around TV. Television decided who got power; it decided what reality meant. Television helps explain why John F. Kennedy occupies a unique place in the American consciousness. Kennedy's ill health (as well as his sex life) today would remove him from presidential consideration, but no other American president has ever looked so gracefully in control of his own body as he did on television. Then, there was his assassination: along with the September 11 attacks, the most compelling television event in American history.

After 9/11 there was some high-minded speculation that the

media now might pay more attention to foreign news. This was followed by the illuminating incident in which Disney executives tried to cancel one of television's most distinguished news programs, *Nightline.* The program was profitable but, according to the executives, it didn't have the right demographics. In the run-up to the Iraq war, MSNBC experimented with a kind of *Nightline*–Lite, hosted by the talk-show veteran Phil Donahue. The issue-oriented program was almost immediately axed.

By the time George W. Bush decided he was going to "take out" Saddam, the spiritual paradigm for American national debate on issues of war and peace was *The Jerry Springer Show*. The standard for news reporting had become "reality" TV, the defining element in the "reality" being its made-for-television quality. Freedom of opinion cannot be said to have been repressed, but it was opinion divorced from reality. In fact, dissent was needed, as part of the entertainment, in order for it to reach its George W. Bush–style "for-us-or-against-us" climax. Only this time the desert island was Iraq, and Saddam Hussein was the one getting booted off the show.

It's useful to think of television as a mirror. Whatever channel we select, what we see is mostly ourselves, but is the backdrop authentic? Or is "Iraq" only a studio prop? During the Iraq invasion, you could see two opposing views of reality by watching Al Jazeera and Fox side by side. Who was telling the truth, and who was lying, including lying to themselves? One test of professional accuracy in reporting, as well as of ethical and competent news analysis, is that the journalist depicts reality in such a way that if the viewer were transported to the place concerned, he would be able to recognize it as the same place as the one he's been shown on TV. By this standard, American coverage of Iraq was a shameful failure. Americans were grossly deceived by the images on their TV screens. Some of them would die as a result.

"It's weird," Captain Burris Wollsieffer, of the Third Armored Cavalry Regiment, told an AP reporter, as his Fox news expectations collided with the Al-Jazeera realities of Ramadi, an Iraqi town where he and his fellow soldiers had expected to be welcomed as liberators. Instead, eight members of his unit were killed.

Captain Wollsieffer and his men had been trained to triumph in a techno-war against Saddam Hussein's elite Republican Guards. Instead they found themselves chasing a young girl who had shot at them into her house, where they found a rifle wrapped in a little red dress. This wasn't how it was supposed to be.

"Iraq was a brittle, oppressive regime that might break easily," Wolfowitz argued at Camp David. That was what, in his judgment, made getting Saddam so "doable." Wolfowitz's notion had spread throughout the administration, the US military, and the American media to become the received wisdom underlying the faith that conquering Iraq would be a cakewalk. The AP report explained what happened next: "Three men in the household were taken for interrogation, but the troops allowed the girl to remain at home when they learned her age. They also seized $1,500 in cash and $1,000 in Iraqi dinars." The report added: "None of the troops saw who fired the weapon, although they found no other suspects in the area other than the young girl."

This wasn't the brittle victory the neocons had conjured up in their briefing papers. "It's guerrilla warfare," as Captain Wollsieffer put it; but in these same events that were taking American lives, it was also possible to perceive a different kind of tragedy in which Iraqis, not Americans, were the victims: A young girl, angered by what she overhears her elders saying about the invaders, sneaks off with the rife, and fires a few stray shots. As a result three men of the family are taken away and the household savings are looted. Later, as Iraqis killed Americans every day, Americans found it hardest to understand why the Iraqis were so ungrateful. They did not connect these deaths and their own bewilderment with the greatest threat to freedom of the press in America, which is not the suppression of information, but its trivialization.

Around the same time Americans were getting killed in Ramadi, a BBC reporter came upon a scene that never made it into the American press. Better than all the "breaking news" flashes with jazzy graphics, it explained the growing resistance in Iraq. On the road north of Basra, the reporter had come upon another Iraqi girl, hysterical by the side of the road. She was weeping over the crushed body of her little brother. He had been run over by some Americans in a Humvee, and they'd kept going. In Iraq, metaphor was becoming reality. A hit-and-run foreign policy was producing actual traffic fatalities as American vehicles converged on Baghdad.

To borrow a born-again figure of speech from the George W. Bush lexicon, it was a matter of reaping what you sow. Using Iraq as a wedge issue had helped George W. Bush do well in the 2002 midterm elections. It had revived his presidency and given him the chance to be something other than an accidental president. This short-term success, however, had created a long-term problem. As a result of the midterm election year international crisis which George W. Bush had generated, Americans actually had to go ahead and conquer Iraq.

Even before US troops crossed the border into Iraq, they began to encounter resistance. In Kuwait, the land Americans had liberated in 1991 from Iraqi oppression, Kuwaitis themselves had to be banned from the northern half of their own country, in order to protect the US forces encamped there from drive-by killings.

Military spokesmen called these killers of Americans the agents of Saddam or Osama, the two faces of evil having merged into one by then. But like the irregulars who would kill so many GIs in Iraq, these attackers were angry locals with guns. Arabs (especially Iraqis) do share certain values with Americans (especially Texans). These include a high regard for their own dignity and independence, and above all, an inclination to jealously guard their right to bear arms.

The fall of Saddam's statue in downtown Baghdad was supposed to culminate the cakewalk. It wound up illustrating how wrong US expectations had been from the start. A small crowd did try to topple the statue. They could no more bring it down than, prior to the invasion, the US-backed Iraqi National Congress and its expatriate businessman leader, Ahmed Chalabi—a Rumsfeld favorite—had been able to topple Saddam himself. So American tanks did it for them.

Even then, this literal instance of "Saddam falling" led to no mass rejoicing. The crowd, instead of growing larger, dispersed. Here, as nowhere else, the Americans had expected jubilation on the part of the Iraqis, as a result of the gift of freedom having been bestowed upon them. What they encountered instead of friendship was reserve shading into hostility. The American soldiers did not yet understand that, thanks to America, specific terror had been replaced by generalized fear.

Before the invasion, Iraqis had only one thing to fear: the wrath of Saddam. Now fear lurked everywhere in many forms: random violence, American mistaken targeting, disease (from lack of clean drinking water). Saddam was gone. So was Saddam's electricity and water supply, along with his food rations and all those "jobs" he'd given people to keep them subservient to him. Following their liberation by American forces, millions of Iraqis found themselves unemployed, hungry, and scared.

The Americans focused on Saddam's falling statue because that event seemed to contain the meaning Americans had set out to impose on Iraq. From another perspective, it was just one more incident in the general wave of vandalism that overtook Baghdad now that the Americans were there. The playbook had called for a prime-time eruption of freedom, but this was different from the Tiananmen Square demonstrations, and the fall of the Berlin Wall. In Beijing and Berlin, no one had looted hospitals.

One consequence of the invasion was a health care crisis in a country that, even under Saddam, had maintained fairly high levels of public health. As problems grew, the new US "administrator" called in seventy Iraqi merchants for a talk. They told him infants were dying of dysentery because the water supply had been polluted, and no oral rehydration salts were available. Supplies in warehouses were not being distributed. The Iraqis also pointed out that the mass unemployment provided an inexhaustible reservoir of young men eager to take up arms against the occupation. US officials responded, according to news reports, by emphasizing to the Iraqis that free enterprise was the key to creating jobs.

The Iraqis now did have the right to criticize their new rulers, both in such meetings and on the street. They exercised it freely and loudly, often in questions shouted at passing American troops. If Americans respected their ancient culture so much, and weren't just here to steal oil, Iraqis wanted to know, how come the only places the Americans guarded had to do with Iraq's petroleum exports? Hadn't anyone in the White House or the Pentagon realized that once Baghdad fell, it might be prudent also to protect schools, hospitals, and libraries, as well as museums?

The answer was: No, no one had thought of that, at least no one with any pull. The State Department had conducted a five million dollar study of the potential difficulties establishing law and order in Iraq might actually involve. The study had been ignored—just like every study or finding that, if taken seriously, might have caused George W. Bush, Cheney, and Rumsfeld to reconsider their decision not only to attack Iraq, but to invade it on the cheap.

Who cared what "studies" said? Secretary of Defense Rumsfeld had already decided that 140,000 troops—not the 250,000 it probably would have required—would be more than enough to do the job. So confident was he that conquering Iraq was going to be a cakewalk he also had decided that US force levels in Iraq would be down from the initial 140,000 to fewer than 40,000 by Christmas 2003. US forces would have been insufficient to secure the country—even if there had been an intelligent, workable plan to administer Iraq once it was conquered, which there never was.

In the ensuing chaos, which was the greater loss for Iraq and humanity—the priceless antiquities that vanished in the looting, or the death of Sergio Vieira de Mello, the UN's special respresentative to Iraq? Many archeological treasures, dating back 5,000 years to the dawn if human civilization, were looted during the early days if the US occupation.

Vieira de Mello, a Brazilian, was killed, along with more than a dozen other UN experts from nearly as many different countries, when the United Nations headquarters in Baghdad was bombed. He had done heroic work in East Timor and many other places. Earlier George W. Bush had told the United Nations it faced a test of its relevance. The presence of Vieira de Mello and his staff had been proof that in spite of the contempt with which George W. Bush had treated it, the UN would continue to do what good it could.

But what about George W. Bush's own relevance? America's duties in Iraq were clear under international law. It was the responsibility of the United States, as the occupying power, both to preserve the cultural heritage and to protect the lives of the people, both Iraqis and foreigners, who had fallen under US military administration. "The United Nations Security Council has not lived up to its responsibilities, so we will rise to ours," George W. Bush proclaimed on the eve of the invasion, but especially after the bombing of the UN headquarters, the American detachment from any sense of responsibility was striking. It was as though such terrible events weren't America's concern. After all, hadn't the United Nations been "against us"?

One thing Iraqis say over and over, now that they are free to speak their minds, is: Thanks for overthrowing Saddam, America. Now go home. But as Rumsfeld, Cheney, and George W. Bush himself made clear, the United States wasn't going to cut and run. It wasn't going home until, among other things, it had unearthed Saddam's weapons of mass destruction—that is to say, maybe never.

"We know where they are," Rumsfeld declared. But to paraphrase Gertrude Stein, when Rumsfeld's inspectors got there they found there was no there there. In the months after the invasion,

US inspectors did make some discoveries. For instance, they came upon some railroad cars buried in sand. They thought these might be the mobile chemical-weapons factories unconfirmed intelligence reports had claimed were in Iraq, but nothing was in them. Never mind. As Cheney and Rumsfeld declared, over and over, the empty warehouses meant nothing. George W. Bush believed the weapons existed, so they would have to be found.

"But my dear Rumsfeld," as Sherlock Holmes might have put it, "can't you understand? That is precisely the solution to the mystery, that there are no weapons of mass destruction." The invasion revealed that the United Nations sanctions—for which George W. Bush and his capos had such contempt—had worked, and worked admirably. Under the pressure of UN sanctions Saddam had decommissioned his weapons of mass destruction. Yet instead of celebrating this happy discovery, the Americans did everything they could to discredit the revelations that Saddam Hussein had no weapons of mass destruction—even when the CIA's own David Kay reported that to the president.

Even if the desired underground caverns full of nasty spores had been found, American forces still would not have gone home. This was because, thanks to the ideological equivalent of "mission creep," America was no longer in Iraq merely to enforce "regime change" or save the world from mass destruction. America was in Iraq now to build democracy there, and then spread it all over the Arab and Muslim world.

It was all in keeping with the reverse–domino theory administration officials had started propounding a few months before the attack. Saddam falling, they predicted, would lead to regime after Arab regime falling to freedom. And once the Arabs were free, they wouldn't disagree with us anymore! It was the repetition of a very old historical pattern. The forces of "civilization" intervene to fight evil (slavery, desecration of the Holy Places, piracy, Saddam). Duty then obliges them to stay on indefinitely because the natives are culturally defective. In the old days the French called it the "mission to civilize." The English called it the white man's burden. George W. Bush called it Operation Iraqi Freedom.

Democracy would be good for the Arabs, but it would be great for America. Once America made the Middle East democratic, all those Arabs and Muslims would stop causing us trouble. This imaginative and original hypothesis raised even more questions about the nature of democracy than it did about Arabs and Muslims.

For instance, why should Arabs and Muslims living under democracy be in any way less inclined to resent foreign domination of their natural resources, including their stupendous oil reserves, than those governed by hereditary rulers or military tyrants? Why should free Arabs want to resist foreign occupation any less than repressed Arabs? The truth is that people in the Middle East don't object to what the United States does because they have bad governments. American actions disgust them because the policies of the US government are so hypocritical, dishonest, and unjust.

"Are Security Council resolutions to be honored and enforced, or cast aside without consequence?" George W. Bush asked, that time he dared the United Nations to prove its relevance. He was perhaps the only person in the chamber unaware that this was the exact same question that Arabs and Muslims (along with many others) had been asking about the UN for forty-five years.

"Iraq has answered a decade of UN demands with a decade of defiance," he continued. In his speech, he did not mention that there was another country in the Middle East that had defied UN demands for even longer. Only Saddam Hussein and Iraq were the recipients of George W. Bush's ire. Ariel Sharon and Israel's decades-long defiance of UN resolutions calling for it to withdraw from territories conquered during the 1967 Six Day War were never mentioned.

In reality, as well as in Arab and Muslim eyes, the American invasion of Iraq was the most spectacular example yet of the double standard the United States has always applied to United Nations resolutions, as well as to the Middle East. Arabs and Muslims—like most other people, including Americans—don't like double standards, so all the talk about this latest foreign military attack on an Arab country being a crusade for democracy made George W. Bush's remarks doubly offensive. It was also a logical absurdity: What conceivable reason could there be for supposing that democratically elected Arab governments would accept injustices that even dictatorships opposed?

The Middle East countries where some sort of evolution to greater freedom was possible (Iran, Syria) were actually the ones to which George W. Bush displayed the greatest hostility. Meanwhile, America's most useful military allies in its new crusade for democracy continued to be military dictatorships and absolute monarchies. The military dictator of Pakistan had played an essential role in making Operation Enduring Freedom possible in Afghanistan. Now hereditary monarchies (Qatar and Kuwait) provided indispensable land, air, and naval facilities for launching Operation Iraqi Freedom. At the same time, the freely elected parliament of the region's most important Muslim democracy, Turkey, refused to authorize US military use of that country's territory for the attack. The Turks, while not Arabs, were as opposed to the invasion as their neighbors, both in the Middle East and Europe. The difference was that, thanks to Turkey's parliamentary democracy, Turkey's actions reflected the wishes of its people.

The ouster of Saddam Hussein had achieved the ouster of Saddam Hussein; that was all. This is not a negligible achievement. Done the right way—that is, in keeping with international law, and with support of the proper coalition of allies—it might even have been an admirable achievement. But doing it the George W. Bush way created countless more problems than it solved. At the heart of the problem was a willful misunderstanding of what US power—indeed any power—can achieve.

The United States does indeed have the power to invade countries like Afghanistan and Iraq, and put their rulers and their armed forces to flight, but Iraq would prove, as Afghanistan had, that creating a power vacuum is an invitation to chaos. There is a difference between regime change and regime destruction. There is also a difference between liberating a country and plunging it into war. In a matter of weeks, Operation Iraqi Freedom turned into a counterinsurgency operation. One of the first attempts at military pacification was named Operation Scorpion. It would have been better to call it "Operation Scorpion Eggs," for with each attack, new fighters against the American occupation were spawned.

The unfounded arrogance of the neocons was based on cultural contempt for the Arabs. They forgot when they decided to start their Iraq war that what they perceive as Arab weakness is precisely what has brought down many a previous conqueror. Arabs are a people whose resistance grows with defeat. This is the great theme of the Middle East—obvious to everyone except the Bush crowd—that every person and power wishing to act rationally there must understand. You can defeat them, humiliate them, steal their oil, their water, their countries. But you cannot get the Arabs to submit, no matter how many of them you kill, no matter how many victories you win. This is the lesson of Algeria, Suez, Palestine, and now, after the US invasion, it is becoming the lesson of Iraq.

Once upon a time, George W. Bush seemed to understand the limitations of power. Does anyone remember the debates during the 2000 presidential election campaign, when he derided "nation building" and scorned "mission creep"? Apparently George W. Bush does not.

While, by the tens of thousands, Americans rode around Iraq in big Humvees, APCs, and tanks, George W. Bush rode his pickup truck around his ranch—more than 1,500 acres of Texas that, like Iraq and Afghanistan, seemed to have fallen to him as if in the nature of things. Bob Woodward describes a preinvasion episode that, on Christian Bible TV, might be titled *George W. Bush Wandering the Wilderness*, only it is the terrain of his mind, as reflected in these surroundings, that seems the true wilderness.

The incident occurred in August 2002. Iraq had not yet been invaded, but George W. Bush had already decided to ignore the fact that there was still no evidence linking Saddam Hussein to the 9/11 attacks, and go ahead with the invasion anyway. He invited Woodward to join him and Condoleezza Rice for a ride around the ranch. After jolting around in the pickup for while, the two men got out, and started walking toward a giant natural rock formation.

Woodward describes the great stone outcropping that loomed up before them as "maybe 40 yards across . . . nearly white in color, shaped like a half-moon, with a steep overhang." Condoleezza Rice doesn't get out of the truck, because she's not wearing the right shoes. So, with only the journalist trailing after him, George W. Bush plunges into the dead landscape toward the weird rock, but it's the autistic landscape of George W. Bush's world vision that is really eerie. This autism isn't psychiatric; it is cultural and political, ideological and intellectual. Bush's mind, it becomes clear as he speaks, is as isolated from the realities of the world as this desolate stretch of his ranch.

"I loathe Kim Jong Il!" George W. Bush had shouted to Woodward earlier. "I've got a visceral reaction to this guy." During their talk, Woodward adds, he "spoke a dozen times about his 'instincts' or his 'instinctive' reactions, including his statement, 'I'm not a textbook player. I'm a gut player.' " The subject of emotions entered the conversation obliquely: "I mean if, you know, if you want to hear resentment, just listen to the word unilateralism," George W. Bush had said. "I mean, that's resentment." "I will seize the opportunity to achieve big goals," he promised Woodward.

Whether Woodward intended it or not, his account of George W. Bush is a portrait of what, under ordinary circumstances, a layman would call, without too much rashness, madness. Yeats might have given us a couplet about this scary man with the power to conquer countries walking to a rock. Woodward simply summarizes his impressions of what he calls George W. Bush's "overall approach or philosophy to foreign affairs and war policy" in one sentence, and that is enough. "His vision clearly includes an ambitious reordering of the world through preemptive and, if necessary, unilateral action to reduce suffering and bring peace," he writes as though that were the most normal attitude in the world for a man occupying the presidency of the United States to have.

Vice President Cheney had already explained what George W. Bush and the rest of them imagined invading Iraq would accomplish in a speech to an organization in which Cheney is not eligible for membership, the American Veterans of Foreign Wars.

"Regime change in Iraq would bring about a number of benefits to the region," Cheney predicted. "When the gravest of threats are eliminated, the freedom-loving peoples of the region will have a chance to promote the values that can bring lasting peace. As for the reaction of the Arab 'street,'" Cheney continued, "the Middle East expert Professor Fouad Ajami predicts that after liberation, the streets in Basra and Baghdad are 'sure to erupt in joy in the same way the throngs in Kabul greeted the Americans.'" The benefits, Cheney predicted, would radiate out from Iraq. "Extremists in the region," he assured his audience, "would have to rethink their strategy of jihad. Moderates throughout the region would take heart. And our ability to advance the Israeli-Palestinian peace process would be enhanced, just as it was following the liberation of Kuwait in 1991."

That was the administration's vision before the Iraq invasion. Here is what George W. Bush said afterwards—after no weapons of mass destruction had been found, after it turned out no Iraqi oil was going to pay for his eighty-seven billion dollar-a-year occupation, after his invasion had unleashed chaos, and embroiled America in a war in which every day Americans were getting killed: "History will remember we made the absolute right decision."

Afghanistan had been one twist of George W. Bush's kaleidoscope. Now, just as he wanted, Iraq was twisted—and once again, in Iraq as it had in Afghanistan, the pursuit of evil produced the vivid image of another young American whose misfortune it was to be at the wrong place at the wrong time as George W. Bush pursued his "war on terrorism."

In the opening stage of the invasion, the TV images of the putative rescue of Jessica Lynch seemed, like Operation Iraqi Freedom itself, to vindicate George W. Bush's take on the world. Brave American soldiers had used our technological supremacy to rescue a good girl from bad people. That was the video millions of Americans will probably remember, in November 2004, as they vote for George W. Bush.

In reality, there had been the usual intelligence failure: The rescue squad charged into a hospital thinking it was a terrorist command post. Instead of Islamist fanatics, they came upon a scene that showed that the Iraqis who had captured Jessica Lynch had behaved with what, if they were Americans, we would call chivalry. Jessica had been injured when her Humvee crashed during an ambush, not in combat. Actually, it hadn't even been an ambush. Lynch and the others had gotten lost, and taken a wrong turn off the road to Baghdad. Near the town of Nasiriya, shooting had erupted.

The Iraqis who captured Jessica, who had been knocked unconscious in the Humvee crash, had saved her life, then made sure she got medical care. As for Jessica's subsequent "rescue," the US troops would not even have known her whereabouts had an Iraqi lawyer not courageously revealed her location. And no "rescue" mission would have been necessary in the first place had US soldiers not opened fired on the Iraqi ambulance when the staff of the hospital tried to reunite her with American forces.

As result of this chaotic turn of events, so typical of warfare as it actually unfolds, the young, blonde, very pretty, and utterly captivating Jessica Lynch became not only a hero, but the Iraq war's first celebrity. Her fifteen minutes of fame flattered America's heroic vision of itself. It also contained revelations audiences preferred not to have televised into their living rooms.

One such revelation related to the different treatment accorded Jessica Lynch and another female member of her unit, named Shoshana Johnson. As Jessica Lynch herself later said, she was a survivor rather than a hero. Shoshana, in the military sense, was the hero of the episode. When Jessica was knocked unconscious, and other members of their group killed, Shoshana had fought, and was seriously wounded resisting capture. Yet Jessica, not Shoshana, was the one who got the lucrative book deal and the prime-time interview with Diane Sawyer. Shoshana, the other female survivor of the incident, who got so much less attention, was black. George W. Bush and people who vote for him, in general, are not supporters of affirmative action. But the truth is, until people started raising a ruckus, Shoshana wasn't in the photos with Jessica Lynch.

It gets worse than that. While Jessica got 80 percent of her salary in disability pay once she got back to the United States, and she started physical therapy, Shoshana, who had been more seriously injured than Jessica, got only 30 percent. The way the Pentagon spokesmen explained it, paying more seriously wounded soldiers like Shoshana less was in keeping with the neocon accounting "reforms" Cheney and Rumsfeld had introduced at the Pentagon. After all, it is only logical to pay someone who no longer is able to fight for you less money than someone who was less seriously injured, and therefore more likely to see active duty again some day.

Then there were the other members of Jessica Lynch's 507th

Maintenance Company who would never, ever, get even a photo op once George W. Bush had welcomed America's newest and prettiest celebrity-hero to the White House. These would include the Americans in Jessica Lynch's unit who had been killed. George W. Bush would never visit their grave sites.

The Jessica Lynch story is like the Iraq war itself. The more you learn, the worse it gets. Within six months, three of the soldiers who rescued her were dead—only one of combat wounds, which he suffered in Afghanistan, not Iraq. One died in a traffic crash after returning to America; another, after coming home, was shot dead at a barbecue. The true heroes of the incident were the Iraqis. They were the ones who actually saved Private Lynch. Their heroism was demeaned as well—their humanity betrayed for a headline and a big book advance.

FIENDS RAPED JESSICA, ran the headline in the New York *Daily News.* The tabloid was only repeating the story being peddled by Knopf, which is considered to be one of America's most distinguished publishers. The venerable publishing house, having paid a million dollars for the right to put Jessica Lynch's name on the front of a book, hired a ghostwriter to manufacture a memoir that would sell. Rape sells, but Jessica didn't remember being raped. She remembered the Iraqi nurse who had sung her lullabies.

It was like the weapons of mass destruction. The lack of evidence was the proof. The author cited "medical records" he claimed showed Jessica had been anally raped. No professional would ever verify them; no copies of the supposed records were ever produced. Iraqi doctors did provide detailed refutations of the charges though, and whether they realized it or not, they—the very ones who had saved Jessica Lynch—were now in the eyes of millions of Americans, like Saddam Hussein, scarcely human at all, "fiends" who had molested a nice American girl who had only come to their country in order to help them.

Jessica herself refuted almost all the claims of mistreatment. She remembered the crash. She insisted on pointing out that—contrary to the Pentagon's original hyped-up claims—she had not fired a single shot as the Iraqis advanced. She recalled in grateful detail the kindness of the Iraqi staff at the hospital. She also refuted the reports she was suffering from "amnesia," although she had been unconscious for three hours—between the time her Humvee crashed and the time she awoke in the Iraqi hospital. And this—the time when Iraqis were saving this unconscious US soldier's life—was supposedly when, according to the book Knopf published with Jessica's name on it—she had been raped and beaten.

Iraqi doctors at the hospital—who had been as charmed by Jessica as Americans later were—found such accusations astonishing. They described how Jessica's captors had brought her to them unconscious and fully dressed. The doctors pointed out that raping an unconscious woman was virtually beyond belief, and that then taking the supposed rape victim to a hospital where evidence of such a crime would surely be noticed by trained medical personnel defied imagination. Besides, she showed no signs of physical mistreatment. "Why would anyone bother to hit me while I was unconscious?" Jessica herself asked, referring to claims in the book that she had been beaten as well as sexually abused.

While Knopf sullied itself in an attempt to recoup its investment on Jessica's misfortune, one of the *New York Times* reporters covering the story, Jayson Blair, was fabricating descriptions of Jessica's family and home in little Palestine, West

Virginia. This was far from the worst of the falsifications Operation Iraqi Freedom had spawned. But in the ensuing scandal, Blair was fired and the executive editor of the esteemed newspaper, Howell Raines, resigned. George W. Bush's decision to act on instinct when it came to lashing out at the enemies of unilateralism had, if only indirectly, helped to produce regime change at the *New York Times,* though even after the big shake-up Thomas Friedman continued to expound upon his belief that out of all this Iraq death, democracy and peace were bound to rise, like beautiful flowers on a grave.

Beneath these great public controversies, there unfolded as always the caprices of individual fate. John Walker Lindh got twenty years as a result of Operation Enduring Freedom. Jessica Lynch would get her million dollars, thanks to Operation Iraqi Freedom. He was denounced as a traitor. She became, through no fault of her own, a heroine-celebrity, but all these two young Americans really were, or ever had been, were orphans of the storm.

As for the villain of the story, long after Jessica Lynch and George W. Bush are forgotten—maybe even after Alexander the Great is forgotten—the name of Saddam Hussein will live on amid the fabled ruins of Babylon. Babylon is famous for the bible story about its Hanging Gardens. It is also where Alexander the Great, having conquered the world from the Adriatic to the Indus, died of fever in 325 BC, at age 34.

Saddam Hussein saw Babylon, as he saw everything else, as a proscenium for the display of his own glory. His original grand conception was to transform Babylon into a theme park honoring himself. The fabled gardens would be reconstructed and renamed in honor of Saddam. Magnificent guest houses, resembling those sketches seen in real estate advertisements for "Mediterranean" villas in Florida, only much larger, would surmount the hills overlooking Babylon. From these residences, Saddam and his children and their families—including the families of the sons-in-law he later authorized his own sons to murder—would be transported to the archeological marvels of Babylon by ultramodern cable cars such as the kind seen at the largest American theme parks and poshest ski resorts.

Fortunately, the UN sanctions came to the archeological rescue. Saddam Land was never built. Importing the cable cars, including the hanging gondolas, the towers for the cables, and the machinery to operate them, apparently might have helped Saddam in some way or another to produce WMDs. In any case it was not allowed. Foreign enemies, however, could not stop Saddam from transforming Babylon with millions of bricks. At Saddam's command, whole districts of ancient Babylon were reconstructed.

Wander among these recently-manufactured ruins, and you will soon see why Saddam Hussein's name will never be forgotten. Most of the bricks are just ordinary bricks. But every fourth or fifth brick is a special Saddam Brick. In florid official Arabic, the inscription on each brick says something to the effect of: "Constructed by the grace of the Mighty and Merciful Saddam Hussein, Beloved of his People" and so on and so forth. Mobs can tear down statues, and if they can't, tanks or bombs can demolish them. But no one will ever be able to remove his name from Babylon.

You would have to tear down every building in Babylon to dislodge them all—and then what would you have? You would have an immense pile of bricks, in a country where bricks endure for thousands of years, with Saddam's name on them.

XIII
Roadmaps to Nowhere

All wars, to one extent or another, are exercises in mass hallucination. Why, otherwise, would perfectly normal people gather together in large groups and walk into cannon fire? Crowds of people firing off guns, dropping bombs, and shooting off artillery shells (that is to say, armies) are very dangerous, but nowhere near as dangerous as an out-of-control political elite in the grip of a shared delusion.

World War I was a catastrophe of elitist decision-making; it remains history's bloodiest war. One of its astonishing features is that the folly of starting it was at least partially visible to those who unleashed it. People ranging from the German Emperor Wilhelm II to British Foreign Secretary Sir Edward Grey, sensed they were acting insanely. Yet swept along by the delusion that unleashing a general war in Europe was the unavoidable course of action, Europe's rulers chose self-destruction. Within five years the czar was dead, the kaiser in exile, and the British aristocracy beset by inheritance taxes and the servant problem. Thanks to Europe's folly, Vladimir Lenin and Mahatma Gandhi, along with the United States of America, would inherit the earth.

One way to see the Vietnam War is as a catastrophe of self-destructive presumptuousness. For Lyndon Baines Johnson, creating the Great Society in America wasn't enough. He had to export it to tropical Asia. His belief in the domino theory transformed his impulsiveness (at least in the eyes of his believers) from a rash scheme into strategic necessity. One consequence of Johnson's folly was an ideological backlash in America that led to the emergence of the neocons, including the key control figures in the George W. Bush administration.

Vice President Dick Cheney is on the surface the most sophisticated of those figures. Scratch the surface, however, and he turns out to be just another loopy Washington mandarin with an *idée fixe*. Even before taking office as vice president in 2001, Cheney showed himself to be as irrationally obsessed with Saddam Hussein as, back in Lyndon Johnson's time, supposedly astute presidential advisers like McGeorge Bundy and Walt Whitman Rostow had been with falling dominoes.

Saddam Hussein was defeated in the 1991 Gulf war, though in the years afterward to hear Cheney talk you'd never know it. "Everything that had been tried before didn't work," Cheney complained, after Kuwait had been liberated and Saddam defeated. In fact, listening to Cheney, it sometimes sounded as though Iraq had defeated the United States, not the other way around. What was to be done? "By a system of elimination—sanctions won't stop him, bombing won't stop him, and so on—you come down to the last resort: Then we'll have to take him out," Cheney was heard to remark at neocon conclaves even before the "regime change" doctrine was formally codified in the January 1998 "Get Saddam" letter.

But what did "stop him" mean by then? Saddam had been stopped in Kuwait. He'd been stopped (though Cheney refused to believe it) from developing weapons of mass destruction. He'd been stopped from posing a threat to his neighbors. After the United States actually stood up to him, instead of coddling him, as it had done earlier, Saddam never attacked anyone again. Thanks to the UN-imposed (and United States and British-patrolled) no-fly zones within Iraq, Saddam had also been prevented from reasserting control over the Kurds in the north of the country.

You couldn't find a more successful example of good old Cold War Republican, John Foster Dulles–style containment than the successful containment of Saddam Hussein. Yet for the neocons, Cheney included, the success of this bipartisan policy, pursued by both George H.W. Bush and Bill Clinton, amounted to surrender on the installment plan.

In the decade separating Saddam Hussein's defeat in 1991 from George W. Bush's inauguration in 2001, the world changed stupendously. The Soviet Union disappeared from our maps; the personal computer arrived on our desktops. From the microchip factories of Malaysia to the online haberdasheries of Wisconsin, globalization changed the way people lived and did business. But, by the time the neocon moment to make history arrived, their squinty little minds still had only one line of focus when it came to "national security."

The Butcher of Baghdad continued to fascinate them more than any of the world's many, much more important opportunities and perils. The notion of "taking out" Saddam Hussein over the years had become for Dick Cheney, in particular, what the Schleswig-Holstein question had been for certain forgotten statesmen of the nineteenth century—the bugaboo that, fed by his obsession, grows to dominate all other concerns.

"Everything that had been tried before didn't work." Ergo,

"we'll have to take him out." This false syllogism reflects the workings of a mind untethered from reality, as well as from its constitutional duties.

In March 2002, six months after the 9/11 attacks, and exactly a year before the Iraq invasion, Cheney visited nine Arab and Muslim countries. Wherever he went, he met leaders of considerable experience. Many of them had important insights they wanted to share; some even had wisdom to impart. As in any region of the world, the notables Cheney encountered also included charlatans, criminals, and rogues. Whatever the moral characteristics of the local regime, the honor guards were drawn up as Air Force Two landed. Following the motorcade to the royal or presidential palace, and the usual ceremonial pleasantries, the attempt to communicate began—and kings and presidents, emirs, and prime ministers alike discovered that while a vice president of the United States was seated on the gilt armchair opposite them, they might as well have been trying to reason with a stone.

As far as Cheney was concerned, these very leaders soon would be consigned to the dumpster of history by the Bush-Cheney reverse-domino theory. As the neocons foresaw it, even long-standing United States allies were nothing but yesterday's headlines—destined to be swept away by the Bush-Cheney tide of democracy that following the attack on Iraq supposedly was going to surge over the Middle East.

Wherever Cheney presented his Iraq war plans, the reaction was the same (though phrased more diplomatically): Mr. Vice President, are you crazy? If sanity is defined as the capacity to distinguish volition from possibility, and then to adjust one's expectations and behavior accordingly, the answer was a double yes.

The reaction of America's best friends to Cheney's Iraq war

scheme was the most telling. No leaders were more pro-American than King Abdullah of Jordan and Prime Minister Bulent Ecevit of Turkey, a NATO ally. "A strike on Iraq will be disastrous for Iraq and the region as a whole and will threaten the security and stability of the Middle East," Abdullah declared, in an official statement issued after his meeting with Cheney. Ecevit called the threat of a US attack on Iraq a "nightmare." He added that it would devastate the Turkish economy.

Cheney had anticipated a triumphal progress across the Middle East as, one by one, he would enlist the countries he visited in the cause of "taking out" Saddam Hussein. But his trip was no diplomatic cakewalk; it foreshadowed the military surprise that would await United States forces in Iraq one year later. Faced with the refusal of reality to conform to his requirements, Cheney did what he had done earlier in the case of anthrax, and what he would later do with weapons of mass destruction. He lied. George W. Bush already had decided to invade Iraq. His "axis of evil" pronouncement, just over a month earlier, had been the curtain-raiser. Now, with Cheney's junket, the profile of the Administration's intentions came into clearer view. If he had had the makings of a competent statesmen, Cheney would have returned to Washington with an honest, that is to say, a very negative assessment of the situation he had encountered, which (had George W. Bush any interest in conducting a realistic foreign policy) would then have led to a broad reconsideration of the plans for attacking Iraq.

But Cheney had no interest in reconsidering anything. The great alarm the prospect of the United States invading Iraq excited everywhere did however cause him to change his tactics, and to claim that "no decision" had been made. Following his visit to Turkey, Prime Minister Ecevit assured reporters that

Cheney "very clearly stated that there will be no military action against Iraq in the foreseeable future."

Ecevit's English was perfect, but if he had examined the transcript of their discussion, he no doubt would have found that Cheney had slipped some qualifiers into the small talk. Colin Powell, whose position of secretary of state gave him as good a vantage point as anyone to observe the unfolding of the Bush-Cheney foreign policy, was more circumspect. Military action against Iraq was unlikely in the immediate future, he remarked, after learning of the latest policy shifts from his usual source, the newspapers.

Cheney's visit to the Middle East coincided with a particularly dangerous moment in the region. The second Palestinian uprising against Israeli occupation had erupted more than a year earlier, and attempts to crush the new intifada had led to more terrorism. Israel was the regional superpower, but Prime Minister Ariel Sharon was afflicted with what might be called "Star Wars" impotence. Israel's armed forces could defeat any Arab army, but not even its nuclear weapons could stop young Palestinians from turning themselves into human bombs. Sharon, as he had twenty years earlier, in his brutal and futile attempts to crush Palestinian resistance in Lebanon, opted to brutalize the Palestinians even more.

Historians may someday remember March 2002 as an even more disastrous watershed than March 2003, when the United States invaded Iraq. Sharon could not provide Israelis with security in their daily lives. But he could go on the rampage against Palestinians on the West Bank, including the Palestinian president, Yasser Arafat. As Cheney appeared on the horizon, that was what he did.

On March 12, the day Cheney arrived in the Middle East,

more than 20,000 Israeli troops swept into the Gaza Strip and reoccupied the West Bank city of Ramallah. This was the most serious blow to the Israeli-Palestinian peace process since the Oslo Accords were signed in 1993. Under any other United States president except George W. Bush, stupendous pressure would have been applied to stop the fighting, and to prevent Sharon's reoccupation of the West Bank. Instead, the United States did nothing. Secretary of State Powell did not swing into action. George W. Bush made no comment. Vice President Cheney continued his "Get Saddam" tour as though nothing had happened.

Cheney finally did touch down in Israel on March 18 for a prescheduled courtesy call. Simply by meeting with Arafat—as United States presidents and vice presidents had been doing, by then, for nearly ten years—Cheney probably could have prevented much bloodshed. Instead he met only with Sharon. Cheney's refusal to meet Arafat was a calculated insult; he had, after all, met with rooms full of other Arab leaders in the course of his trip. The chief effect of this insult was to incite further Palestinian violence while even further reducing the ability of Palestinian moderates to curb it.

Cheney may not have told Sharon he could go on attacking the Palestinians with impunity, but the Israeli prime minister acted as if he had. Within days of Cheney's departure, President Arafat was a prisoner in Ramallah, unable to travel within the Palestinian territories, or to attend a scheduled Arab League meeting in Lebanon. On March 29, Israeli tanks assaulted Yasser Arafat's compound. Forced to take refuge underground in a basement, Arafat if anything seemed to enjoy returning to his old life as the Palestinian leader Ariel Sharon could defeat, but never kill.

History was repeating itself in another way. Demonizing Arafat did not stop the Palestinian attacks on Israelis. The wave of suicide bombing grew worse. Terror was redescending on the Occupied Territories and, within Israel itself, people were more terrorized than ever before. Vice President Cheney did not let any of this distract him from the only thing that mattered to him: launching a war against Iraq.

The workaday prose of the following press report conveys the nature of the diplomatic disaster created by Cheney's first major foray, as Vice President, into foreign affairs: "Almost all the countries Cheney has visited refrained from supporting action against Iraq, insisting that the Palestinian-Israeli conflict should be resolved instead." Not a single country Cheney visited in the end would provide troops for the Bush-Cheney war. Instead every nation he visited (except Israel) would oppose it, and almost all refused to let their territory be used for the attack.

When it came to diplomacy, Cheney was a dud, but his failure to lift a finger to stop Palestinians killing Israelis and Israelis killing Palestinians was more than incompetent; it was scandalous. As he flew around on Air Force Two, the last tattered shreds of the Oslo peace accords were blown away and what Prime Minister Sharon correctly described as a "long and complicated war that knows no borders"—the horrible war of double terrorism afflicting all the inhabitants of the Holy Land—erupted. Whatever the long-term consequences of having started the Iraq war turn out to be, the consequences of having failed to stop this new and dangerous Israeli-Palestinian war are bound to be dire for Israelis, Palestinians, and Americans alike.

Cheney's triumphal tour had turned into a circuit of shame. His behavior had been callous, irresponsible, and contrary to United States' national interest, but was it also something else?

When it comes to the Middle East, it is as though there are two United States policies—and two George W. Bushes. It's the wimpy George W. Bush, not the conqueror of Baghdad, who concerns us here. He may be the scourge of NATO and the terror of the UN Security Council, but when it comes to two particular countries, George W. Bush might as well be a little lamb.

One of those two countries is Saudi Arabia. On September 11, 2001, the United States had been attacked by citizens of Saudi Arabia who were members of an organization led by a citizen of Saudi Arabia, Osama bin Laden. Earlier, the United States had fought the first Gulf War in order to protect Saudi Arabia from Iraqi attack, as well as to liberate Kuwait. Going back to the time of Franklin D. Roosevelt the United States has strongly supported Saudi Arabia. No one else in the White House, however, has been quite so solicitous of Saudi feelings as George W. Bush. He never said so much as boo in response to the manifest failure of the Saudi government to make its citizens desist from unleashing mayhem in other countries.

Meanwhile, in response to those attacks, George W. Bush moved nearly a quarter-million U.S. troops to the Gulf region. He confronted the United Nations and ignored the pleas of the Pope. But never once did he issue any kind of admonition to the Saudis. It nonetheless would have seemed appropriate for the authorities of Saudi Arabia to take some effective measures at least to protect Americans living in Saudi Arabia from being attacked.

This they did not trouble themselves to do, as became evident on May 12, 2003, when terrorists bombed residential compounds in Riyadh where many foreigners lived. Scores of foreigners, including seven Americans, were killed, but George W. Bush expressed not the slightest disquiet following the event. Vice President Cheney did eventually speak out. "We've had significant cooperation, of course, from the Saudis with wrapping up members of Al Qaeda, especially since last May 12th, when they were hit in their own terrorist attack," Cheney declared and then, as usual, altered the facts—in this the numbers of Americans killed—to suit the spin, "and two Americans were killed." They apparently did not do enough wrapping. Scores more foreigners have been killed in attacks focused on foreigners in Saudi Arabia since then. The point here isn't the Saudi failure to stop terrorism, a difficult task anywhere. The point is the evidently bottomless indulgence the Saudis can expect from the Bush-Cheney administration—even to the extent, in Cheney's case, of misrepresenting the numbers of Americans killed, and in George W. Bush's case, of never criticizing them whatever happens.

The other country George W. Bush almost never criticizes is Israel. However, during that same month of March 2002, he did ask Sharon to release Arafat from house arrest, and permit him to attend that Arab League meeting in Lebanon. This appeal had no effect; Arafat remained a prisoner.

After several more weeks of Sharon escalating the "war that knows no borders," George W. Bush issued another polite request: "I ask Israel to halt incursions into Palestinian-controlled areas and begin the withdrawal from those cities it has recently occupied." Yet again there was no result, so days after that, George W. Bush said, "My words to Israel are: Withdrawal without delay." Again nothing happened; in fact, more than two years later, Israeli troops are still where they were in Spring 2002. Whether or not, as George W. Bush later put it, Saddam Hussein was allowed to defy UN resolutions "with impunity," Ariel Sharon is free to defy United States injunctions so long as George W. Bush is in charge at the White House.

American politicians are traditionally spineless when it comes to curbing Israeli extremists, yet after taking another look into the neocon policy-proposal archives, it's impossible to see Bush's failure to halt Palestinian-Israeli violence as simple gutlessness. For at the end of this particular neocon paper trail lies another of those ideological tirades that seemed merely nutty—until it was turned into a blueprint for what George W. Bush is actually doing in the world.

For the leader of a supposedly anti-intellectual, "outsider" administration, George W. Bush has let his actions be guided to an astonishing degree by Washington insider bureaucrats who like to spell out what they intend to do, in advance, on paper, in ideological treatises. One of the more colorful of these "defense intellectuals"—that is to say, neocon radical agitators—is a jowly man with a taste for tailored suits and broad-brush invective named Richard Perle.

All these years that George W. Bush has been failing to take any serious steps to revive the Israeli-Palestinian peace process, it turns out, he hasn't simply been doing "nothing." He has been implementing a course of action that Richard Perle and a collection of like-minded policy radicals proposed long ago. The key document in this instance is a 1996 manifesto titled "A Clean Break: A New Strategy for Securing the Realm." What Perle actually proposed to break was any possibility of comprehensive peace in the Middle East—replacing it, instead, with a situation of unending chaos and destruction in which Israel becomes an unbridled free-enterprise war machine.

Originally, Perle's policy proposals were made for an Israeli government—not for a US government to implement. To the extent George W. Bush has made Perle's "Clean Break" the basis for American action, it is a case of the United States pursuing extremist policies that even today many of Israelis find offensive. In that sense, George W. Bush hasn't been acting in the United States national interest; he has not even been pursuing a "pro-Israel" policy. (What is "pro-Israeli" about a course of action that keeps Israelis, as well as Palestinians, perpetually traumatized by violence?) He has been implementing an extremist agenda, concocted by neocon Americans, which even the right-wing Israeli government of the time, headed by Benjamin Netanyahu, did not adopt when Perle presented it.

Like Wolfowitz's "Defense Policy Guidance," Perle's "Clean Break" is, morally as well as strategically, a shocking document. Wolfowitz, in his proposals, abandons the moral and ethical bases of American action in the world. Perle goes further. From his perch at the American Enterprise Institute in Washington, DC, he sneers at everything Israelis like David Ben-Gurion, Golda Meir, Yitzhak Rabin, and even Menachem Begin have accomplished.

"Israel has a large problem," "A Clean Break" begins. "Labor Zionism, which for seventy years has dominated the Zionist movement, has generated a stalled and shackled economy. Efforts to salvage Israel's socialist institutions—which include pursuing supranational over national sovereignty and pursuing a peace process that embraces the slogan, 'New Middle East'—undermine the legitimacy of the nation and lead Israel into strategic paralysis and the previous government's 'peace process.'"

It's the kind of statement only an ideologue could make. Between 1925 and 1995—the seventy years during which "Labor Zionism" supposedly botched everything up—the Jewish "homeland in Palestine," authorized during World War I by the British government in the Balfour Declaration, grew from a collection of

Jewish settlements into one of the world's most powerful nations. Over the same period the Jewish population increased from a few hundred thousand to about five million. Under "Labor Zionism," Israel fought and won three wars. It became a nation that—whether they love it, or whether it terrifies them—no one on this planet disrespects, except for Richard Perle, that is.

From the Palestinian perspective, of course, this triumph of Zionism has been a catastrophe. The odd thing is that Perle is none too delighted with the way the establishment of a Jewish homeland has worked out either, since those contemptible "Labor Zionists" not only refused to put the neocons' pet economic theories into practice, but had attempted to make peace as well.

From this point of view, even attempting to make peace is a sign of decadent deviationism from the path of neocon ideological correctness. Or, in Perle speak: "That peace process obscured the evidence of eroding national critical mass—including a palpable sense of national exhaustion—and forfeited strategic initiative." From there it was straight to hell in a handbasket: "The loss of national critical mass was illustrated best by Israel's efforts to draw in the United States to sell unpopular policies domestically, to agree to negotiate sovereignty over its capital, and to respond with resignation to a spate of terror so intense and tragic that it deterred Israelis from engaging in normal daily functions, such as commuting to work in buses." In other words, the search for peace is the cause of war and, as Perle sees it, the way to get the buses running on schedule again is to plunge the entire Middle East in unending conflict.

In place of the peace process, Perle proposed that Israel adopt what, five years later, became George W. Bush's "regime change" strategy. Only Perle's "Axis of Evil" has a slightly different cast of characters than the one the Bush-Cheney administration later chose to confront. In "A Clean Break," Syria, not Iraq, is Public Enemy Number One. The centerpiece of Perle's policy was "weakening, containing, and even rolling back Syria." Though invading Iraq was fine, overthrowing Saddam Hussein is only a way station on the road to Damascus. As Perle puts it, "This effort can focus on removing Saddam Hussein from power in Iraq—an important Israeli strategic objective in its own right—as a means of foiling Syria's regional ambitions."

Even for a neocon policy proposal, "A Clean Break" is fanciful. Egypt—Israel's most important neighbor—is never mentioned. It is proposed that Israel install a member of Jordan's Hashemite dynasty on the throne of an Israeli-reconstituted Kingdom of Iraq because, we are assured, "the Shia venerate foremost the Prophet's family, the direct descendant of which—and in whose veins the blood of the Prophet flows—is King Hussein." Moving right along, the paper predicts that "Were the Hashemites to control Iraq, they could use their influence . . . to help Israel wean the south Lebanese Shia away from Hezbollah, Iran, and Syria."

This ignores the fact that the Hashemites are Sunni, not Shia, and that the last Hashemite king of Iraq was torn apart by a mob in 1958. Also unlikely to enhance the plan's chances of success is Perle's proposal that Israel "cut itself free immediately from at least US economic aid and loan guarantees, which prevent economic reform." A rare touch of prudence does parenthetically intrude in this connection: "[Military aid is separated for the moment until adequate arrangements can be made to ensure that Israel will not encounter supply problems in the means to defend itself.]"

Israel, according to Richard Perle, will not be entirely alone as it unseats Saddam Hussein's Iraq, destabilizes Syria and, with the help of its new friend and ally, the as-yet unchosen new king of Iraq, outfoxes Hezbollah in south Lebanon. "Work closely with Turkey and Jordan to contain, destabilize, and roll-back some of [Syria's] most dangerous threats," Prime Minister Netanyahu is instructed. What Perle proposed to Netanyahu, in a perhaps unintentionally revealing choice of words, was a "'natural axis' with Israel on one side, central Iraq and Turkey on the other, and Jordan in the center [to] squeeze and detach Syria from the Saudi Peninsula."

We have seen the reaction of Turkey and Jordan, nearly seven years later, to Dick Cheney's comparatively modest scheme to "take out" Saddam. Why those two nations should have signed on for an extremist Israeli-militant neocon crusade to destabilize the Arab world Perle never explains.

Among the key extremists associated with the George W. Bush administration, Richard Perle is generally considered the most offensive. What seems to pique critics most is that no other figure manages to convey quite the same degree of contempt for those who presume to disagree with him, or even ask him a simple question. During the summer of 2003, for example, Perle consented to give an interview to the BBC about the potential role of the United Nations in Iraq. Earlier, in one of his polemics, Perle rejoiced in what he foresaw—erroneously, as usual—as the demise of the United Nations, which pleased him even more than the upcoming discovery of Saddam's vast cache of weapons of mass destruction, which he also treated as a foregone conclusion.

Summer 2003 was not a happy time for the world body. The United Nations had been scorned by the George W. Bush administration. UN employees in Iraq had been killed. During the BBC interview, Perle gloated as he suggested that, if it wanted to play a role in the reconstruction of Iraq, the United Nations Development Program should turn itself into a profit-making organization: Then (ha, ha) see if all those lazy international bureaucrats can compete in the open marketplace with feisty United States firms like Halliburton for contract work in Iraq.

It is Perle's fusion of ignorance and arrogance that makes him so much fun to hate. On occasions such as that broadcast his voice oozes rather than drips contempt. He seems genuinely unaware that he is making an ass of himself. Talking to the BBC, he seemed to have entirely forgotten that even if the various United Nations development and relief organizations had privatized themselves, they would have been prevented from competing with US companies.

However, it is the repulsiveness of Richard Perle's ideas, not his manners, that needs to concern us here. If no peace agreement is ever reached between Israel and the Palestinians, and generations to come are forced to live with the same stresses of hostility and violence, to some extent it will be because the noxious ideas Perle has propagated have become the settled policy of both Americans and Israelis.

The view Perle presents of the Arabs is bizarre, but weirdest of all is his view of Israel. He blames the "peace process" and "Labor Zionism" for Israel's "palpable sense of national exhaustion" as well as its economic difficulties. It does not seem to occur to him that when one nation, Israel, for more than thirty years denies another nation of approximately equal population, the Palestinians, the same rights it values for itself, the result is quite likely to be "national exhaustion." How reoccupying the Palestinian territories while also launching offensives against Iraq and Syria is going to revive Israel's economy or its spirit goes unexplained.

Perle and his co-authors don't seem troubled in the slightest by the effects of permanent warfare on the Israeli psyche. They do not refer in any way to the most consequential act of terrorism in Israel's history, the assassination of Prime Minister Yitzhak Rabin by an Israeli—not a Palestinian—fanatic in 1995. It was Rabin's killing—not any failure of "Labor Zionism" or the "peace process"—that led to Netanyahu coming to power and gave Perle his big chance to announce that "Israel has the opportunity to make a clean break."

Even the wording of his policy proposal's title implies a renunciation of Zionist values as well as a permanent denial of Palestinian rights. The goal Perle proposes that Israel achieve as result of "A Clean Break" is "Securing the Realm." That is, the goal no longer is to establish the borders of a secure and democratic state of Israel, but to take and keep whatever Israel wishes to arrogate to itself, regardless of the rights of others. There is not a single suggestion in Perle's proposal as to how to create a society in which Israelis as well as Palestinians can live as peaceful human beings. Intellectually this bellicose scheme of regional domination leads Israel exactly to where it finds itself today—in retreat, behind Sharon's Wall. Reading "A Clean Break," you realize it is not for nothing that Perle was called the "Prince of Darkness."

The history of "A Clean Break: A New Strategy for Securing the Realm" runs parallel to the history of "Defense Policy Guidance." Netanyahu ignored Perle's approach, just as President George H.W. Bush rejected the Wolfowitz-Cheney proposals. Then in 2001, a few weeks after George W. Bush moved into the White House, Ariel Sharon became prime minister of Israel.

Even before gaining power, Sharon had made his own "clean break." In late September 2000, he precipitated a crisis in Israel that would produce as much trauma for that country as the 9/11 attacks, a year later, would for the United States. Sharon, leading a crowd of hard-line supporters, marched right into the holiest of the Muslim shrines of old Jerusalem. The greatest of the Palestinian nightmares—and it is also the dream of the most extreme Israelis—is that Israelis some day will drive all the Palestinians out of the country, destroy Islam's third holiest shrine, the Dome of the Rock, and put in its place what Israeli zealots call the third Jewish Temple.

Sharon's deliberate provocation shocked Palestinians, and the direct result of Sharon's march into their holiest sanctum was the outbreak of the second Palestinian intifada. Sharon had provoked the gravest crisis in Israeli-Palestinian relations since the Lebanon invasion. He also, as he had intended, outflanked his Israeli political rivals on both the right and the left. After fending off a comeback attempt by Benjamin Netanyahu, he defeated Prime Minister Ehud Barak in elections in February 2001, and only a few weeks after George W. Bush was inaugurated in Washington, became prime minister of Israel.

Ever since Dick Cheney's March 2002 visit to Israel, the United States has had two different policies when it comes to seeking peace between Israelis and Palestinians. As is often the case with George W. Bush, there is the official policy, or what might better be called the cover policy—in this case the "Roadmap to Peace," which Colin Powell, Tony Blair, and George W. Bush himself mention all the time.

Then there is the policy that consists of what the administration is actually doing—which, in this case, as in so many others, is what Dick Cheney wants the United States to do. On the surface it all seems like a terrible muddle. Powell is always saying one thing while Cheney does another. Yet once you become familiar with neocon proposals like "A Clean Break," it is clear that George W. Bush follows the intelligible pattern of doing what Cheney, Sharon, and Perle want. What makes doing this easier for him is that what the pro-Sharon neocons want is for the United States to do nothing—that is, to leave Sharon free, militarily, to create "new facts" in the Palestinian territories, which is neocon-speak for avoiding the kind of negotiated "peace settlement" they detest.

What is happening is clear, but why is it happening? More than a year before the Iraq invasion, according to reports circulating in Israel at the time, Cheney told Sharon "We are doing this first and foremost for Israel." Implementing Perle's plan for turning Israel into a militarist state uninterested in permanent peace and beholden to no one—certainly not the United States—cannot be described as beneficial to Israel. Today its economy is more "stalled and shackled" than ever. The "palpable sense of national exhaustion" has not disappeared. And far from regaining it, Sharon has "forfeited strategic initiative" to the extent that all he can think to do now is build his wall.

All this hardly can be described as acting in the United States' national interest either: It is a violation of America's security interests. Why pursue a course of action that only creates greater danger for Americans, as well as greater suffering for Israelis and Palestinians? It is simplistic, but the explanation that best fits the facts is that all this is what a bunch of neocon loonies want—and George W. Bush has let them do it.

To this day, whether it is Iraq or Israel, George W. Bush has not taken advice from anyone with competence in Middle East affairs. No one has obliged him to surround himself with national security incompetents; he could have consulted others. For instance his secretary of state, Colin Powell, could have educated him on the realities of foreign policy and introduced him to the basics of war-making. This would not have been unprecedented. Under previous administrations, U.S. secretaries of state have played a role in the formulation of foreign policy, but in George W. Bush's Administration, the secretary of state fulfills a different function. Colin Powell personifies America's marginalized voices of reason.

Powell had the qualifications to help George W. Bush avoid making a mess of things. He is an American soldier-diplomat in the grand tradition of Dwight Eisenhower, George C. Marshall, and—before he was mythologized—George Washington. Powell's superb record of achievement may conceivably help explain why George W. Bush, having chosen a secretary of state of such eminence, instead relies on Dick Cheney, a geopolitical nincompoop and Yale dropout, when it comes to the most vital decisions. Going back to his own C-average days, George W. Bush's reaction to excellence has always been a little like his gut reaction to Kim Jong Il. Of course he doesn't loathe Powell; he just routinely treats the secretary of state's attempts to inject rationality and realism into the proceedings with utter disrespect.

When he was named secretary of state, Powell was one of the most highly respected Americans in public life—more respected than Bush himself, to say nothing of the shadowy Cheney. Today Colin Powell is the least consequential secretary of state since the unfortunate William Rogers, whose functions Henry Kissinger entirely usurped when he was Nixon's national security adviser.

Powell's marginalization flows in part from the fact that he lacks the character traits and career track of the people George W. Bush naturally likes and trusts. Unlike most of the people George W.

Bush chooses to have around him, Powell had not spent the previous twenty-five years either avoiding military service, ingratiating himself in the closed worlds of the Republican and neocon power elites, or making himself rich through government contracts. This has turned out to be a decided disadvantage for him when it comes to trying to make George W. Bush understand things. Repeatedly, Powell's entirely reasonable proposals—for instance, to actually make a sincere effort to the help the Israelis and Palestinians make peace—have not only been thwarted by Cheney and Rumsfeld, but treated as a joke.

George W. Bush has demoted Powell into the smiley face of his and Cheney's ultra-radical vision of a world polarized for or against the United States. While Powell deploys his considerable intelligence and world-famous charm in the attempt to make what the United States is doing appear rational, Cheney plays the Cheshire cat in the Bush wonderland of strategic fantasy, fading in and out of view as expedient. When the game of global golf played with pink flamingos appears to be going well, Cheney is all over the place. When the going gets tough he disappears, and Powell is summoned like a cleaning service after a fraternity party.

The result is that while Colin Powell is liked wherever he goes, no one trusts him. Whether "for us" or "against us," foreign leaders know that whatever Powell does or promises will be repudiated if anyone with real influence in the George W. Bush administration says so. Meanwhile they dislike George W. Bush himself as much they detest Cheney (Rumsfeld, in spite of himself, never fails to be amusing). But whichever high-ranking American gets off the plane, leaders all over the world can count on one thing: Even on those intermittent occasions when George W. Bush appears to be trying to do something constructive, nothing will come of it. As one diplomat remarked following the Aqaba summit in June 2003, "Even when they try to be serious, they don't know what serious is."

Peace is something you make with your enemies. For that reason, peace conferences from which one of the principal adversaries is excluded seldom if ever produce results. That turned out to be the case with the resultless Aqaba summit of June 4, 2003. Like George W. Bush's "Mission Accomplished" appearance on the aircraft carrier off California a month earlier, his mirage-like appearance at Aqaba in southern Jordan was a George W. Bush photo op. This was "Lawrence of Arabia" country. There, in the blinding sun and shimmering heat of the desert summer, all four of the putative peacemakers stood smiling for the cameras, weaving the kind of serious dark suits that soak up the heat: George W. Bush of the United States, Ariel Sharon of Israel, King Abdullah of Jordan, and, instead of President Yasser Arafat, "Prime Minister" Mahmoud Abbas of the Palestinian Authority.

The dark suits were there to create the illusion of seriousness. Arafat's absence gave the game away. Abbas, better known as Abu Mazen, is an interesting, honorable veteran of the Palestinian struggle for a homeland, but he is at best the Colin Powell of the Palestinians. If you really want peace with the Palestinians, you must go to the boss—and this George W. Bush absolutely refused to do under any circumstances.

Colin Powell by then knew better than to suggest that George W. Bush so much as take a phone call from Arafat, one of the pivotal figures of Middle East war and peace. Tony Blair also had discovered how futile it was to get George W. Bush to open his mind to the simplest thing anyone truly interested in making peace in the Middle East must be willing to understand: You make peace by being an honest broker, not by demonizing one side and pandering to the other.

The valuable assemblage of details in Bob Woodward's book, *Bush at War*, provides us with a scene where Tony Blair tries to jolly George W. Bush into dealing with Yasser Arafat at least a little bit. The date is November 7, 2001. The Afghanistan invasion has been a tactical triumph. The question is what to do next. One could say George W. Bush was at a crossroad, except that he never really considered going in any other direction than on to Baghdad.

Hoping to nudge George W. Bush in the direction of reason, Tony Blair adopted the tactics of the courtier. He delicately suggests that Yasser Arafat "still could be engaged in security and confidence-building steps with the Israelis, however small. He seemed to be a necessary evil." But as Woodward observes, "Bush increasingly viewed Arafat as just evil."

As is often the case, George W. Bush allowed the appearance of a debate over policy to continue long after he had let Cheney determine what was actually going to happen.

Cheney had made the decision to cut Arafat out of the action during his stop in Jerusalem in March 2002. Cheney had used the tactics of an accomplished Washington maneuverer to achieve his purpose. Of course he had never explicitly said: "Not only am I not going to meet Arafat, I'm going to do all I can to humiliate him and insult his people, and then blame him and the Palestinians for the fact that Sharon and the Israelis, with my support, keep attacking them. When Arafat objects to this, I will then blame him for our failure to make peace in the Middle East. When, as is utterly inevitable, all this produces a new cycle of violence, including Palestinian suicide attacks on Israelis, I will not only blame it all on Yasser Arafat. I will proclaim that all this proves my initial refusal to deal with him was right."

To the contrary, Cheney said that while he would not meet Arafat this time, he might return to the Middle East to meet him if the Palestinians did certain things. From then on, it was a matter of asking the Palestinians to jump through a series of higher and narrower hoops. Of course, nothing could be done in any event until Iraq was conquered, and democracy triumphed there. But afterward? One of the final hoops was that the Palestinians create the previously nonexistent office of prime minister, and fill it with someone Ariel Sharon liked.

Arafat would remain confined to his bombed-out compound in Ramallah while peace was made at Aqaba. The dark-suit photo op thus recapitulated the illusion that has kept the Palestinian-Israeli conflict going for three generations now. This illusion is that if an Israeli prime minister (Sharon) with the backing of the Americans can get a traditional Arab ruler (Abdullah) to hold a meeting at which a Palestinian near-nonentity (Abbas) is obliged to sign a series of capitulations, then Israel will at last have peace.

There was another reason this supposed first stop on the roadmap to peace had been postponed for so long. According to Israeli sources, "Sharon was hoping that a decisive American onslaught against Iraq would demoralize the Palestinians and force them to concede defeat and put an end to the intifada." Leaving aside its lack of human understanding, there is the simple illogicality of the proposition. For more than thirty years decisive Israeli onslaughts into their own towns and homes had not "demoralized the Palestinians and forced them to concede defeat." Why should a far-from-decisive American onslaught on a country hundreds of miles away change any of that now?

George W. Bush's Iraq war nonetheless did get Air Force One pointed in the direction of Aqaba. By then, there was no way George W. Bush could avoid such a meeting, without entirely abandoning the pretense that the United States wanted everybody in the Middle East, not just Arabs, to respect UN resolutions. The spin for the moment was that having taken out Saddam, George W. Bush now finally would turn his undeniable powers of single-minded persistence to the problem of restarting the Israeli-Palestinian peace process. Reaching for a Texas simile, George W. Bush himself spoke of "riding herd" on the Israelis and Palestinians as America guided them down the roadmap to peace. It seemed that, after nearly two and a half years in office, George W. Bush finally was going to focus on his responsibilities as a peacemaker—or to put it another way, to start doing what Al Gore, or almost anyone else, would have started doing on Inauguration Day.

As was only to be expected, nothing much happened at Aqaba. The roadmap to peace had barely been unfolded, though once the photo op was over, something completely predictable did happen. Palestinian radicals launched more suicide bombings. Sharon, in an equally predestined lashing out, turned his assassination helicopters loose on the West Bank and Gaza.

And that was it—the end of George W. Bush's involvement in the peace process! That, other than an occasional new photo op, was also the end of the roadmap to peace. At that completely predictable first moment in any peace process when the extremists try to grab back the initiative from the moderates, George W. Bush went AWOL. Rather than swinging into action, and bringing the full might of America's military power and moral authority to bear on both sides, as must be done if any peace effort is to have any chance of success, he disengaged.

It was all the Palestinians' fault, of course, but to show them he was not one to hold grudges, George W. Bush held up another hoop. If the Palestinians ceased resisting the Israeli occupation while also getting rid of Yasser Arafat, while making sure no more terrorist attacks occurred, George W. Bush hinted, he might be willing to give them another chance. How the Palestinians—having removed from power their one leader with uncontested national authority—could be expected to provide Israel with better security than Sharon could, especially after Sharon had destroyed most of the infrastructure of the Palestinian Authority, he did not explain.

While lecturing the Arabs on their need to become democratic, George W. Bush goes on refusing to have any dealings whatsoever with the one Arab leader who was, without any doubt, democratically elected. Unlike George W. Bush himself, Yasser Arafat was chosen by a majority. He won in a free election whose honesty and accuracy was verified by international observers, including former president Jimmy Carter.

George W. Bush's view of Arab democracy has turned out to be like his view of American democracy. It's a fine thing so long as you and people like you win the election. And if other people win? Back when there was someone willing to talk peace with him, Arafat won a Nobel Peace Prize as a result of his negotiations with Yitzhak Rabin. But for more than three years George W. Bush has refused even to talk to him because, as he explained to Tony Blair, the Palestinian president in his opinion is "evil."

As always, after assembling the facts of what George W. Bush does, the question remains: Why? It is beyond dispute that when it suits his convenience, George W. Bush is capable of denying anything, especially to himself. Even in the case of 9/11, he chose not to get it. Since September 2001, he has devoted his presidency to trying to prove that 9/11 somehow happened—in America, on his watch—because tyrants ruled faraway countries. In the case of George W. Bush and the Israeli-Palestinian conflict, once again, ideology, IQ and political tactics have been fused into a seamless evasion of responsibility.

Whether we are dealing here with gullibility or guile, or some combination of them, we are certainly dealing with character, and what we can tell for certain is that George W. Bush, when it comes to Israeli security and Palestinian dignity, has been a shirker.

It is not easy to predict what the consequences of the Iraq war will be. The consequences of George W. Bush's failure to lift a finger on behalf of peace between the Israelis and Palestinians are already discernible: A new generation of brutalized Palestinians already faces a new generation of traumatized Israelis, and if all goes truly badly, the history of the Israeli occupation will repeat itself in Iraq. No modern military triumph was more "decisive" than Israel's victory in the 1967 Six Day War. Yet more than thirty-five years later, where are the solutions this military "solution" was supposed to produce?

The invasion of Iraq may turn out to be only a sidebar to the bigger story of George W. Bush's abnegation of American responsibilities in the Middle East.

XIV

The Pathetic Affair of Tony Blair

As the old saying goes, England, having lost an empire, failed to find a role. But the saying is wrong. Having lost its empire, Britain—or rather Britain's prime ministers—did find a role—as America's fluffer.

As George W. Bush peevishly strode toward his defining moment beside the Euphrates, Tony Blair's United Kingdom followed along, wagging its tail all the way to Iraq. In the neocon schema of US hegemony, allies do not play a policy-making role; they serve a policy-implementation function. The Brits started calling their prime minister "America's poodle" when it became clear that, so far as Blair was concerned, his master's voice emanated from the White House.

In their capacity as America's model allies, the British get to die, as well as obey. More than fifty British soldiers have died in connection with Operation Iraqi Freedom. Twenty of them were killed by those resisting the Iraq invasion and occupation, mostly irregulars, not Saddam's troops. But in the case of another twenty British fatalities, Americans were the cause of death. Twelve British soldiers were killed by American fire. Another eight were killed in a US helicopter crash. Three more British troops were killed by their own "friendly" fire as US forces headed to Baghdad and the British took control of southern Iraq, including the city of Basra.

The first British subject to be killed inside Iraq was a journalist, not a soldier. Terry Lloyd, 50, an award-winning television correspondent, was killed by US fire. Next to die was the crew of a Royal Air Force Tornado fighter. According to press reports, Flight Lieutenants Kevin Barry Main and David Rhys Williams, "father of two," were shot down by a US Patriot missile battery, a notoriously inaccurate spinoff of "Star Wars" research and development.

"UK troops are furious at Americans for killing another British soldier," read reports the following day. The most recent death occurred when a US Thunderbolt tankbuster aircraft attacked British tanks. "Lance Corporal of Horse Steven Gerrard, 33, who was injured in the attack, said the vehicles were all clearly marked as coalition forces and even had Union Jack flags flying," one British newspaper reported. The attacking US plane had thermal sights programmed to enable the pilot to distinguish friendly from enemy tanks. "Combat is what I've been trained for," Gerrard said. "What I have not been trained to do is look over my shoulder to see whether an American is shooting at me." He added, referring to the American pilot, "I believe he was a cowboy."

No cowboys were involved in the next friendly-fire incident to claim British lives. It happened when a British Challenger II Tank was attacked by another British tank outside Basra. One of the British dead was Cpl. Stephen John Allbutt, a father of two who had survived combat during the first Gulf War in 1991. Before the first actual British battle deaths occurred, in what was described as a grenade attack on the Faw peninsula, at least a dozen British soldiers and airmen had been killed by Americans, by each other, or by collisions on land or in air.

The circumstances surrounding the death of the very first British soldier to be killed on the ground in Iraq are illuminating. Like so many others, Sgt. Steven Roberts was a victim of the "cakewalk" illusion—the belief that once the Americans and the British crossed into Iraq, the invading troops would be welcomed, rapturously, as liberators. No one had trained them to deal with sullen crowds. Precisely because it was not a battle death, it foreshadowed the way hundreds of Americans would also be killed.

British spokesmen originally made it seem that Sergeant Roberts had been killed by an enemy sniper. But troops who witnessed the event later informed Roberts's widow that no Iraqi had fired at Roberts. The sergeant was apparently killed when British soldiers started firing at a hostile Iraqi crowd in the town of Zubayr, southwest of Basra, and hit him instead.

Sergeant Roberts's widow, Samantha, later accused the Blair government of lying when it claimed her husband's death was an isolated incident. She was right on several counts. Far from being exceptional, this was the way most US and British soldiers in Iraq would die—not in battle with Republican Guards, but in hostile encounters and, soon, in armed attacks involving angry local people. In another sense, Sergeant Roberts's death was a prototype for what would follow. At the beginning of the war the Blair spinners, like their US counterparts, were as insistent in their denials of any significant popular resistance as they were in their later claims that the resistance was being crushed. Roberts's death was a sign of bitter things to come.

Afterward, British pathologists determined that his wound would not have been fatal had he been wearing the proper combat gear. "Sergeant Steven Roberts had been issued with life-saving body armor," an official investigation later determined, "but was ordered to give it up because his regiment was short of equipment." Tony Blair had sent British troops into war without the proper equipment.

At first this seemed to make excellent PR. During the initial stage of the invasion, the British got a lot of favorable TV time for themselves, even on the US news channels, by emphasizing to film crews that British troops didn't require fancy protection like the Yanks because they had a quite different approach to dealing with the locals. Unlike the American GIs, British troops weren't going to ride around in armored personnel carriers, wearing full body armor, isolating themselves from the people they had liberated. The British would take off their helmets, and win over the Iraqis with friendly foot patrols. It was one of Tony Blair's big sells to the media and, especially, the Americans: The British success in Northern Ireland, as he perceived it, would provide a model for solving Iraq's problems.

"It's very hard to put into words how this makes you feel," Mrs. Roberts said later, after the details of what actually had happened to her husband were pieced together: "Incredibly angry and I'm disgusted at the way this has been handled."

She added: "He was everything to us. He was a soldier but he was a human being, a husband and a son, but that seems to have been totally forgotten."

British prime ministers love toadying to American presidents, imagining it gives them "influence." This illusion goes back to Winston Churchill and his groveling "Former Naval Person" messages to Franklin D. Roosevelt. FDR and all subsequent presidents have let British prime ministers sleep over in the White House—and then gone on to do exactly whatever they please. Every British prime minister dreads being abandoned by the Americans. Every American president knows full well that the Brits will always tag along, even into the mouth of hell, and if they don't, who cares? In its capacity as dominant ally, there are no limits on the demands the United States is entitled to make. The "special relationship" involves no reciprocal privileges for the British, however.

Imagine yourself passing the postprandial port in the drawing room of some stately home of England. You are playing a jolly game of "Special Relationship." Up comes the following question: What do Prime Ministers Harold Macmillan, Margaret Thatcher, John Major, and Tony Blair all have in common that they do not have in common with Anthony Eden and Harold Wilson?

Prime Ministers Eden and Wilson had the temerity to act independently of the United States, and were suitably humiliated. All the others cozied up to their American counterparts closer than a lonely tick to the inner lining of a hound dog's ear. What they principally got for it was the thrill of knowing that when they telephoned the White House, Jack or Ronnie or George would probably take the call.

In 1956, when Eden was prime minister, the British, French, and Israelis invaded Egypt and in the process clogged up the Suez Canal. They did this for the same reasons George W. Bush now tells us he has invaded Iraq: Nasser was evil; the Arabs were a nasty lot. Letting the Egyptians run their own canal would pose a Threat to Civilization. President Dwight Eisenhower was not amused, and that was the end of Anthony Eden. Eden's successor, Harold Macmillan, proclaimed the end of British imperium. The British would become butlers to the Americans or, as Macmillan obsequiously announced, "We will be the Greeks in their Roman

Empire." The classically educated Macmillan, a future chancellor of the University of Oxford, failed to mention that those philosophical, cultivated Greeks with whom the Roman emperors loved to discuss the meaning of life were slaves.

In the following decade, Harold Wilson incurred Lyndon Johnson's wrath for not sending British troops to Vietnam. They fought alongside us in Korea, LBJ raged. Why not Vietnam? It was an early version of the Afghanistan-Iraq question that got George W. Bush so het up when allies who'd supported the United States in the first Gulf War had the effrontery to oppose him over the second. Whereas the famously weaselly Wilson kept Britain out of an immoral, disastrous American war, it would become the invariable policy of Tony Blair to support George W. Bush whether right (Afghanistan) or wrong (Iraq).

A question that never seems to be asked inside 10 Downing Street is: What does all this worming to the Americans get us? When a situation arises in which the British might get something dear to them at the cost of some small inconvenience for the United States, the British invariably get shafted. Kennedy betrayed Macmillan on the Skybolt missile. "Ronnie" went wobbly on Thatcher when it came to her war in the Falklands. The grand tradition continues with George W. Bush's humiliating treatment of Tony Blair. Total value of reconstruction contracts awarded to US firms, after the invasion of Iraq, mostly on a noncompetitive basis and to corporations with close ties to the George W. Bush administration, including the Halliburton Corporation: $2.2 billion. Total value of reconstruction contracts allotted to British firms, following Tony Blair's faithful and costly support for the Iraq invasion: Zero.

News reports that those arrogantly insubordinate French wouldn't get so much as a crepes suzettes concession when it came time for America to mete out the goodies in Iraq were correct. They failed, however, to point out that the humbly subordinate Brits weren't getting a farthing's worth of the action either. Just like the French, Germans, Russians, Canadians, and all those others who had been "against us," the British were prohibited even from bidding on the first big reconstruction projects.

Why were the British barred from making money, as opposed to getting killed in Iraq? According to US law, letting British companies help rebuild the country would endanger "the essential security interests of the United States." The US government must specifically ordain otherwise before any British firm can so much as tender a bid. For that to happen, Tony Blair had to specifically petition the Americans for a waiver from this nonsensical ruling, and hope for the best. In his haste to service George W. Bush's Iraq invasion needs, he had forgotten to ask the Americans to please do him that tiny favor.

British Anger As Port Contract Goes To US Firm, ran one London headline when it turned out that while it was OK for the British to pay, financially as well as in human blood, for driving Saddam's forces out of the key port of Umm Qasr, no British firm would be allowed to particpate the port's reconstruction. Not to worry: Britain still had a role to play. British troops would remain in Umm Qasr to provide security for the US firms as they reaped their windfall.

Of course when such tiffs arise, a British prime minister, thanks to the "special relationship," can take positions a French president never could. In addition to crawling on his hands and knees to the White House, a prime minister can also seek to win American favor in other uniquely British ways, such as turning Buckingham Palace into a bed & breakfast. More than eight months after Sergeant Roberts's death, Tony Blair finally got something to show for it. "Washington is to give British firms the right to bid for multi-million dollar reconstruction contracts in Iraq as a reward for Prime Minister Tony Blair's loyalty over the war," the *Times* of London reported in November 2003.

Britain's most authoritative newspaper described the decision of the George W. Bush administration to expand its definition of free-market competition in Iraq to the extent of including the British as "a major shift in policy." The announcement of this diplomatic breakthrough, it added, had been timed to correspond with the upcoming state visit to London of George W. Bush and his wife Laura, during which time they would be accorded the privilege of a sleepover at Buckingham Palace with the Queen.

Someone high up among the Americans had apparently vetted the Brits before taking this important step. "British firms are excellent firms and I'm sure they will be able to bid competitively," a US official described as "a leading Bush administrator" was quoted as having graciously commented. The US official who actually decided whether Britain got its "essential security interests" waiver or not turned out to be Paul Wolfowitz. Nearly nine months after the Iraq invasion, he finally promulgated his select list of "Countries Eligible to Compete for Contracts Funded with US Appropriated Funds for Iraq Reconstruction." Just as the *Times* had predicted, the United Kingdom was on it.

But Tony Blair's reward for "loyalty over the war" had also been conferred on countries which had refused to let the United States use their territory for the attack (Turkey). It had been extended to countries that had opposed the invasion (Egypt). It turned out that—when it came to Iraq construction projects meted out by Paul Wolfowitz—the United States also had special relationships with Albania, Eritrea, Bulgaria, and the Marshall Islands.

Nondemocracies on the privileged list (to describe them diplomatically) included Ukraine and Azerbaijan. The Anglo-American tradition of shared respect for human dignity, to judge from Wolfowitz's listing, extended to Rwanda. The tiny South Pacific Kingdom of Tonga got the same special exemption Britain did, though no plans were announced for America's First Couple to be house guests of the royals down there. The complete list of nations benefitting from America's "major shift in policy" (a. k. a. the Tony Blair Loyalty Award) follows:

Afghanistan
Albania
Australia
Azerbaijan
Behrain
Bulgaria
Colombia
Costa Rica
Czech Republic
Denmark
Dominican Republic
Egypt
El Salvador
Eritrea
Estonia
Ethiopia
Georgia
Honduras
Hungary
Iceland
Iraq
Italy
Japan
Jordan
Kazakhstan
Kuwait
Latvia
Lithuania
Macedonia
Marshall Islands
Micronesia
Moldova
Mongolia
Morocco
Netherlands
New Zealand
Nicaragua
Norway
Oman
Palau
Panama
Philippines
Poland
Portugal
Qatar
Romania
Rwanda
Saudi Arabia
Singapore
Slovakia
Solomon Islands
South Korea
Spain
Thailand
Tonga
Turkey
United Arab Emirates
Uganda
Ukraine
United Kingdom
Uzbekistan

Wolfowitz was frank enough not to invoke the "special relationship" when explaining why Britain had merited inclusion in this select group. Britain, according to the deputy secretary of defense, was there because it belonged to that category of countries which either could already be counted on to do America's bidding, or—in hopes of sharing the profits from this and future wars—could eventually be induced to do so. "Limiting competition for prime contracts will encourage the expansion of international cooperation in Iraq and in future efforts," was the way Wolfowitz put it.

There is a sometimes sleazy as well as seedy side to the "special relationship." Unlike the United States, Britain has no written constitution. Its various spy organizations, including those in charge of domestic snooping, are less stringently regulated than the CIA and FBI. This allows British prime ministers to help out American presidents in ways that under US law could be construed as criminal offenses. Back in 1992, Prime Minister John Major took advantage of that happy lack of legal restraint to strengthen his own special relationship with President George H.W. Bush. Eager to help Bush the elder in his ultimately unsuccessful re-election campaign, Major sent him a secret dossier British spies had somehow cooked up on a certain former Yank at Oxford named William Jefferson Clinton. The secret dossier revealed that the Democratic candidate for president, while living in England twenty years earlier, had worn his hair long, attended anti-war demonstrations, and taken a trip to Moscow, which at that time was still headquarters of the worldwide Communist conspiracy.

Major's attempt to curry presidential favor by getting British spy agencies mixed up in US partisan politics demonstrated how little self-respect a British prime minister can have in his dealings with Americans. Not until Tony Blair formed his own very "special relationship" with George W. Bush, however, was it clear how truly supine a British prime minister could be.

In the course of his ineffectual pandering to George W. Bush in the run-up to the Iraq war, Blair demeaned himself, lost the respect of his own people, and incurred the contempt of the rest of the world. Then, afterward, as the wicked web which he had woven tightened around him, the British prime minister shifted his fire away from Saddam Hussein. He started lashing out against the one remaining British institution which still commands universal respect now that the royal family's sexcapades have so diminished their stature in the eyes of the world. Blair attacked the BBC.

The tragic events in Iraq that followed the invasion had not ruffled Tony Blair's aura of utter certitude, but crisis gripped 10 Downing Street when the British Broadcasting Corporation reported in June 2003 that the Blair's allegations about Saddam Hussein's supposed weapons of mass destruction had been "sexed up." Prime Minister Blair and his director of spin, Alastair Campbell, professed themselves shocked—shocked!—that an organization of such repute had indulged in such a lewd lapse from propriety.

"Sexed up" was too genteel a euphemism for what actually had been done to the truth, but it was enough to set Blair and Campbell off on a ferocious vendetta. Before they were finished trying to settle scores with the truth-tellers, the BBC correspondent who broke the story, Andrew Gilligan, was hauled before a Foreign Affairs Select Committee and the BBC itself was excoriated in an official report. Blair, via the Hutton report, managed to make it seem that the BBC, not he and his government, had foisted a false impression on the British public.

Neither then nor later was there any doubt about the truthfulness of the BBC report, which was that the Blair government had recklessly spread unfounded (and, as it turned out, false) allegations concerning the military dangers posed by Saddam Hussein.

The furor centered on two of the most ridiculous of the Blair fabrications. The first, in the official words of the executive summary of the accusations issued by the prime minister's own office, was that the Iraqi dictator had "tried covertly to acquire technology and materials which could be used in the production of nuclear weapons [and] sought significant quantities of uranium from Africa." In short, invading Iraq was necessary to stop Saddam from getting nuclear weapons. (During this period just before the invasion, both US and British officials went even further in other briefings, alleging that Saddam Hussein's weapons development was so advanced that he would have deliverable nuclear weapons soon if there was no invasion.)

The second official public contention concerned Saddam Hussein's ability to use biological, chemical, and nuclear weapons. As Blair's executive summary put it, "We judge"—"we" in this case being Tony Blair and the British government—"that Iraq has: continued to produce chemical and biological agents [and has] military plans for the use of chemical and biological weapons." Immediately following this highly dubious judgment, some spinner at 10 Downing Street interjected the following allegation, which no intelligence agency anywhere ever substantiated, either before or after the invasion: "Some of these weapons are deployable within 45 minutes of an order to use them."

These and a number of other sensationalist and, as it turned out, groundless accusations were issued by the prime minister's office in two separate sets of "intelligence findings." The first of the "dodgy dossiers" was released in September 2002. The second came in February 2003, a month before the invasion. Both were clearly intended to win support for an invasion of Iraq, even as both the United States and Britain went through the motions of trying avert war at the United Nations. At the time it was widely noted as curious that allegations of such gravity were being issued by Blair's director of communications (to give Campbell his official title), rather than by the Ministries of Defense or Foreign Affairs, or by any of the British intelligence organizations. It became even more noticeable, in the months following the invasion, that virtually all these various allegations issued by the British prime minister's office turned out to be false.

On both sides of the Atlantic, intelligence professionals were muttering that the politicians—most notably Campbell in Britain and Cheney in the United States—had "sexed up" inconclusive intelligence reports and even invented allegations in an attempt to manufacture support for the war. But who in British intelligence had snitched to the BBC?

It turned out that an intelligence analyst in the British Ministry of Defense named Dr. David Kelly had been Gilligan's source for the BBC story that the Blair government had transformed inconclusive intelligence findings into political propaganda. For reasons that still remain incomprehensible, but which no doubt have something to do with the personal arrogance and political blindness that seem eventually to afflict all denizens of 10 Downing Street, Blair and especially Campbell were outraged at this rather obvious revelation. Odder still, Blair and Campbell apparently convinced themselves that the

BBC report somehow could be discredited by exposing Kelly to public vilification for having told Gilligan the truth—for when the BBC protected its source, the Blair government blew Kelly's cover.

Persecuting Gilligan didn't alter the facts, and mistreating Kelly certainly did not distract attention from Blair's "dodgy dossiers" and their dubious contents. The vendetta did add an unnecessary death in Britain to those that already had occurred in Iraq. Apparently unable to cope with the harassment, Kelly left his home in the village of Southmoor to go for a walk. His body was later found in a wooded area two miles away. Both wrists had been slit. Police said the defense intelligence analyst had bled to death, the result of what the British press carefully termed "an apparent suicide."

"David's professional life was characterized by his integrity, honor and dedication to finding the truth, often in the most difficult of circumstances," his wife Janice said in a statement made shortly after his body was recovered. She added: "Events over recent weeks made David's life intolerable and all those involved should reflect long and hard on this."

Tony Blair cannot be blamed for an act of suicide, but his government's response to the BBC report was the latest incident to call into question his own capacity for responding proportionately to stress. A supposedly astute politician like Blair should have seen from the start that no mole inside the intelligence agencies had been needed to prove that his allegations against Saddam had been "sexed up." The lead paragraph of the dossier Blair's own office issued had clearly been edited by an experienced political pen for maximum political impact. Like the entire report, it was deliberately misleading.

> **Executive Summary**
> 1. Under Saddam Hussein, Iraq developed chemical and biological weapons, acquired missiles allowing it to attack neighboring countries with these weapons, and persistently tried to develop a nuclear bomb.

These allegations, presented in this way, seemed to prove, as Blair himself argued again and again, that Saddam Hussein was not merely a nasty dictator, but an immediate and growing menace to the safety of the world who had to be disarmed immediately if millions of human lives were not to be imperiled. Tony Blair's support for George W. Bush's insistence that action against Saddam Hussein could not be delayed even for several months, as UN investigators continued their work, was at the heart of the diplomatic crisis the Iraq war plan provoked at the United Nations and the deep divisions it created in NATO.

Someone with at least a passing knowledge of Iraqi affairs was likely to notice that the allegations in paragraph one of Blair's executive summary did not refer to what Saddam Hussein was doing currently. They were a rehash of what he had been doing twelve or twenty years ago.

Saddam Hussein, for example, had indeed in the past "persistently tried to develop a nuclear bomb," or at least tried to develop facilities that could have produced some of the components of a bomb, but Blair knew he had never had any success at it after Israeli pre-emptive airstrikes destroyed the Iraqi nuclear facilities near Baghdad more than twenty years ago, in June 1981. Though the contentions in the dodgy dossiers were presented in such a way as to give the impression that they were official findings based on new and verified British intelligence, no intelligence agency has ever provided any evidence that Saddam Hussein subsequently posed a nuclear threat. At the time Blair issued his condemnation of Saddam Hussein, the worst nuclear proliferator by far wasn't some "rogue state." It was George W. Bush's and Tony Blair's close ally in the war on terrorism, Pakistan.

While any moderately well-informed person could tell just by reading it that Blair's dossier had been "sexed up," the target audience for this prime ministerial disinformation was the gullible. Even more sensationalist "executive summaries" were spoon-fed to the British tabloid press. Every casual visitor to Tony Blair's official website was invited, in an eye-catching sidebar, to mouse-click for news about the 45-minute missile threat, and Saddam's uranium hunting in Africa. "Welcome to the 10 Downing Street website," Tony Blair's default page chirped. "Read the dossier on Iraq's weapons of mass destruction, published in September 2002 by the UK government."

As the select committee of investigation later observed, in a classic instance of British understatement, Blair's claims were "more assertive" than the evidence warranted. In another bravado bit of Brit bureaucratese, the allegations about the attempted uranium purchases in Africa were adjudged, in particular, to be "very odd."

In one of his last computer messages, Dr. Kelly had written of "many dark actors playing games." They may have been dark actors, but the game turned out to be a farce. Leaving aside the Kelly tragedy, and Blair himself (whose own reputation was far more besmirched by this pathetic affair than the BBC's), the chief victims of Downing Street's disinformation turned out to be Tony Blair's great pals over in Yankland—Dick Cheney, Donald

Rumsfeld, Condoleezza Rice, Colin Powell, and George W. Bush himself.

"The British government has learned that Saddam Hussein recently sought significant quantities of uranium from Africa," George W. Bush announced in his 2003 State of the Union Address. George W. Bush could have quickly calmed the controversy and dispersed the ridicule that followed this assertion had he been willing, at least on this one particular occasion, to let the buck stop with him. Instead he and Condoleezza Rice spent weeks trying to get the CIA to take the fall. Why was the CIA guilty? It had failed to stop Bush, at Rice's behest, from putting Blair's unfounded allegation in his speech. In an echo of Blair's pursuit and persecution of Kelly, Ambassador Joe Wilson, the American diplomat who had informed the Bush administration that the Saddam-uranium tales were fanciful, was also subjected to public attack.

As the world slipped toward war, official US statements were increasingly littered, as if by mouse droppings, with Tony Blair's nuggets of disinformation. A month after George W. Bush embarrassed himself, it was Colin Powell's turn to get Blair doo on his fingers. The occasion was a final US appeal to the United Nations for support in the upcoming invasion of Iraq. By then Powell was the last US official who had credibility with the international community. Had he presented incontrovertible evidence that day at the UN that Saddam truly did present a clear and present danger, the United Nations Security Council, that late, still might have swung its support behind the United States.

As Colin Powell strode to the podium at the UN, people remembered a crucial earlier moment in the history of international peacekeeping efforts. More than forty years earlier, Adlai Stevenson had provided photographic evidence that the Soviet

Union had installed missiles in Cuba. Stevenson won the world to America's cause that day. Could Colin Powell do it again? Powell, just as Stevenson had, used enlarged photos, projected dramatically into the darkened Security Council, in his attempt to demonstrate that Saddam posed a danger to world peace. He also played telephone intercepts which he claimed proved that Iraqi officers, on Saddam's orders, were trying to hide weapons of mass destruction.

The recorded telephone dialogue between Iraqi officers was so ambiguous that even to the casual ear, it was clear that it proved nothing or, to put it more accurately, could be made to seem to prove anything. Among all the thousands of hours of intercepted Iraqi telephone calls, was this the most incriminating evidence US intelligence could produce?

Powell seemed on somewhat firmer ground when he showed the Security Council photographs of two trucks moving around the Iraqi desert. Although the Iraqis claimed the two trucks carried nothing more sinister than hydrogen for inflating balloons, these photos did seem to show that Saddam was up to something. What was it?

According to Powell, these were "mobile production facilities used to make biological agents." Assuming a confidential tone and conversational manner as he addressed the world body, the US secretary of state continued: "Let me take you inside that intelligence file and share with you what we know from eyewitness accounts. We have firsthand descriptions of biological weapons factories on wheels and on rails. The trucks and train cars are easily moved and are designed to evade detection by inspectors. In a matter of months, they can produce a quantity of biological poison equal to the entire amount that Iraq claimed to have produced in the years prior to the Gulf war."

Powell didn't say who had produced that particular "intelligence file," but the trail led to Tony Blair. As Blair's executive summary had put it, "We judge that Iraq has . . . developed mobile laboratories for military use, corroborating earlier reports about the mobile production of biological warfare agents."

No quantities of biological poison were found after the invasion. Nor were any mobile labs discovered, but for George W. Bush the wish was, as always, tantamount to the fulfillment. "Yes," he told reporters at the end of May 2003, more than two months after the invasion, "we found a biological laboratory in Iraq which the UN prohibited." His serene assurance that proof had been found caused specialists and reporters to take a fresh look at what had happened since first Blair, and then Powell, had made their assertions.

Powell's two trucks, it turned out, were found. When American and British investigators examined them, they discovered Saddam had been telling the truth. They also found a reason why the two trucks might have seemed so identifiable to Tony Blair's "intelligence advisers," who by then seemed chiefly to have been drawn from the staff of his director of communications. They were "part of a system originally sold to Saddam by Britain in 1987," reported the *Observer*, under the headline, SADDAM'S TRUCKS WERE FOR BALLOONS, NOT GERMS. It added: "Tony Blair faces a fresh crisis over Iraq's alleged weapons of mass destruction, as evidence emerges that two vehicles that he has repeatedly claimed to be Iraqi mobile biological warfare production units are nothing of the sort." Yet again had Tony Blair's bottomless insistence on being helpful embarrassed the Americans, and brought into question his own character, as well as his capacity for judgment.

If it is pardonable for people in Britain to see George W.

Bush as an example of "mad cowboy disease," it is equally understandable that Tony Blair might seem to some Americans like a character from some over-the-top *Monty Python* skit. The unedifying spectacle of Blair first fabricating "intelligence," and then trying to use the might of the British government to punish those who pointed out the claims were fake is too sordid to be funny. On the other hand, how not to laugh when it turns out that some of Blair's most extensive allegations, far from being new, or even the findings of British intelligence, actually date back more thirteen years—and were plagiarized (Americanisms and all) from the PhD thesis of a California grad student named Ibrahim al-Marashi? A White House intern could have come up with the same (and probably much more convincing) evidence against Saddam with a 30-second Google search.

It may not be illegal for a British politician to create false intelligence reports for the purpose of misleading public opinion, but in the United States it is a criminal—that is to say, an impeachable—offense for a president or any other official of the United States to use US intelligence reports which have been generated for such purposes. But why then, is it not an impeachable offense to use spurious intelligence reports manufactured by a foreign government?

From late 2001, when it secretly decided to attack Iraq, until March 2003, when it launched the invasion, the George W. Bush administration faced consistent difficulty whenever it attempted to get the CIA and other agencies to provide proof that the attack was justified. We also know that whenever the CIA would not or could not verify some allegation George W. Bush wanted to make, Tony Blair did it for him.

Perhaps someday documentary evidence will emerge indicating whether this trans-Atlantic partnership in deception was a conscious collaboration. What we know for sure is that Tony Blair, like a world-class butler, had the knack of arriving tray in hand, "intelligence finding" on the tray, seemingly without the master of the (white) house even having to ring.

It was Blair's knack for anticipating George W. Bush's propaganda needs that truly made his support for the uranium tale "very odd." No US intelligence agency would support the allegation. The American envoy sent to Africa for the very purpose of verifying it came back and informed the administration the accusation was false. No problem for George W. Bush, and his need to scare Americans into believing Saddam might attack them with nuclear weapons: "The British government has learned that Saddam Hussein recently sought significant quantities of uranium from Africa," the unelected president announced. Thanks to Tony Blair, George W. Bush was consistently able to make claims which would have violated the law had he purported they were backed by US intelligence findings.

In the case of Saddam's supposed efforts to obtain uranium from Africa, he went beyond simply using a Tony Blair allegation when the CIA would not corroborate his claims. In this case, he and Condoleeza Rice disregarded the findings of an American official, Ambassador Joe Wilson, who had been sent to Niger specifically to look into the allegations. Wilson reported that the allegations were false, and that Saddam had not sought to buy uranium there. Faced with the definite conclusion by an experienced American official, George W. Bush chose to propogate Tony Blair's groundless assertions instead.

Blair and those around him indirectly confirmed that his allegations had been generated for the convenience of his American friends. This revelation emerged as the Blair government defended itself from criticism by resorting to the time-honored

PR technique of refuting a charge by admitting it. Poppycock! Rubbish! Blair mouthpieces sputtered—while mentioning in passing that one of the dodgy dossiers had indeed been "published last February to coincide with Blair's 'war summit' with President George Bush in Washington." They conceded as well that Blair's earlier "mishmash of intelligence reports, student work and publicly available briefings by *Jane's Intelligence Review*," as one intelligence source described it, had been presented in such as way as to create "the impression that it was all based on fresh intelligence." Oh, and while we are rejecting utterly any talk that Tony Blair and his government did anything even slightly improper, let's slip in the mention that, to be sure, the dodgy dossier had been "used to fill a 'political vacuum' ahead of Colin Powell's presentation on the weapons to the United Nations Security Council."

Anyone seeking to understand why world events have unfolded as they have during the presidency of George W. Bush must consider the mystery of why Tony Blair—the leader of a significant nation possessing the material qualifications for sovereignty—chose, at the exact historical moment when Britain might have actually exerted some influence for good in the world, to act like a camp follower. Before he attached himself to Bush, Blair appeared to be an authentically independent leader with a role of his own to play in the world. Blair's toadying to the Americans disappointed many in Britain. It was an even greater disappointment to those Americans who imagined the prime minister would help contain George W. Bush's excesses. But Blair's behavior came as no surprise to the Europeans, especially, of course, to the French. From their perspective, Blair was simply doing what the English have been doing since the Hundred Years' War: keeping Europe divided.

A generation ago, Charles de Gaulle vetoed Britain's entry into the Common Market. England wasn't ready to be a part of Europe, he said; maybe it never would be. De Gaulle predicted that someday there would come into existence a united Europe stretching from "the Atlantic to the Urals." This was a conception that could, but did not necessarily, exclude Britain, and which definitely foresaw the collapse of Communism, and Russia's loss of its Caucasian and Central Asian dependencies. De Gaulle's doubts about England proved to be prescient.

Over the decades, the veneer of England has changed. You can drink Beaujolais nouveau in Birmingham, and find fresh ducks' breasts for sale in Hungersford. But if there had been any doubt about England—or at least its governing elite, including Tony Blair's "New Labor"—retaining a profoundly hostile attitude toward the possibility of becoming European, Blair's behavior proved that Perfidious England remains the inveterate enemy of a united Europe.

The mystery here is that Blair, by dividing Europe instead of working to keep it united, threw away a historic chance to exalt his own, and Britain's, role in the emerging power arrangements of the twenty-first century. George W. Bush's unilateralist foreign policy, especially his disdain for America's European allies, give the European Union—which is supposed to have a shared foreign policy—the chance to act like an emerging independent power. More than a chance, it was an opportunity. No previous challenge had united the people of Europe more than George W. Bush's scheme to invade Iraq. It wasn't just in France or Germany. In Britain itself there was overwhelming popular opposition to the Iraqi invasion.

The British are skeptical of the euro. They don't like the bureaucrats in Brussels, but by a two-to-one ratio they agreed with the Italians, the Spanish, the Germans, the French, and virtually all the Europeans who believed that this time, Europe must check American arrogance and impetuousness with a constructive policy of its own. Forging a united European alternative to Bush's Iraq war was a kind of Europeanism the majority of the British public could have supported.

This unanimity of public opinion gave European leaders the opportunity for the first time to provide an independent, friendly alternative to an American policy they and the people who had elected them did not support. What makes his rejection of those possibilities truly odd is that these very same circumstances also gave Tony Blair, who favors closer integration into European Union, including British adoption of the euro as its currency, a tremendous chance to further his own European objectives. In the process, he could have done more than simply advance his own agenda at the expense of the opposition Tories and "Euroskeptics." He could have raised British influence to new heights in both the United States and in Europe. Instead Blair wound up demeaning his and Britain's status on both sides of the Atlantic.

Another factor could have worked greatly to Tony Blair's advantage. In Washington, George W. Bush didn't care about the mass demonstrations against the war, or about Democratic opposition in Congress. He knew instinctively that the people waving antiwar placards—however well-behaved and middle class—would only shore up his support in American-flag-decal country. Similarly, Democratic opposition would play straight into his wedge-issue electoral strategy for both the midterm Congressional elections and the 2004 presidential campaign.

The only opposition Bush truly had to fear in the run-up to the Iraq invasion—other than from his own father—never materialized. Had Colin Powell resigned, or Blair held out the option of not sending British troops to Iraq, even George W. Bush and his capos would have had to rethink their impetuous scheme. In the process, Powell would have turned himself, very possibly, into a future president. Tony Blair would have joined Nelson Mandela as a figure of stupendous global authority.

Powell's decision to stay loyal to the administration, while misjudged, was understandable. He was a soldier. He owed his job to George W. Bush. He was a loyal American. But Blair didn't owe anything to George W. Bush. All he had, and was, he owed to Britain and the British people.

Tony Blair could have been an effective statesman in his own right, but only if he had possessed the courage to act as an independent foreign leader, not as a third-tier member of George W. Bush's entourage. For that was what the prime minister of the United Kingdom had chosen to be, and having made that choice, he found himself far from the top in the White House pecking order. Blair was in no way as influential as Cheney or Rumsfeld, or even as Wolfowitz and Rice.

Going down another echelon or two, was Blair's influence even comparable to that of Richard Perle and the talk-show radicals? Blair claimed he had gotten George W. Bush to agree that once Saddam was taken out peace between the Israelis and Palestinians would be the next tough-guy act. But after a month or so of talking about it, and then one single meeting, at Aqaba, dedicated to restarting the peace process, George W. Bush walked away, as usual. The advocates of giving Ariel Sharon a free hand prevailed. The Sharon wall went up, just as the Sharon tanks had earlier gone into Ramallah.

Tony Blair could have done great good. He could have helped a united Europe to take a historic step forward. He could have helped America save itself from a very serious blunder. He could have saved the lives of a number of good British people, and also saved his own Exchequer hundreds of millions of pounds. Instead, faced with the appalling prospect of actually having to disagree with George W. Bush, the British prime minister threw all those chances away.

Tony Blair himself seems unlikely ever to explain this failure of moral vision and political nerve. Yet one explanation for his behavior that fits the facts of the mystery is that when you scratch Tony Blair's telegenic "Cool Britannia" persona, all you really find underneath is that old English fear that the jungle begins at Calais. And if the Yanks won't save us from all those garlicky foreigners, who will? Blair has said as much a number of times while attempting to justify his policy of dependence on the United States to domestic audiences in the United Kingdom. The following is from his speech to his annual party conference in October 2003.

"Britain should be in there," Blair said, speaking of his support for the US invasion of Iraq, "not because we are America's poodle, but because dealing with it will make Britain safer." He continued: "It's not so much American unilateralism I fear. It's isolation. It's walking away when we need America there engaged."

There it was—that old British fear of being left in the lurch, combined with that old British condescension toward the bumptious Americans. If we don't make a show of going along with these Yanks on their periodic rampages, they'll huff off, back into isolationism, and whatever will we do then? But if we do jolly them, then America, as Tony Blair put it, would be there "fighting to get world trade opened up. Fighting to give hope to Africa." In his speech to the party conference, the prime minister who had mistaken British-made balloon-inflating devices for Iraqi weapons of mass destruction expressed the classic delusion of the courtier. Because he had appointed himself George W. Bush's little voice of sanity, America, now that Saddam had been taken out, would be "changing its position for the future of the world, on climate change." Because he, Tony Blair, was there to keep George W. Bush from acting like a total and absolute lout, America also would be "staying with it in the Middle East, telling Israel and the Palestinians: Don't let the extremists decide the fate of the peace process, when the only hope is two states living side by side in peace."

And when the courtier's dream of power is rebuked by reality? There always remains the option of denial. "On weapons of mass destruction, we know that the regime has them, and we know that, as the regime collapses, we will be led to them," Tony Blair insisted in April 2003, even as invading US and British forces failed to find any weapons of mass destruction. Even after the facts were verified, Blair continued telling interviewers, "We have already found two trailers, both of which we believe were used for the production of biological weapons."

After nine months of fruitless searching, Blair remained in denial. On December 16, 2003, Blair made the following statement in an interview with the Arabic service of the BBC: "INTERVIEWER: Forgive me to ask you, are you still confident that they may be found? PRIME MINISTER: I am confident that the Iraqi Survey Group, when it does its work, will find what has happened to those weapons, because that he had them, there is absolutely no doubt at all."

Beneath the absurdity, as always, lay the guile of the spin. Consider the following quote. It comes from Tony Blair's official website: "There is no doubt about the chemical program, the biological program, indeed the nuclear weapons program. All that is well documented by the United Nations. Now, our priority, having got rid of Saddam, is to rebuild the country. So the focus at the moment is on the humanitarian and the political reconstruction of the country. The threat from weapons of mass destruction, obviously with Saddam out, is not immediate any more."

In the end there is not really a contradiction. The Tony Blair with the clever, professional wife, who helped gentrify Islington in North London, who vacations in Tuscany and Aquitaine, who is at his best both classy and classless is exactly the self-same Tony Blair who, the moment George W. Bush decides he's going to invade Iraq, is also just another spineless Brit politician who snaps to attention whenever America snaps its fingers.

So Tony Blair fled from his rendezvous with history. Into the shadow of America's pant leg Blair fled, and clung—and if anyone dares to suggest that this judgment is too harsh, let them honestly answer the following question. If things had been the reverse—if Europe had wanted to liberate Iraq from Saddam, and George W. Bush had been dead set against it—would Tony Blair have been for or against the invasion?

XV

Weapons of Mass Delusion

In diplomacy there are the many small things that should not be said because they are false. Then there are those immense things that a well-meaning statesman should never mention because they are true. Secretary of Defense Donald Rumsfeld's famous comment about "old Europe," made less than two months before the Iraq invasion, falls into that second category. In this case, telling the truth deeply offended countries which, until then, had been considered important US allies.

Cheney, earlier, with his comment about not letting UN inspectors back in Iraq, had let the cat out of the bag when it came to the administration's intentions concerning weapons of mass destruction. With his swipe at "old Europe," Rumsfeld provided an equally telling glimpse of the neocons' geopolitical agenda. At the time his comments were ridiculed on both sides of the Atlantic as an inadvertent gaffe by the guy whose job it was to run wars, not calibrate diplomatic nuance. Everyone knew Rumsfeld was a loose cannon, said the spinners. The opposite was true; Rumsfeld was exactly on target. What he said all too accurately revealed how the George W. Bush administration intended to apply the Middle-Finger Foreign Policy to erstwhile allies. Iraq would be used as a wedge issue to preclude the emergence in Europe, as Wolfowitz had put it so long ago, of a "potential alternative" to United States supremacy, even on a regional basis.

The timing and scene of Rumsfeld's comment, even if not contrived deliberately, were perfect for giving the Europeans the jab. His comment came on January 22, 2003, as the Bush administration, having discovered that NATO and the European Union would not support them in Iraq, were working hard to shatter the unity of both organizations, and piece together a "coalition of the willing" from the splinters. Rumsfeld made his "old Europe" remark in Prague, showcase of the new Europe. A reporter asked him about "European opposition" to the Iraq invasion plan, and Rumsfeld seized the moment.

"You're thinking of Europe as Germany and France," Rumsfeld rejoined. "I don't. I think that's 'old Europe.'" He then laid out the administration's strategic vision for Europe: "If you look at the entire NATO Europe today, the center of gravity is shifting to the east. And there are a lot of new members. And if you just take the list of all the members of NATO and all of those who have been invited in recently—what is it, twenty-six, something like that?"

Continuing on in his signature stream-of-consciousness manner, Rumsfeld then made the comment that more than any other made the rupture between George W. Bush's America and Europe irreparable. "Germany has been a problem, and France has been a problem," Rumsfeld said. Then he added: "You look at vast numbers of other countries in Europe. They're not with France and Germany; they're with the United States."

After Rumsfeld left, Colin Powell rushed around Europe with his diplomatic mop and pail, but it was Rumsfeld, not the secretary of state, who had defined George W. Bush's Europe policy, which was to exploit Europe's divisions, not help heal them. The Europeans reacted with the kind of shock that comes when you can't quite believe what someone has just told you yet you know it's true. The French finance minister said he was "profoundly vexed." The German foreign minister took issue with the word "problem." "Our position is not a problem, it is a constructive contribution," he said, as though George W. Bush had ever shown any interest in "constructive contributions" to the Iraq debate.

The French environment minister, who had more than one reason to be vexed, when asked, started a sentence that began: "If you knew what I felt like telling Mr. Rumsfeld—" Then she stopped. Various allied officials already had called George W. Bush a "fool," an "idiot," and (most useful, in terms of its political spin back in America) gone so far as to use the word "Nazi" in sentences containing his name.

Such comments entirely missed the point. George W. Bush's objectives may have been moronic, but he and those around him had the intelligence and determination they needed to achieve them. What, even now, the Europeans do not entirely seem to understand is that dividing Europe was not merely a means to an end so far as George W. Bush was concerned. As much as "regime change" in Baghdad itself, dividing Europe was a policy imperative. The reaction to Rumsfeld's comments showed the policy was working. For in international as well as domestic politics, what better proof is there that a wedge issue is working than that it gets people mad at you?

There truly is an "old Europe" that, until Rumsfeld stuck his verbal wedge in there, had been coexisting, more or less amicably, with the new Europe that began to emerge after the fall of the Berlin wall. The old Europe had started, in the 1950s, as a bloc of nations that steadily dismantled the trade barriers dividing them. Free trade was only a first step toward fulfilling the dream of a united Europe extending far beyond the original Six (France, Germany, Italy, and the Benelux countries), as the founding members of the common market were called. By the time Rumsfeld made his comment, the grouping had renamed itself the European Union. It also had expanded to include fifteen countries stretching from Finland to Portugal, and from Ireland to Greece. Even at that size, it remained mostly a rich man's club. But by the time George W. Bush started taking his "for-us-or-against-us" approach to the world, the balance of power and also the way things are done in Europe, had started to shift.

Over the next few years, at least ten more nations will join the European Union. NATO also will greatly expand. The new members of both organizations will include such countries as Romania, Cyprus, Lithuania, and Malta. The days when "Europe" was a stroll down the Champs-Elysée, or a performance of Verdi at La Scala, or a scenic Rhine cruise, are gone. Poor people are pouring into rich countries. Polish farmers now want subsidies French farmers fear losing. The euro and the unified European market have made some things (computers, VCRs) cheaper, while making many other things more expensive than ever. Europe is becoming more like America in ways some Europeans, especially in "old Europe," are not sure they want. Meanwhile, many of the new members, especially those in Eastern Europe, are less interested in European unity than they are in using membership in the European Union (as well as NATO) to maximize their independence—an opportunity the George W. Bush administration would most adroitly exploit.

The motor and soul of "old Europe" (which is still very much in business) is the fusion of French and German interests. The two countries coordinate their domestic as well as foreign policies. On some occasions, when the chancellor of Germany cannot attend an important conference, the president of France speaks for both countries, or the other way around. Two nations that three times in less than 100 years drenched Europe in blood today live in peaceful symbiosis. This deep friendship between the two old enemies truly is a special relationship. Particularly in the United States, where it is scarcely noticed all, the French-German fusion is one of least appreciated as well as one of the most noble international accomplishments of the post–World War II era.

Acting as one gives France and Germany stupendous power within Europe. They will remain very important whatever form new Europe takes, but in the "old Europe" almost nothing could be done without French-German support. This was a European fact of life that small countries, and even large ones like Italy, Spain, and Britain, had no choice but to accept. But what about the new Europe? With so many new members piling on board, will the French and Germans still control the tiller, even when they want to pilot Europe on a different course from the United States?

Arrogance and self-importance are far from being alien traits in either France or Germany. The truth is, if you aren't French or German, or happy to let them take the lead on practically everything, this admirable French-German amity can be a pain in the neck. To put it another way, the European "Union" is still much more an expression of principle than it is a reality. Everything it does (especially when the French and Germans make it happen) is done over the opposition, and incurs the resentment, of at least some of its members. At least one of those members—Britain, whether under Blair or Thatcher—is almost always looking for an excuse to gum up the works. If it weren't for the traditional European commitment to policy-making by consensus, respect for opposing views, and civility in deliberation, wedge-issue politics might have torn Europe apart long ago.

At first all this didn't seem to have much bearing on George W. Bush's efforts to polarize world politics. In Europe, as practically everywhere else, everyone opposed his attempts to disrupt efforts to deal with global warming and his efforts to block treaties banning land mines. In both the old and new Europe, as everywhere else, the reaction to his attempt to transform the war on terrorism into a war against Saddam Hussein was also uniformly negative. Had there been a European referendum on supporting George W. Bush's invasion of Iraq, the proposal would have been overwhelmingly defeated. But the European "Union" is still a collection of sovereign states with independent governments, which from time to time, even in democracies, ignore the will of the people who elected them.

As the United States turned Iraq into a successful wedge issue there, the European Union was split in a way reminiscent of the way, earlier, the American Electoral College had been split. Who cared what the voters wanted, so long as George W. Bush got his way? Two officials were in overall charge of implementing the George W. Bush policy in Europe. Donald Rumsfeld (not Colin Powell, for obvious reasons) coordinated the overall onslaught, especially when it came to splitting off from "old Europe" the countries of eastern Europe. The other official in charge of implementing American policy in Europe was Tony Blair. His good offices, in this instance, would be considerably more helpful to George W. Bush than his dodgy dossiers were.

Because, for present purposes, he was a "European," Blair was useful in lining up Western European countries like Spain and Italy for George W. Bush's "coalition of the willing." The prime ministers of Spain and Italy didn't care about Iraq. As their actions showed, they didn't care about their peoples' overwhelming opposition to the Iraq war either. But both saw their role in the world as something grander than supporting players on a European stage where France and Germany were always the stars. They, too, could become featured actors on the world stage.

Rumsfeld—precisely because he was secretary of defense, not secretary of state—was ideal when it came to encouraging East European countries like Poland to defy Germany and France. Here, too, the basis for support was not agreement that invading Iraq was a reasonable thing to do. It was political expediency, as currently defined. Supporting the Iraq invasion gave the leaders of Spain and Italy the chance to give the French and Germans a neighborly kick in the shins. For the East Europeans, so recently liberated from Soviet domination, and with the memory of Nazi aggression still vivid as well, Rumsfeld's invitation to join the American "war against terrorism" in Iraq was an ideal chance to defy both of their historical oppressors—both Germany and Russia. Besides, no one was asking these countries to do any dying in Iraq—though they would be welcome to do a little well-paid guard duty after the "cakewalk" was finished, and all was peaceful and happy. The Italians and Romanians and Spaniards and Poles and Bulgarians arriving home in coffins from Iraq would come only later.

While Blair was helping Rumsfeld split Europe, the French were doing what they always do. This consists of supporting the United States when it is right and opposing America when it is wrong.

The French truly are among America's best friends. They would be even better friends if US officials let them, but they are not the kind of friends who chat over the backyard fence while hanging out the laundry. The French are like those very nice friends who have that elegant penthouse apartment with the parquet floors and the maid's room. You send them DVDs; they send you important books you know you should really read for Christmas. Even though they are a little formal, you can count on them to tell you what they think—and, when they have you to dinner, the table is so elegant and the conversation is always so lively! Robert Frost certainly wasn't thinking of the French when he said good fences make good neighbors, but in their case, it happens to be true.

If the French on occasion are wise, it is because their past foolishness has provided them with so many opportunities to learn. France hasn't won a major war on its own at least since the time of Louis XIV. That's why that giant arch in Paris is called the *Arc de Triomphe*. To call it the Victory Arch would be absurd.

Beginning in the 1700s, France lost Canada; it lost India. It lost, in Haiti, the first successful war of liberation by a nonwhite people against a European colonial power. That didn't stop France from fighting and losing future colonial wars in southeast Asia and north Africa. One of those French colonial wars—in Vietnam—led to US involvement in what's usually described as the first defeat in American history (though we hadn't been exactly victorious in the War of 1812). The single most famous defeat in battle since World War II—Dien Bien Phu—is a French defeat. So is the most famous of all military defeats: Waterloo.

The French know full well that were it not for the British, the

Canadians, and above all, the Americans, the Germans never would have been driven from French soil in 1945. World War I was different. It is intellectually possible for a Frenchman to argue that France won—or at least that it certainly contributed the most—to the Allied victory in World War I, but not emotionally. Who would want to describe the ultimate outcome of that horrendous bloodletting as a "victory" for anyone?

To this day every village in France has its memorial to the dead lost in the horrible slaughter of the Western Front. In some places every boy and man went to their death in the trenches. The memorials simply say: "To Our Children." After the second world war, both countries decided the solution truly was for the two countries to unite—though not in the way either Napoleon or Hitler had tried to do it. De Gaulle's special relationship with Germany was his supreme achievement.

While victories are unusual, triumphs abound in French history, even if they are not quite so boundless as the French themselves imagine. In part this is because the French are so much better at winning the peace than they are at winning wars. It is also because the French, as much as the Americans, are masters at self-illusion. Consider the thirty years after France's liberation by foreign forces from its foreign conquerors in 1945. Having lost World War II, France went on to lose the Indochina and Algeria wars. It also lost its immense empire in Africa. For the first time, it indisputably lost great power status.

During this same period the Fourth Republic collapsed. France, had de Gaulle not come to the rescue, might have found itself on the brink of civil war. In 1968, the country was convulsed with civil disorders, which was just about the last time that France did anything to set the world on fire. Most people who are not French would look at the 1945–1975 period, shrug, and remark: *C'est la vie.* The French, however, refer to it as *Les Trente Glorieuses*—the thirty years of glory.

Such are the some of peculiarities and a few of the idiosyncrasies of the French, who in symbiosis with their German soulmates, still constitute one of the three or four most important nodes of political, economic, and military power in the world—after the United States itself, which remains in a one-nation superpower league of its own. The experience of this long history of defeat and triumph has made of France the sort of ally that, if America really did like having allies, it would love.

France always has a lot of ideas, as well as a certain amount of money and armed forces to contribute, and isn't timid in the slightest about going off with us on some foreign military expedition, so long as it agrees with the objective, and is well-represented in the chain of command. In the end, France usually supports us. When it doesn't, that is often a helpful warning sign. Last but not least, France doesn't cost the United States anything. France pulls its own weight. If the entire world were made up of countries like France, America's biggest overseas military expense would be the Marine guards at US embassies. On the other hand, Cheney, Rumsfeld, and Wolfowitz would all have to work for a living.

One of the sadder things about George W. Bush's presidency is that he could have had so many interesting conversations with experienced world leaders, and hasn't. Imagine if he had asked Nelson Mandela to show him Africa, rather than dashing from one palm-fringed photo op to another telling the Africans what they should do. His trip might have amounted to something more than a string of neocon (in this case, mostly neo-confederate) soundbites.

Chatting once in a while with the president of France,

Jacques Chirac, could also have saved George W. Bush trouble in Africa, and embarrassment elsewhere. Chirac, if George W. Bush had bothered to ask him, could have let him know that Tony Blair's uranium tales were a plate of tripe because the French are heavier on the ground in Africa than any other Western power. But in George W. Bush's world, a friend is someone who feeds you falsehoods, so long as they are the falsehoods you want to believe. (Come to think of it, that's what he does in his own capacity as "friend in chief" of the American people.) What about people who tell you the truth? George W. Bush has let us know how we should regard such people time after time.

When France disagrees with the United States, Americans ask: Why do the French always disagree with us? Instead of complaining that they're against us, yet again, in Iraq, it would be more fruitful to ask: How come the French did support us in Afghanistan?

Jacques Chirac was the first foreign leader to reach Ground Zero. "In these terrible circumstances, all French people stand by the American people," he declared, while the air around was still thick with debris. Had George W. Bush wanted friends, Chirac was the kind of European friend he would have found congenial. For one thing Chirac, unlike Tony Blair, was ideologically untainted with socialism and liberalism. Though it could come from a George W. Bush campaign biography, the following statement is taken from one of Chirac's own political résumés: "Standing for lower tax rates, removal of price controls, strong punishments for crime and terrorism and the privatization of businesses, Chirac [first] ran for president in 1981."

A conservative who had studied in the United States (like George W. Bush, Chirac did some graduate work at Harvard),

Chirac also has experience when it comes to rising to history's unexpected challenges. In 2001, when the French electoral system—in a malfunction as stunning as the snafu in the US Electoral College that made Bush president—made the French racist and fascist, Le Pen, one of the two final candidates for president, Chirac unified the country in statesmanlike manner, and won eighty-five percent of the vote. An event that could have dangerously divided France and injected great bitterness into its political life was turned into an amicable and impressive display of moderation and national unity.

Bush presented Chirac with a similar challenge, on an international scale. Once again Chirac rose to the occasion. Having supported George W. Bush for all the right reasons in Afghanistan, he opposed him for all the right reasons on Iraq. There was never any question that George W. Bush could win the war of bullets and bombs, if he chose to launch his virtually unilateral attack. But Chirac and France won the war of reasonable discourse. It was a German official who actually summed up the outcome, though he was also speaking for France and many other countries by then: "You never made your case."

As the desperate, futile search for weapons of mass destruction ultimately showed, there had never been a case to make. And—call it "anti-Americanism" or simply character—the French, along with the Germans, were not going to go to war simply because George W. Bush said so. They weren't alone. Standing with France and Germany in opposition to the Iraq invasion were Russia, China, India, Canada, and more than 100 other countries. "Old Europe," as things turned out, still had some cards to play.

It also had some cards not to play. Following the Iraq invasion, the US dollar went into free fall. Back in 1992, it had risen. One reason was that after the first Gulf War the Europeans contributed billions of dollars to help the US war effort. Now they were keeping their euros at home. The money George W. Bush's divisiveness had saved them was a sum incomparably greater than any profits lost by being excluded from Paul Wolfowitz's list of countries allowed to bid for contracts in Iraq.

In America the international opposition to the United States was widely misconstrued as a triumph of French intransigence. Almost everywhere else, it was regarded as a triumph of French reasonableness. After Iraq did turn into the quagmire its opponents warned it would be, and the number of Americans killed in Iraq kept mounting, there was something else to consider. No young French (and German) soldiers were getting killed in Iraq. What possible answer could George W. Bush or Tony Blair have given if, at the first Christmas after the Iraq invasion, some mother actually had gotten close enough to grab either of them, and say: "Why did you really get my son killed?"

Chirac and Schröeder don't need to be evasive. They can truthfully tell their people: "We Germans and French no longer kill for no reason." Meanwhile, George W. Bush, having sent his fellow Americans to their deaths, shirks their funerals. There are no photos of him next to a coffin with an American flag on it in the newspapers or on TV. An Internet search reveals how successfully the White House media management folks have been in visually detaching George W. Bush from the American deaths his war is producing. An image search elicits the following message: "Your search—'Bush coffin flag'—did not match any documents." The search "Bush flag" produces 502 hits, the majority showing him patriotically backed by immense American flags while he salutes or holds his hand over his heart.

In the end George W. Bush's "coalition of the willing" was a motley assembly, which is the way the neocon radicals like it. The problem for them with organizations like the UN and NATO is not that allies sometimes oppose us. The problem is that allies are allies. The pundits' laments that the US-induced splits on the Security Council and within the European Union are "mistakes" which now need to be corrected miss the point. The success of the whole strategy behind "coalitions of the willing" depends on creating division. Only division can provide the United States with the utter freedom of action that is the real strategic goal of the George W. Bush foreign policy.

Go back and look again at Wolfowitz's list of "Countries Eligible to Compete for Contracts Funded With US Appropriated Funds for Iraq Reconstruction." You are looking at wedge-issue politics in the process of assuming geopolitical form. This unilateral detachment of US war-making from traditional alliances operates in two directions. The absence of many of America's traditional treaty allies from Wolfowitz's list means that the United States no longer has to waste its time reasoning with them. It is finally liberated from "constructive contribution" and is free to do exactly what it wants.

Replacing treaty alliances and collective security with "coalitions of the willing" provides other advantages, including the illusion, useful in the 2004 election year, that "coalition" forces are taking the causalities in Iraq, night after night. It also serves the deeper purpose of helping to prevent regional alternatives to US hegemony from emerging in reaction to American unilateralism. France, Germany, and Russia may have stood up to America, but notice on Wolfowitz's list how Spain, Italy, Ukraine, and, of course, Britain compensate for the loss of those countries' support. Thanks to Iraq, it will be a long time before Europe has a unified foreign policy of its own.

In this strange new world disorder, in which US freedom of action, and nothing else, is the great strategic goal for which wars are provoked and Americans are sent off to die, the relationship of allies to the United States comes to mirror the postindustrial relationship of American workers to the corporations which employ them.

Think of "old Europe" nations like France and Germany as experienced executives and unionized workers. Following the hostile takeover of America, Inc., after the 2000 elections, the new management doesn't want to pay the costs, and above all it is uninterested in maintaining the kind of social benefits necessary to keep France on the management team and Germany loyal and productive. It fact it wouldn't mind getting rid of them altogether.

Though the new board of directors still has a few distinguished holdovers from an earlier, more collegial era in executive management, it is dominated by asset-strippers and greenmailers, who have decided the time has come to show who's in charge now. It's time for some union-bashing or, in this case, some Euro-UN bashing. It works! France resigns and Germany takes early retirement. Now we can hire all those undocumented workers who never talk back, go on strike, or ask us to honor a contract (treaty).

In this new schema of neocon unilateralist US force projection, America's own cross-cultural fighting force—the multihued members of those racially, ethnically, and sexually integrated military units you see dying every night on TV—are like temp workers. In fact that is exactly what the National Guardsmen suffering most in Iraq are in relation to America's professional armed forces: temps you hire when you don't want to expose top-grade employees to industrial accidents.

Temps—National Guardsmen—don't have expensive pension rights. If they do manage to get home alive and uninjured from Iraq (or anywhere else George W. Bush, Cheney, Rumsfeld, and Wolfowitz decide to send them), you don't have to pay, promote, educate, or house them. You just dump them back onto the local labor market.

Getting rid of traditional allies serves a similar purpose. Since, in the end, all the United States really wants now is to prevent any other power from being able to block, or even disagree with whatever it decides to do, it no longer really wants traditional allies anymore. On a shifting basis, though, it does need "platforms" for projecting US power, and "local hires" to man them. It's also nice to hire troops from low-income countries to soak up the kind of casualties Americans don't like to take. This is precisely what Secretary Rumsfeld proposed doing with India and several other nations, but they proved to have too exalted an idea of their sovereignty to accept such a deal.

Now look again at Wolfowitz's list. The list is not entirely made up of camp followers and microstates, but two of the more respectable countries on it are the Philippines and Australia. The Philippines, though a remarkable democracy, never has psychologically recovered from the experience of having been an American colony. Australia, when it comes to foreign policy, might as well be. When the leader of the Australian opposition, resorting to the insouciant and expressive Assuie dialect, described his country's support for George W. Bush as "arselicking," he was simply describing the habitual Australian approach to relations with the United States going back to the Vietnam war era and beyond.

What about the other countries on the list? The only thing almost all of them have in common is that—before George W. Bush decided he was going to invade Iraq—they had nothing in common. Some countries on the list, like Australia and the Philippines, clearly aspire to full Tony Blair–style status. Others (Denmark, the Netherlands) are wedge-issue candidates, if only in Paul Wolfowitz's mind. Other countries are there because they are orphans (Tonga). Others seem to be proto-bulwarks against the dreaded Wolfowitz bugaboo of "regional aspiration" (Uzbekistan as well as Singapore).

What truly links all the diverse countries on the Wolfowitz list is that this is a "coalition of the willing" without even the pretense of reciprocity or mutual respect. You're on that Wolfowitz list because Wolfowitz put you there. Get out of line, and you're off. And please do not annoy us with your opinions. This approach to foreign policy may be tactically convenient, but it raises a strategic (and moral) question: Why would any self-sufficient nation with a self-respecting leader demean itself by entering into such a humiliating, unequal relationship? And why should any decent member of the community of nations remain America's friend once the United States starts treating it that way?

The case of Canada also demonstrates how George W. Bush has degraded America in the eyes of the world, while creating enmity and, unfortunately, probably also storing up future dangers. Iraq shows it's dangerous to be America's enemy. Canadians have found it is dangerous to be George W. Bush's friend.

On September 11, 2001, the United States had no better friend than Canada. As Barbara Crossette writes, the Canadians that day "came to the aid of the United States with almost reckless haste. The Canadian government decided within 45 minutes of the attacks on the World Trade Center and Pentagon to allow all inbound trans-Atlantic and trans-Pacific flights diverted from the United States to land on Canadian territory, fully aware that there could have been more terrorists in the air."

The Canadians exposed Montreal and Vancouver to possible attack in order to help protect New York and Washington from further trauma. Yet George W. Bush's solicitude for his Saudi friends' desire to flee the United States that day was never matched by any apparent gratitude for what the Canadians had done. After the attacks, Canada supported the invasion of Afghanistan. It sent 2,500 of its soldiers there—the equivalent of the US sending 30,000 troops. This faithful Canadian support for the US war on terror led to the incident that caused Canadians, including their government, to fundamentally reassess the nature of their relationship with George W. Bush and the United States to an extent unthinkable in the past.

In April 2002, a dozen Canadians soldiers were hit and four of them killed when the American pilot of an F-16 fighter-bomber attacked them without warning during night training exercises. That was not the watershed event. That came the day after the Canadians died, when George W. Bush didn't offer a word of sorrow or regret. The death of the Canadians had been a lead item in the United States, but it was the dominant breaking news event in Canada. TV crews followed George W. Bush to his five public events that day. He did not mention the Canadians once. When a Canadian journalist called out a question to him, giving him the opportunity to make an impromptu expression of regret, he said nothing, and walked out of the room.

The next day, after public complaints from members of the Canadian government, George W. Bush did make the following comment: "I want to say publicly what I told Jean Chrétien the other day about how sorry I am that Canadian soldiers lost their lives in Afghanistan. It was a terrible accident."

That was it. Canadians parsing this statement noticed it contained no acceptance of responsibility. As always, when things went wrong, George W. Bush's response was personal denial and damage control. Besides, hadn't he already phoned the Canadian prime minister?

The ensuing headlines in Canada showed how George W. Bush had managed to alienate America's most important ally—and trading partner, and neighbor, and friend. SHOCK AND GRIEF GIVE WAY TO ANGER ran a typical headline. "We went to help out the Americans with their war—and they used us for target practice," said a front-page editorial in Canada's major national newspaper, the *Globe and Mail*.

Canada, like many other countries that supported the US in Afghanistan, declined to sign on for the Iraq attack. It did try until the very last moment to help the US find a diplomatic way to avoid the war. Canadian opposition was founded on the George W. Bush administration's failure to make a convincing case that the attack was justified, or even legal under international law. Lingering Canadian distress at Bush's attitude did not play a role in the decision, though by then people north of the border had started noticing that George W. Bush seemed to have stopped mentioning Canada when he listed America's friends.

CANADIAN ANGER OVER SNUB GETS SUPPORT, the headline ran, in December 2003. It referred to Wolfowitz's exclusion of Canada from his list. Washington insiders said Canada should have known what to expect. "It's naïve and simplistic at best if Canadians were taken aback by this," one of them remarked. "Can you imagine the reaction on Capitol Hill if the Defense

Department opened up prime contracts to countries that gave them nothing but grief about Iraq?" (Faced with the flak, the administration eventually announced that the Canadians could bid on some contracts later.)

Such an estrangement between the United States and its closest neighbor once upon a time would have been a cause of disquiet in Washington, as well as an important news event. But it was scarcely noticed. When it comes actually to protecting America's national security, the question remains: Was winning Baghdad worth losing Canada's respect?

Except for the need to fight terrorism, of course, the invasion of Iraq reflected most of the changes that had overtaken America since George W. Bush was made president. But as much as the news management out of Baghdad, what had happened to America's relations with Canada was an indication of how successfully the technology of mass communications had been transformed from a source of information into a tool for the manipulation of public opinion, at least in the United States.

Back in 1991, the great victor in the first Gulf War seemed to be the truth. Suddenly, back then, it seemed the world was entering a new era in which people everywhere could see and understand war with their own eyes. In the latest Gulf war the great victor was media manipulation. Even when it was proven beyond a doubt that Saddam Hussein's weapons of mass destruction had never existed, the fact that the war had been fought for a lie no longer seemed consequential.

"What difference does it make?" answered George W. Bush, in a Christmas interview after the capture of Saddam Hussein, when it was pointed out to him that no weapons of mass destruction had been found.

XVI

Saddam to the Rescue

THAT SOMBER FIRST POST-9/11 THANKSGIVING of November 2001, as Americans gathered together in the company of their loved ones, and reflected on the recent tragedies that had befallen their nation, who could have imagined that by Thanksgiving 2003, George W. Bush would be holding up a plastic turkey in Baghdad?

Actually, the stage prop he displayed to the cameras was made of various inedible substances, including plaster of Paris and silicone, but what became known as the Plastic Turkey episode at Baghdad airport was, along with the "Mission Accomplished" photo op on the aircraft carrier, a defining moment of the George W. Bush presidency.

The video feed, as planned, was heroic: Air Force One stealthily transporting America's Commander in Chief into the heart of Iraq while the press corps at Crawford dozed. As always, the timing was dictated by TV scheduling. George W. Bush flew halfway around the world so that, along with the traditional Thanksgiving football games, Americans could watch him, on this most American of all holidays, sharing a turkey dinner with the troops on the frontlines of freedom.

It would have been nice if some real turkey dinners had arrived with George W. Bush in the capacious hold of Air Force One, but he had not flown all that way to feed the troops. America's men and women in uniform had been rounded up before dawn to help him—in this instance with his 2004 presidential election campaign, in an event that had been orchestrated to avoid any interaction with reality.

Instead of turkey and the trimmings, the troops in the hall where the Bush in Baghdad Thanksgiving photo op was staged ate MREs (Pentagonese for "Meals Ready to Eat"). Besides, it was 6 A.M., Baghdad time, when this particular "dinner" was served. Still, it was a wholesome and dramatic symbol of the American Way of Life triumphant in the erstwhile Heart of Darkness. At least it was until the details leaked out.

Could it possibly be that the media manipulation mastery was wearing thin? After his November 27 touchdown at the former Saddam Hussein International Airport, people started making George W. Bush–plastic turkey jokes, though not for long. One way or another, George W. Bush is always exempted from the consequences of his action. Three years earlier, on December 11, 2000, Chief Justice William Rehnquist issued his Florida election nullification order like a hired magician pulling a rabbit from a hat at a little boy's birthday party. Now, on December 13, 2003, former President Saddam Hussein emerged from a hole in the ground near Tikrit to restore George W. Bush's standing in the opinion polls.

"This is a great day in your history," the American provisional ruler of Iraq, Paul Bremer, told the Iraqis after Saddam was captured. It was certainly a red-letter day for George W. Bush's image managers. For the time being, the mounting death toll was forgotten as America celebrated this latest triumph over evil as though it were a Christmas gift from the Almighty. Amidst the media exultation, it was left to a small Vermont newspaper to point out what the big-league media seemed to have forgotten.

"We're missing the point," began an unsigned editorial in the *Brattleboro Reformer* published a couple of days after Saddam's capture. "Amidst the giddy party mood spawned by the capture of deposed Iraqi leader Saddam Hussein, it's important to interject a sobering fact: Saddam Hussein is not Osama bin Laden."

Having made that salient, by now almost entirely ignored point, the editorial continued: "Despite an overwhelming paucity of evidence to support himself, President Bush has been disturbingly successful at hoodwinking the American public into believing that Saddam Hussein was somehow connected with the murderous assault on Americans on Sept. 11, 2001." Giving its readers no surcease from the truth, in spite of the holiday season, the editorial went on: "The hullabaloo over Hussein's weekend capture, the cowboy rhetoric over the United States' superior military and intelligence capacity, again cloud some critical facts. First, the mastermind behind 9/11 remains at large. Second, and more importantly, bin Laden will have more recruits than he needs lining up for suicide missions so long as US policy continues to fuel the Muslim and Arab belief that ours is a foreign policy dictated exclusively by self-interest."

As the show-business bible, *Variety*, might have put it, back during its headline-writing heyday: STIX NIX BUSH BLITZ. Of course, it didn't matter. The *Brattleboro Reformer* was a voice crying out in the wilderness metaphorically as well as literally. So far as most Americans were concerned, the capture of the scruffy ex-dictator proved that their unelected president had been right all along. After the capture, there was a double-digit jump in approval of George W. Bush's handling of events in Iraq, from 45 to 59 percent. His overall approval rating rose from 52 to 58 percent.

Americans were not the only ones gratified by Saddam's capture. Osama bin Laden was delighted too. According to a tape recording that the CIA confirmed was bin Laden's, Saddam Hussein had gotten his just deserts. In Osama bin Laden's exact words, "the capture of their former comrade in treason and collaboration with America" showed other Arab leaders that "their turn is coming." In American eyes, however, Osama and Saddam —like the terrorists who had attacked America, and the Iraqis who were now resisting the US occupation—were one and the same. If they'd ever been aware of it, almost all Americans had entirely forgotten that, before the first Gulf War, Saddam had been supported not merely by the United States, but by many of the same US officials who were now his captors, including Secretary of Defense Rumsfeld.

Meanwhile the killing continued. IRAQI TEENAGERS CHEER AS AMERICAN BLOOD FLOWS, ran a typical wire service headline, this one from Reuters. When a bomb exploded, wounding two Americans as they drove through Baghdad in their Humvee, local boys surged out of their houses—not to help the wounded Americans, but to cheer, as though Iraq had scored a goal over America in a soccer game.

"This is good. If they ask me, I will join the resistance. The Americans have to die," said a fifteen-year-old kid who identified himself as Ali Qais. "They are just here to steal our oil." Around the same time, in the fabled city of Samara, US troops killed more than fifty-four Iraqis when a firefight turned into a massacre. Iraqis insurgents had fired on the Americans, but when the Americans retaliated they shot up a kindergarten and a mosque, and also fired on civilians trying to evacuate the wounded.

The neocon seers were unperturbed by these distressing events because many of them occurred in what they had started calling the Sunni Triangle. This was a section of central Iraq where lots of Sunni Muslims lived. To hear them spin things, the Sunni Triangle was like the Bermuda Triangle—a mysterious black hole where things inexplicably happened—so, they claimed, such incidents didn't mean much. The problem with this convenient analysis was that the killing was going on all over Iraq. From the Kurdish north, where the Americans had initially been welcomed as liberators, to Basra in the south—which, under British occupation, more and more resembled war-torn Belfast—all kinds of Iraqis were turning against the occupation.

A year earlier, if you had predicted that after the cakewalk to Baghdad, Americans in Iraq would be getting killed every single day in encounters like those, the George W. Bush apparatchiks would have laughed at you. If asked what effect so many Americans getting killed would have on George W. Bush's political fortunes, many commentators would have predicted the end of his presidency. Instead, as a result of the mounting American death toll overseas, George W. Bush only seemed to become a more serious person in the American public's eyes—more "presidential."

There remain many dissenters. Still, for millions of Americans, these endless, needless deaths proved America was "strong." One dismaying revelation of the Iraq invasion was how quickly the war became a normal part of daily life for the American people. After a few weeks, the deaths and casualties ceased to shock people. Americans getting killed in Iraq became a routine part of the nightly news, like shootouts in the inner city.

It now took an usual combination of circumstances for an American death in Iraq to be connected with a face, a life, an actual person like Chief Warrant Officer Aaron Weaver. Weaver, 32, was a passenger aboard a US helicopter shot down during a medical evacuation in January 2004. His death was notable, so far as the press reporting was concerned, because he was both a cancer survivor and a survivor of the famous "Blackhawk Down" incident in Somalia, the one that provided the inspiration for the movie. He was on his way to a medical checkup in Baghdad when, in the manner of the old John O'Hara short story, "Appointment in Samara," he finally had his rendezvous with death.

Weaver's death elicited the kind of human interest a similar fatality in a commercial plane crash would have. There was no sense that his death was avoidable or needless, or that anyone, including George W. Bush, should be held accountable for it. This pointed to the greatest of all the mysteries of George W. Bush's peculiar ascendancy: the passivity of the American people. The usurpation of their democratic rights did not stir them in 2000, nor did deaths like this one in Iraq. Were they confused or merely indifferent?

"Bush misled every one of us," Senator John Kerry lamented in June 2003, as it became clear that every pretext for the Iraq war had been fraudulent. Even Republicans like George W. Bush's own former treasury secretary, Paul O'Neill, eventually acknowledged that Bush and Cheney had begun plotting their Iraq invasion within days of taking office in January 2001—not in response to the 9/11 attacks eight months later. But had there ever been a political class more willing to be gulled? Kerry's own address to the Senate during the Iraq war debate had been stirring—but, as much as any of Bush's perorations, it had been aimed straight at the TV cameras. After orating no, Kerry voted yes; he went along with George W. Bush and his war.

The difference between the first Gulf War and the second was the difference between a just war and an unjust war—not the difference between being patriotic or not. Yet only one member of the US Senate who had voted yes for the first war was courageous enough to vote no to the invasion of Iraq. Senator Bob Graham of Florida was a ranking member of the intelligence committee, as well a popular former governor of Florida, a state bound to be crucial again in the 2004 presidential election.

Graham believed the war on terrorism should be fought against terrorists, and kept pointing out that George W. Bush's "war on terrorism" was a farce. Graham felt he could do a better job than George W. Bush, so he joined the Democratic race for president.

The point Graham kept trying to make during his brief presidential campaign was not a terribly subtle or controversial one: Instead of fighting fake terrorists, we should combat the real ones. His kind of truth-telling, however, was apparently too disconcerting for Graham to be taken seriously as a presidential candidate in the national press. His campaign collapsed soon after the *Washington Post* dubbed him "The Most Dangerous Man in Washington." More dangerous than Rumsfeld? Than Cheney? Than George W. Bush himself? In the Kingdom of Spin, telling the truth had become a terrorist act.

If ever an event proved character was destiny, Saddam Hussein's capture was it. He'd lost his palaces, but he'd found his hole. The billions were gone, but he still had 750,000 dollars in cash—and he still knew how to use people, how to exploit a situation.

Over the decades he had perverted Baath socialism, the cause of Arab unity, Islam, and many another noble cause and ideal. Anyone foolish enough to imagine that Saddam Hussein, at this late date, was going to redeem himself with martyrdom clearly had underestimated his still formidable survival skills.

What American official, sitting through those tortuous meetings with Saddam in the past, where even the slightest pleasantry had to be communicated through translators, had suspected he really understood everything that was being said in English, that Saddam also could speak it quite well? Now, as the Americans ripped open his burrow, he called out in an English so clear the US GIs in the heat of such an operation could clearly understand it: "My name is Saddam Hussein. I am the president of Iraq and I want to negotiate."

Finally, Saddam Hussein had uttered the magic words that, if he had deigned to use them in the past, could have saved countless lives. But, this time it was Saddam Hussein's own skin, so having called out the magic words, he scrambled up and out of his hole into the bright light of his new career, displacing Slobodan Milosevic as the world's most famous war criminal. He might eventually face the death penalty, but it would only be after years of publicity. So far as the immediate future was concerned, Saddam would continue to enjoy the gratification of remaining at the center of events. His status and living conditions would be much altered, but his overthrow and capture actually had enhanced the possibility, rare for such a dictator, of his dying a natural death.

"It is important that we kill or capture Saddam Hussein," Bremer had noted, months earlier, when it seemed he might never be run to ground. There was more to that observation than it might seem. Before the war, as US intelligence sources later confirmed, Saddam had actually prevented Al Qaeda terrorists from operating out of Iraq. After the invasion, he tied down 140,000 US troops in Iraq. Meanwhile a variety of terrorist organizations set up shop in the country, and began killing Americans there. It is a revealing transformation. Before the invasion Saddam hadn't been a threat to America. After it, Saddam became a major drain on US military resources that would have been better used fighting terrorism.

In the guise of pursuing that objective, George W. Bush had led America back into deep waters while adding a touch of Texas to that old New England impulse to harpoon evil. Have you seen the Great White Whale? Ahab cries out in *Moby Dick*. On Voice of America, they offered cash bounties for the Great Dark Saddam. There was even a US government website—rewards forjustice.com—where you might win up to thirty million dollars by telling the Americans what they couldn't find out on their own.

The billion-dollar spy satellites and communications intercepts had come up dry in to the search for Saddam, his sons and henchmen. Old-fashioned bounty hunting, it turned out, worked better. Saddam's sons were finally caught and killed after someone revealed their whereabouts in return for a multimillion dollar reward, "payable into any bank account in any currency anywhere."

After a shootout in the northern city of Mosul, which was the last place US intelligence agency had expected to find Saddam's sons, their reconstituted corpses were displayed on Iraqi television. In this way the Americans, apparently unknowingly, reinstated an Iraqi political tradition. Back in 1963, the body of an earlier Iraqi dictator, Abdul-Karim Qassim, had been exhibited on television, propped up on a chair, so all the world could see who was no longer in charge in Iraq.

So far as the dark arts of "intelligence" are concerned, the lesson here, while unedifying, is useful. Millions in hard cash work better than billions in high-tech when it comes to tracking down evildoers. We don't know the full truth yet, but boots on the ground—not high-tech gadgets—led Saddam's pursuers to his spider hole. When it comes to the real spy world, bribing sleazy informants and hunting down adversaries like animals is often the best way to go. These are not pretty truths, but they are truths nonetheless. Another truth is that even the most tawdry tactics are futile if the guy in the Oval Office will only listen to what he wants to hear.

Neither boots on the ground nor bribes could produce Saddam's weapons of mass destruction because they never existed, as George W. Bush and Tony Blair had every reason to know before the invasion.

After the first Gulf War in 1991, Saddam actually destroyed his WMDs, as the UN resolutions demanded. Then, for more than ten years, he prevented the world from verifying it. This was the essence of Saddam's paranoia—also the secret of his hold on Iraq, and one of the reasons his every foray outside of Iraq was a catastrophe.

Why, having destroyed his weapons, did Saddam Hussein then do everything he could to prevent the UN inspectors from actually proving it? So far as domestic terror politics in Iraq was concerned, it made perfect sense. If Iraqis ever once sensed that Saddam could be forced into giving up anything by anyone, who knows what his opponents might be emboldened to try? The double game Saddam played with the weapons inspectors helped him keep his own people in line. He denied he had the weapons, but of course every Iraqi was certain Saddam was lying (even though he wasn't). They also knew he had used poison gas against the Kurds. What was to stop him from using it against demonstrators in Baghdad, if that day ever arrived?

The result outside Iraq was that powerful foreigners—eventually including George W. Bush—also believed Saddam had kept his weapons of mass destruction, and was prepared to use them. As his attacks on Iran and Kuwait showed, Saddam had no understanding of the world just beyond Iraq's borders, let alone any understanding of the possible long-term consequences of his charade in the United States. Probably Saddam calculated that his foreign enemies would eventually lose interest in him. Possibly he imagined that the Americans, thanks to their magical technology, knew full well the double game he was playing, and therefore understood he no longer posed a threat. He may even have worked on the assumption that so long as he did not actually commit any new acts of aggression, he would be safe to go on ruling Iraq—and taunting the inspectors—forever. Perhaps it was too late when Saddam finally realized that in the form of George W. Bush—as opposed to George H.W. Bush—he had met his match.

It is now public knowledge that work on biological, chemical and nuclear weapons in Iraq ceased with Saddam's defeat in the 1991 war. While continuing to claim otherwise, US officials had begun a kind of image manipulation metamorphosis even before Saddam was captured. For those who were keeping track of George W. Bush's and Tony Blair's attempts to spin allegation into evidence, a tell-tale event was the revelation that the chief US weapons hunter, a CIA officer named David Kay, was resigning his position and leaving Iraq.

"My reading is that it's a serious part of downgrading the whole procedure," a British academic, Paul Rogers, told a reporter from the magazine *New Scientist* in autumn 2003. As he saw it, the George W. Bush administration had already decided to shift its public relations stance away from weapons of mass destruction. He predicted that in the latest rewriting of history, the Bush Administration would start "focusing on the atrocities carried out by Saddam Hussein as the key reason for going to war. They've made a transition with the truth and my guess is they're pretty well convinced there's nothing serious to be found," Rogers said.

"While that may be totally different to what we were told eight months ago," he added, "that is the new line." All the new line required to make people start forgetting the old line was Saddam in the dock. Soon after these astute observations were published, Saddam was extracted from his spider hole near Tikrit. The world watched—agog and forgetful—as the former dictator had the inside of his mouth examined by a US medic.

If Saddam at least had the satisfaction of having fooled George Bush and Tony Blair, Fidel Castro was one of the winners of the Iraq war. Muammar Qaddafi of Libya has done pretty well out of it too.

During the 2000 elections, Cuban-American voters deserted the Democrats in large numbers and voted Republican, attracted by George W. Bush's astute manipulation of the symbols of patriotism. The Cuban belief that Bush would be tougher on Castro than Gore was one of the reasons the Florida election was so close. The decision to use Guantanamo Bay as a prison camp, however, guaranteed that George W. Bush would not do a thing to inconvenience Castro. That is what George W. Bush continues to do—nothing—as Castro persecutes dissidents and stomps down what small democratic openings existed before the Bush-Cheney administration took office.

Following the attack on Iraq, Libya's dictator Col. Muammar

Qaddafi decided it was time to plea bargain. Qaddafi and Libya posed no real threat anymore, but in the past Qaddafi had engaged in state-supported terrorism. He was behind the 1988 Lockerbie bombing. Fifteen years later, many American families are still grieving. Qaddafi needed help to come in out of the cold; Tony Blair, as always, was delighted to be helpful. With George W. Bush's approval, Qaddafi copped a plea that left everyone satisfied except the victims of Qaddafi's terrorism, and those who believed the Libyan people should have some say in the governance of their country.

Under the deal, none of Qaddafi's many crimes, including the kidnapping and murder of exiled Libyans, would be punished. At the same time George W. Bush got to boast that his attack on one Arab dictator had caused another to quake in his boots. Qaddafi's dysfunctional weapons systems, which international experts said had never posed a threat in the first place, would be dismantled by competent international experts under (wonder of wonders!) United Nations supervision.

This was an entirely desirable outcome, but it was risible to claim that invading Iraq was a necessary prerequisite for any of it happening. The former British foreign minister, Robin Cook, who resigned from Tony Blair's Cabinet because of Blair's dissembling, scathingly described the hypocrisy of it all. Tony Blair and George W. Bush, Cook pointed out gleefully, were now trying "to justify the invasion of Iraq on the grounds that they have indeed found weapons of mass destruction—but in Libya. Their novel defense," he went on, "appears to be that their strategy was right and it was only a minor detail that they invaded the wrong country. They must not be allowed to get away with it."

If the Iraq war had influenced Qaddafi's behavior, it had also diminished George W. Bush's strategic options. Faced with the growing resistance in Iraq, the United States did not appear likely to provoke war with Iran, that neighboring member of the Axis of Evil. It also seemed less likely that George W. Bush would attack Syria—though a crusade against Syria remained the sweet dream of the Perle faction within the neocon congregation.

The indirect lesson—whether anyone in the White House noticed it or not—is that it is often better for the world's only superpower to let others take the lead. The United Nations International Atomic Energy Agency was doing excellent work in Iran. China, instead of a rival, was turning out to be useful in dealings with North Korea. The broad strategic lesson of George W. Bush's rampant unilateralism, in contrast, is overwhelmingly negative. Not only was Iraq a fiasco but the interjection of US military power into regional conflicts is in and of itself destabilizing. This is most evident in Pakistan as Musharraf seemed to face an assassination attempt every time he went out for drive.

Everybody knows what the worst-case scenario in Pakistan would be and nobody knows how to prevent it, so all we can do is hope for the best. And if hoping for the best turns out not to be effective? A militantly Islamist Pakistan armed with nuclear weapons would be both the George W. Bush nightmare come true—and, to a certain extent, a self-fulfilling prophecy.

Even without a friendly rogue regime to give them nuclear or biological weapons, the new enemies George W. Bush has made for America could strike at any time because those new enemies are everywhere. As late as September 12, 2001, what people around the world wanted to be, more than anything else, was American. Now there are millions who believe the world would be better if America were destroyed.

Can we make some profiles of the kind of person who might

be trying to culture nerve gas or make a dirty bomb—a little like those pictures of crime suspects people put together on detective shows? That is impossible, because the people who do horrible things so frequently turn out to be so different from what we expect. We imagine Serb hit squads or bearded Islamic clerics on the loose. We wind up with Timothy McVeigh and nihilists who run up big charges on their credit cards before flying jets into the World Trade Center.

We can make some educated guesses, however, about the kind of person George W. Bush has turned against America all over the world. He is young. He hates injustice; he hates hypocrisy, and in the America he equates with George W. Bush, he sees sickening excesses of both. He hates those who kill people for no reason. The lies he hears emanating from America have disgusted him. So has the double standard. In this description of the George W. Bush–generated Enemy of America, it is proper to use the masculine pronoun because, at first, the great majority of such people are likely to be young males, though plenty of girls and women will join them.

This new enemy of America is intelligent and adept with technology. The same America he despises has placed in his hands—via the PC and the Internet—access to knowledge he can use to do America great harm. It's a case of US military spending inadvertently empowering the powerless. To protect the Internet against nuclear attack, the US Defense Department, which created the Internet toward the end of the Cold War, deliberately made it uncontrollable—and therefore not destroyable—by a single strike. Now that same Internet, by conferring on individual humans immense powers even nation-states did not have until recently, has for the first time made it possible for small groups, even individuals, to attack the United States.

Suppose we located some of these people and tried to reason with them. What could we tell them? We could tell them that America is full of good people, that America, in spite of its lapses, is a good country. We could say: Look at the crimes Americans have never committed the same ones committed by countries and governments you do not hate. Do not single us out just because America for the moment happens to the world's most powerful country. Others have done worse during their moment of hegemony.

Maybe some of these ardent young men would say: Yes, I will not hurt you Americans, after all. But how to answer the ones who say: You had your chance. You could have elected better leaders. You could have controlled how your money is spent. You could have had a foreign policy based on justice. You are a democracy, aren't you?

We could answer some of that. But what would be our counter-argument when this Enemy of America said: You at least could have patrolled your own borders, instead of going on the rampage 5,000 miles away. But you didn't, so we already have it—the weapon you fear most—inside America. It is in the hold of a ship pulling into New York or San Francisco or Boston harbor. It's fastening its seat belt at LAX and ORD and EWR. It's in an RV driving at this moment down, or up, Pennsylvania Avenue. What would you say when the earnest young terrorist in the seat next to you on the airplane, grabs you by the throat and shouts: If I cannot have justice, I will have vengeance. You will not listen, America, but as you now are going learn again, you can be hurt. You can feel pain.

Maybe then, at last, you'd have a persuasive argument—or at least a good exit line. Thinking of the speech from the White House that would follow this soon-to-erupt event, and how your death is about to help give George W. Bush a bump in the polls, you could lean over to your fellow passenger and say: OK, pal, if you're so determined to give George W. Bush another four years in the White House, be my guest.

The George W. Bush-centric universe is like Ptolemy's old pre-Copernican system. Cycles spin upon cycles, but the overarching cycle is the diversionary tactic which fails, creating the need for another turn of the wheel. The result is a perpetual motion machine in which each cycle begins with some startling event, such as a declaration of war on evil, and winds up with passing the buck. The result—whether the test is getting into Harvard Business School or getting past 9/11—is that it doesn't matter how George W. Bush scores. Guile is the main propellant, but good fortune—such as the capture of Saddam Hussein—also regularly intervenes to keep him going.

On September 11, 2001, for instance, the Al Qaeda terrorists killed thousands in America, but they saved George W. Bush's political career. Until then not only was George W. Bush an unelected president but it was widely assumed he would never be elected legitimately when he ran again. This, though few noticed it, seemed to fit him safely into an exceptional category of presidential aberration in which even violations of democracy in America wind up proving the democratic rule.

Leaving aside Rutherford B. Hayes and his stolen presidency, only three men have ever assumed the presidency after losing the popular vote. They are John Quincy Adams (1825–29), Benjamin Harrison (1885–89) and George W. Bush (2001–?). It provides an interesting perspective on the oligarchic tendency in American politics, and also the democratic resistance it faces, that these three unelected presidents were also the only presidents in US history to be the sons—or in Harrison's case, the grandson—of a previous president.

In all three cases, being born into a presidential family helped one of its sons get nominated for president. But it wasn't enough to actually get him elected, and having gotten into office under these curious family/Electoral College circumstances, it was not enough to keep them in office. Adams and Harrison were defeated in both the popular vote and in the Electoral College the second time around. The question America will answer in 2004 is whether George W. Bush repeats this pattern, or transcends it.

George W. Bush seemed safely on the road to electoral oblivion before 9/11. Objectively, the security lapses that day still provide the greatest grounds for his transformation an from accidental president into an ex-president. But subjectively? The upwelling of patriotism and love for America and its institutions, including the presidency, gave George W. Bush a second chance. He used it, at home, to fight the reforms that might make America less vulnerable to future attack, and to accelerate his program of expanding government for the benefit of the rich. As a result his popularity again eroded, but the Iraq invasion once again revived his fortunes. When the folly of that adventure started to become apparent, Saddam came to the rescue.

The timing of Saddam's capture was not ideal for George W. Bush. It would have been better for it to have come closer to the 2004 presidential election—though Osama bin Laden is still out there, and thus potentially of great utility. Capturing Saddam did not help the US pacification effort in Iraq, and as Americans continue to die there, Iraq more and more become like those military coffins that have to be kept out of George W. Bush's photo ops.

It was time to attach the name of George W. Bush to some

other new great crusade, but what? World hunger was growing, but so was American obesity. He'd already promised to eradicate AIDS in Africa. There was no need to promote energy sanity, even if he were willing to consider it. The hydrogen car he announced in the State of the Union address after the one on the axis of evil was going to make America energy independent, and save the ozone layer too. Something bigger than war, disease, and preserving the planet was needed this time.

Following Saddam's capture, George W. Bush announced that the United States was going to conquer the solar system. Not only would Americans return to the moon, they would fling themselves to Mars. His Mars proposal was to serious science exactly what his Iraq invasion scheme was to serious diplomacy—utter lunacy. One thing human beings had learned from forty years of the space race was that it was so much better to probe the universe with our intellect and our amazing scientific instruments. Our flesh, our blood, and our hearts are best left here on the fleshy Earth—and, as usual, wisdom was lost on George W. Bush. First step to Mars: Abandoning the superb Hubble telescope, one of America's true glories in space. As in Iraq earlier, rejecting knowledge was fundamental to George W. Bush's scheme of conquest.

Conquering Mars, if it ever happens, will be like conquering Iraq on an interplanetary scale—not only much harder and more costly than he pretended but equally pointless. But as George W. Bush put it in his Christmas interview: "So what difference does it make?" As old spins slowed, new ones were always there to be added. This presidential election year will be no exception.

Whatever the spin, the key to winning is going to be more and more money, stupendous amounts of money. Victory will also involve waving flags and creating division, but whatever it takes, this time he intends to win.

XVII

Systemic Dysfunction in America

CAN A POWERFUL NATION also be a good nation? Americans started pondering that difficult question long before the United States actually did become powerful. The question arose, in part, because it was so evident that the new Republic—"the new colossus" it sometimes was called—ultimately would dwarf the kingdoms and empires of the Old World. Even before US territory extended beyond the Mississippi River, Americans started to believe they were fated to be a great transcontinental nation. Jefferson's purchase of the immense Louisiana territory in 1803, followed by the Lewis and Clark expedition to the Pacific Northwest, turned belief into growing certainty.

North America, people very early on began to sense, would only be the beginning of America's "manifest destiny." As early as 1835, more than 110 years before the Cold War pitted the United States against the Soviet Union, Alexis de Tocqueville picked up on this dawning certainty of almost limitless US power when he predicted that the destiny of the whole world ultimately would be decided by two powerful continent-countries, Russia and America. "Their starting point is different, and their courses are not the same; yet each of them seems to be marked out by the will of Heaven to sway the destinies of half the globe," he wrote. What made America different from Russia and all other countries—in the eyes of Americans, if not others—was the belief that America would not just be powerful, but good. The felicitous consequences of this triumph of virtue which Americans believed their country embodied, Americans believed, would radiate far beyond the borders of the United States and change the whole world by inspiring other people to liberate themselves. That is why Thomas Jefferson and the other Founding Fathers proclaimed that "All men"—not just Americans—were "endowed by their Creator with certain unalienable rights." Their ambition was to devise a way to put universal principles of liberty into practice, but how to be equal to such a task?

Faced with their twin beliefs that America was destined to be good and that power was evil, the Founding Fathers did not pretend that Americans were somehow exempt from the temptations that corrupt people of other nationalities. To the contrary, they worked from the premise that Americans—including American presidents—are every bit as likely to abuse power as a Roman emperor or king of England. To contain that danger, they devised a system of government in which American good would be preserved by imprisoning evil—that is, power—inside a constitutional system rather in the way a genie is contained in his bottle. The way to prevent abuses of power at home, they believed, was to check power by balancing power. They designed a constitutional system that made sure—so long as it was respected—that no single politician, faction, or branch of government would ever get enough power to oppress the majority. But what about the use and abuse of American power outside of the United States?

President John Quincy Adams, at the time he was James Monroe's secretary of state, gave the practical arguments for not shedding American blood on foreign soil a moral—indeed an evangelical—underpinning. Once America started down the road to foreign military intervention, Adams prophesied, even if its overseas wars were fought for the best of motives—even if the purpose was to liberate others—America would find herself sinking into a moral, as well as a strategic, abyss. In part because her motives were so good, he warned, America "would involve herself beyond the power of extrication, in all the wars of interest and intrigue, of individual avarice, envy, and ambition which assume the colors and usurp the standard of freedom."

Addressing a great crowd in the new capital city of Washington on July 4, 1821, Adams warned that the more the United States used its growing power in the attempt to confer freedom on others, the more it was likely to corrupt its own spirit and compromise its own liberties. More than seventy years before the Statue of Liberty was built, Adams portrayed America as a beacon of democracy, radiating hope and liberty into a dark, oppressed world as it stood above and outside the fray. What if, instead, America tried to make the world free through force?

"The frontlet upon her brow," Adams declaimed, as though describing some grave moral tarnishing, "would no longer beam with the ineffable splendor of Freedom and Independence; but in its stead would soon be subsituted an Imperial Diadem, flashing with false and tarnished luster the murky radiance of dominion and power."

In Adams's analysis, the use of power was in and of itself corrupting. America's reliance on power, as he foresaw it, would make her forget her commitment to liberty. Having set out to liberate others America would find herself corrupted by her own reliance on force. "The fundamental maxims of her policy," he predicted, "would insensibly change from liberty to force." For the sake of America's own goodness, Adams urged, she must not go abroad "seeking monsters to destroy. She might become the dictatress of the world," he conceded, but "she would no longer be ruler of her own spirit."

Most Americans (including most American presidents) continued to believe right into the twentieth century that the best way to deal with that potential threat to American goodness was to heed Adams's warning, and steer clear of the corruptions and depravities that would inevitably flow from US involvement in overseas wars and foreign power struggles. The framers of the Constitution had also foreseen the danger of foreign wars. They deliberately made it impossible for the president to start a war on his own, by making it necessary for both houses of Congress, as well as the president, to approve any declaration of war. War, as the Founding Fathers of the American Republic saw it, and as they intended the war-making provision of the US Constitution to ensure for all time, was not to be an ordinary tool of statecraft—no mere "continuation of diplomacy by other means" as the Prussian military theorist Clausewitz argued. In their American Republic of goodness, war was to be a very last resort. No amount of constitutional tinkering, however, could change the reality that the United States, a nation founded on distrust of power, was destined to possess immense power whether it used it or not.

Until World War II, most Americans continued to agree with John Quincy Adams that it was best to remain in virtuous aloofness from foreign struggles. After all, the United States had not been founded in order to become another Rome or Britannia—to replace the jaunty republican cap of freedom with "an Imperial Diadem." Or was this America's destiny, after all? That question, that nagging doubt, has been running through American debates about foreign wars, and whether the United States should fight them, for 200 years.

Twice in American history the question of power and evil as it relates to US involvement in foreign wars has become paramount in the national debate; each time it has driven the country to the point of a national nervous breakdown. One of those times, as everyone knows, was the Vietnam war era. The other, nearly forgotten, occurred during a period even more fateful for the United States and its people. Upon taking office in 1845, President James Knox Polk decided American virtue was not producing the anticipated results fast enough. After nearly seventy years of independence, America's territory still did not extend to the Pacific Ocean, so Polk resolved to fulfill America's "manifest destiny" through use of force. To this self-appointed task Polk applied the stratagems of hypocrisy and deceit, abetted by the tactics of the coward and the bully.

Polk had what today we would call a hidden agenda for his presidency. He started to fulfill it upon taking office by betraying his campaign pledge to go to war with Great Britain if the British didn't accept US ownership of the whole of the Pacific Northwest. The disputed territory was called "Oregon," but this vast area included what today is the Canadian province of British Columbia, as well as the states of Oregon and Washington. It stretched from Nevada and California all the way up to Alaska and the Yukon.

A war with Britain for control of all of Oregon would have been popular—so popular, indeed, that if he hadn't promised the voters such a war Polk probably would have lost the election. But Polk was one of the most astute judges of power in American presidential history; once in office, he tailored his actions to fit the realities of power. Great Britain was a powerful country with the world's most powerful navy, so Polk cut a deal with the British. "Fifty-four-forty or fight!" had been the war cry that won him the presidency. But instead of getting Oregon up to fifty-four degrees and forty minutes of north latitude—the southern tip of Alaska today—Polk settled for the forty-ninth parallel, a line lying just north of Seattle. He gave up US claims on everything north of that line. This amounted to about half of the disputed territory. As a result, a vast part of North America remained under British colonial rule. What would have been an uninterrupted US Pacific coastline extending from the Columbia River all the way to the Bering Sea is today interrupted by Canada's Pacific coastline. The name of the lost territory—British Columbia—to this day rebukes the idea that the triumph of American republican virtue over those corrupt Old World empires was somehow inevitable, or ever complete, even in North America.

President Polk's pusillanimousness with the powerful British cost the United States half of Oregon. He made up for it by stealing half of Mexico. What historians call President Polk's "war intrigue" was a brilliant design, brilliantly executed. By first avoiding war with Britain, and accepting far less territory than he had been elected to get in the Northwest, and instead attacking America's weak southern neighbor, Mexico, and seizing the northern half of its territory, all the way from Texas to California, Polk increased the territory of the United States by more than one million square miles. He also cleft the American soul.

Then, as later, the moral outrage—the sense that an American president had betrayed America's values, indeed corrupted the meaning of America itself by tricking the nation into an unjust war—was especially strong on campus and, eventually, in Congress. "When a whole country is unjustly overrun and conquered by a foreign army," protested a Harvard student named Henry David Thoreau, "I think it is not too soon for honest men to rebel and revolutionize. What makes this duty the more urgent is the fact that the country so overrun is not our own, but ours is the invading army." This contrived presidential attack on Mexico, its congressional opponents soon realized, was also aggression against the US Constitution. "Allow the president to invade a neighboring nation whenever he deems it necessary," a junior Illinois congressman named Abraham Lincoln protested, "and you allow him to make war at pleasure. Study to see if you can fix any limit to his power."

The protesters protested, but the president got his war. The ruthless use of American power got him his conquests. Victory over Mexico was never in doubt, but Americans would have to live and die with the consequences of this change in maxims from liberty to force. It was the Mexican war's strongest supporters who eventually suffered the most. Polk's twin expansions of United States power—northwest into Oregon and southwest into Mexico—had been deliberately symmetrical, an attempt to balance sectional interests within the United States. In Polk's design, the North was meant to be assuaged by the peaceful acquisitions in the Northwest, the South gratified by his conquests in the Southwest—and the slave states of the South, at first, were delighted by Polk's attack on Mexico.

One reason Southerners supported war against Mexico so enthusiastically was that they believed seizing those vast stretches of foreign soil would lead to "an extension of the area of freedom"—by which they meant the freedom to practice slavery. In the territories seized from Mexico, they imagined, slavery would flourish and—thanks to the "three-fifths of a person" provision of the US Constitution rewarding slavery—the South's political fortunes would prosper too. More slave states, they believed, would mean more proslavery members of the House of Representatives and, every four years, more proslavery votes in the Electoral College too.

But Arizona and California, it turned out, were no more suited to the expansion westward of the slave economy than Oregon or Washington were. Polk's Western conquests had the opposite result of what the proslavery forces hoped. The creation of new states shifted the national balance of power permanently and massively against the South. Outnumbered and outvoted by the growing roster of new states opposed to slavery, the slave states, in their fear and frustration, increasingly turned toward secession. And when the South did attempt to leave the Union, there were plenty of seasoned American military men ready to fight on both sides in the Civil War. Grant, Lee, and most of the other famous generals, on both the Union and Confederate sides, had learned war while fighting in Mexico. Within thirteen years, the war to "extend the area of freedom" at Mexico's expense led to Americans killing each other by the hundreds of thousands, once again in the name of freedom.

Through war and peace, whoever was president, the growth of US power was inexorable. By the beginning of the twentieth century, the United States had surpassed Great Britain in economic output, to become the richest nation on earth. Following Teddy Roosevelt's seizure of Panama, and his and Woodrow Wilson's numerous military interventions in Latin America, the United States was a regional, indeed a hemispheric, power. Even before that, the US victory in the Spanish-American War had shown that the United States, whether Americans realized it or not, was a world power—or would be, if it chose to use its power on the world stage. Even so, the tradition that involvement in the struggles of the Old World would sully America's goodness, as well as be a waste of American money and lives, remained very deeply ingrained in national beliefs and politics. President Wilson had a hard time getting the United States into World War I. Had the Japanese not attacked Pearl Harbor in 1941, it is difficult to imagine how President Franklin Roosevelt would have gotten the United States into World War II.

The reverse is even more difficult to imagine. Trying to envision a twentieth century in which the United States did not become the decisive world power—in which Americans did not fight and defeat Germany and Japan in the struggle for control of Western Europe and the Pacific basin—is like trying to imagine a world without nuclear weapons. People can remember a time when they didn't exist, but it's impossible to imagine what the future—that is, the present—would have been without them.

Whatever the "might have beens," after World War II the United States finally, irrevocably, did abandon the idea that, except under the most exceptional circumstances, it must hold itself aloof from the outside world's rivalries and conflicts. Indeed, from then on there seemed hardly a confrontation or conflict—from Berlin to the Congo, and from Beirut to the Taiwan Straits—in which the United States did not immerse itself. Why did it do this? Historians and economists can provide many different varieties of explanations as to why the United States became the interventionist super power it is today. But at each crucial stage in the expansion of the global power of the United States, neither America's leaders nor the American people understood, explained, or justified their actions in terms of the reasons historians and economists use to explain why things happen.

Instead, at every step, the justification for this immense projection of US power across the globe was the necessity of fighting evil—an evil personified by evil men, an evil which Americans were morally entitled, indeed morally obligated, to resist. Evil—whether it took the form of Nazism or Communism, and whether Hitler, Stalin, Mao, or any of a host of minor villains was its current personification—provided the rationale for the United States becoming embroiled, as John Quincy Adams put it, "beyond the power of extrication" in foreign conflicts almost everywhere.

The widespread notion that the world outside America is evil had not changed. What had totally changed was America's belief in how it should comport itself in the face of that supposed evil. In 1821, John Quincy Adams had used a rhetorical device to make his point. America "well knows," he claimed, that she should not go abroad chasing monsters. By 1961, another Massachusetts and Harvard man, John F. Kennedy, was claiming that America knew something else—that Americans must, and willingly would, "pay any price, bear any burden, fight any foe, to defend the cause of freedom and ensure the success of liberty around the world." Kennedy's lock, stock, and barrel repudiation of the Founding Fathers' approach to foreign affairs thrilled a nation, and a generation that, within eight years, would be torn asunder by anti–Vietnam war protests.

In his farewell address delivered a few days before Kennedy's inaugural speech, the outgoing president, Gen. Dwight Eisenhower, delivered a different kind of message. He reflected upon how much and how fast the United States had changed. He talked to his countrymen about how that change had created a new kind of danger. "Until the latest of our world conflicts," Eisenhower recalled, referring to the American participation in World War II, "the United States had no armaments industry. American makers of plowshares could, with time and as required, make swords as well." But World War II, the Korean War, and especially the Cold War had changed that. The United States, Eisenhower went on to note, now had "a permanent armaments industry of vast proportions. Added to this, three and a half million men and women are directly engaged in the defense establishment. We annually spend on military security more than the net income of all United States corporations," the outgoing president reminded his countrymen.

As Eisenhower now emphasized, for the first time in its history the United States had an economy—and therefore a society and a politics—in which war, notably the development and production of increasingly sophisticated weapons of mass destruction—provided the livelihood for millions of people on a permanent basis. "This conjunction of an immense military establishment and a large arms industry is new in the American experience," he said. "The total influence—economic, political, even spiritual—is felt in every city, every state house, every office of the federal government."

Then Eisenhower sounded the warning that would give his 1961 farewell address, like Adams's July 4 speech in 1821, a permanent place in the American debate about the interrelationship of liberty and force. "In the councils of government," Eisenhower urged, "we must guard against the acquisition of unwarranted influence, whether sought or unsought, by the military-industrial complex." One hundred forty years after Adams issued his warning, Eisenhower perceived that, thanks to the creation of a permanent American war machine, the dangers Adams foresaw were becoming reality. His warning about this was quite explicit. "The potential for the disastrous rise of misplaced power exists and will persist. We must never let the weight of this combination endanger our liberties or democratic processes." Then Eisenhower, in his own fashion, reminded Americans that the price of liberty is eternal vigilance: "We should take nothing for granted. Only an alert and knowledgeable citizenry can compel the proper meshing of the huge industrial and military machinery of defense with our peaceful methods and goals, so that security and liberty may prosper together."

Eisenhower's comments indicated how extraordinarily America had changed even within the eight years of his own presidency. He had come into office in 1953, at the height of the McCarthy–Cold War anti-Communist hysteria—at a time when Americans believed the greatest threat to their liberties and their goodness came from the agents of a foreign evil. Now he was leaving at the dawn of the 1960s with a warning that Americans faced a new, very different kind of peril—from an "enemy within," though not the kind of enemy whose telephones J. Edgar Hoover was tapping. The danger to America, as Eisenhower described it, came from the kind of patriotic fellow Americans you might meet in "in every city, every state house, every office of the Federal government." It came from the city councilmen who give the local military subcontractor a tax break, from the alert congressman who agilely insures, each year at budget time, that his district gets a bigger piece of the military pie, and from that civic-minded crowd of good citizens who—every time their town or county or state is threatened by the closure of a military base—rally to make sure it doesn't happen. America's liberties, Eisenhower's farewell speech made clear, were now threatened by a whole political as well as economic class of Americans who had never seen war, never served in a war, but who now prospered by insuring that even in peacetime, the United States spent more and more on "defense" whoever was President—whether or not any external threat to the country existed. Eisenhower's warning attracted attention at the time, but nothing to compare with the rapture that Kennedy's promise to "fight any foe" aroused soon afterward.

Eisenhower's departure from power and Kennedy's arrival in power marked a watershed—though not the "the torch has been passed" moment that lives on in US mythology. With Kennedy as president, US war spending and war-making became entirely untethered from any actual threat to the United States, and from any actual ability to defend America as well. The untethering worked both ways. The Vietnam war would be a war fought for no reason having anything to do with the "defense" of the United States. But the groundwork would also be laid for 9/11 because what the United States spends on defense has so little to do with actually defending America, thanks to the "unwarranted influence" of the proponents of unaccountable military spending "in every city, every state house, every office of the federal government."

Adams and Eisenhower, it's important to note, did not fear war. They feared that what Eisenhower called "the acquisition of unwarranted influence, whether sought or unsought, by the military industrial complex" would, in Adams's words, deprive America of what no foreign enemy could take away from it: the "ineffable splendor of Freedom."

Even back in the 1820s, this perpetual talk, by Americans, about America incarnating liberty could be as mystifying, and irritating, to foreigners as it is today. It was the same back in John Quincy Adams' day, when it came to his effusions about the "ineffable splendor of Freedom." "What about your millions of African slaves?" the Russian ambassador to the United States exclaimed as he listened to John Quincy Adams orate on that same Fourth of July, 1821. Adams, having issued his warning against America fighting foreign wars for freedom, then went on to purport that the creation of the American Republic, unlike the establishment of the kingdoms and empires of Europe, had been a triumph of pure freedom "in which conquest and servitude had no part." This was too much for the Czar's representative in Washington. "How about your 2 million black slaves who cultivate a great expanse of your territory for your particular and exclusive advantage?" the Russian diplomat asked. "You forget the poor Indians whom you have not ceased to spoil," he chided Adams in the margins of his printed copy of the address.

Where most Americans perceive a triumph of liberty, others have always seen a much darker history beneath the endless rhetoric—a long, unfolding pageant of American usurpation in which the selfish use of power is robed in hypocrisy and outright lies. H.L. Mencken, for one, would have hissed John Quincy Adams and slapped the Russian ambassador on the back, had he been there to listen to Adams's speech. Writing a century later, Mencken pointed out that Americans had acquired their country by "butchering innocent savages and swindling them out of their land," then built it up by the sweat of kidnapped Africans and indentured laborers. Wars of conquest had completed "the extension of the area of freedom" which genocide and slavery had begun. "The Mexican and Spanish Wars I pass over as perhaps too obscenely ungallant to be discussed at all," he wrote. Mencken went on to quote President Ulysses S. Grant's comment on the Mexican

War: "It was the most unjust war ever waged by a stronger against a weaker nation."

As Lyndon Johnson's Vietnam war adviser, Walt Whitman Rostow would put it, in more temperate tones, there was "a double bar-sinister which cut across the fabric of American life"—the twin original sins of the "African slave trade" and the "decimation of the Indian." Throughout their history, Americans have preferred to ignore that history. Blinding themselves with the shining glory of their own supposed goodness has been one of the most effective ways of doing it.

Equating power with good, so long as it is American power, has had an additional benefit for Americans: Besides helping them to avoid any recognition of their own defects, it automatically makes those who resist us "evil." So just as by extending slavery Americans "extended the area of freedom," they also didn't kill Indians or steal land from Mexico. Instead, Americans conquered "the frontier." As for slavery, the nation did confront that dark circumstance straight on once. Before the Civil War was finished, more Americans had been killed than in any other war—more than in Vietnam, Korea, World War II, and World War I combined.

Americans not only believe in the perfectibility of the world, at times extended to include even such places as Iraq; they believe the past is perfectible too. That's one reason James Knox Polk has been almost entirely air-brushed out, although he was incontestably the most important US president between Jackson and Lincoln. Imagine an America without Hollywood, the Golden Gate and Las Vegas—as well as without *Dallas*, *Dynasty*, and the Grand Canyon. You are imagining what America would be, or rather not be, if Polk had not stolen northern Mexico. For one thing, Richard Nixon and Ronald

Reagan, along with Lyndon Johnson and the two Bushes, would have been ineligible to serve as president, due to their foreign residency.

James Knox Polk's ruthless use of American power not only changed power relationships within the United States, especially between the slave states and the rest of the Union, it also forever changed the nature of relations between the United States and the outside world, starting with its Latin American neighbors, who thenceforth were increasingly subject to US domination. America's role as a Pacific power (Pearl Harbor, Hiroshima, Vietnam) also became virtually inevitable as a result of his action.

Equally important, Polk pioneered the tricks of the trade of the imperial presidency. Long before George Bush claimed that Saddam Hussein had weapons of mass destruction in order to justify his invasion of Iraq, Polk created the paradigm for presidential war, including systematic deception of Congress and the public. Perhaps if Americans remembered Polk better, they would know themselves better. They certainly would have more insights into how others perceive them.

The American obliviousness when it comes to Polk—that is to say, to the role of power used unjustly in American history—amounts to a kind of historical "spin." Read some American history books, especially the books used to teach history in US schools, and you find they have been churned out by historical spin doctors. The result, inculcated into generation after generation of Americans, is an idea of America, and of how it came to be what it is, that is as fake as a Dick Cheney interview on PBS, as divorced from reality as a George W. Bush address to the United Nations.

This "brainwashing" about America's goodness and the

resultant evil of all whom we decide are "against us" is all the more effective because it is self-inflicted. A 2003 poll, for instance, shows that 69 percent of Americans believe Saddam Hussein "was personally involved in the September 11 terrorist attacks"—although not even George W. Bush has purported that. Even many Americans who oppose George W. Bush no doubt believe that the US invasion and occupation of Iraq has something to do with "freedom." These beliefs exist not only in defiance of reality, but independent of it.

A military historian would ignore all that. Looking back at what has happened since George W. Bush took office, he would explain events in terms of the global balance of power, or the lack of one. With the collapse of the Soviet Union, and the channeling of European and East Asian energies into nonmilitary pursuits, he would point out, no external counterweight to the exercise of US power remained. From this perspective, Bush, Cheney, and Rumsfeld have been able to act as they do because there is no one to stop them. Power, like all forms of energy, tends to extend itself until it either meets resistance or is exhausted. Thus George W. Bush was able to invade Iraq in 2003 and get away with it for the same reason James Knox Polk was able to attack Mexico in 1848 and get away with it. By 1848, the United States was already "the world's only superpower" so far as its southern neighbor was concerned. Mexico couldn't defend its vast, thinly populated territories—and as much as they fretted and disapproved, the Europeans weren't about to come to Mexico's assistance. It was also a help that back then, Mexico, like Iraq 155 years later, was ruled by an unpopular dictator and involved in a longstanding dispute with the United States.

There are regional as well as global imbalances of power. History, including recent history, shows us that when such an imbalance becomes a chronic condition, the strong abuse the weak. This was the case when it came to relations between the Soviet Union and the countries of Eastern Europe following World War II. In the Western Hemisphere, the United States has been by far the greatest military power for more than 150 years; the history of Latin America reflects that chronic imbalance. Most Americans are vaguely aware of how Teddy Roosevelt "took" Panama; they are almost completely unaware that the history of military aggression by the United States in Latin America continues in our day. In recent decades alone, the United States has intervened—clandestinely or openly—in Guatemala, El Salvador, Honduras, Nicaragua, Panama, Cuba, Haiti, the Dominican Republic, Grenada, and Chile. It has done this in order "stop Communism" or to "build democracy"—but whether the president is a human rights advocate like Bill Clinton (Haiti) or a national security hard-liner like Nixon (Chile), US intervention has been unceasing.

Since World War II, the United States has extended its Latin American model of behavior to much of the rest of the world, especially the Third World. Within the United States, among Americans, the debate about such interventions is always a debate about right and wrong. Rightly or wrongly American power goes on filling power vacuums, whatever the moral circumstances—even when the Communist "threat" used to justify such intrusions disappears, and cartoon-character menaces like the "axis of evil" have to be created because real Hitlers aren't around anymore. America's approach to the world is perpetually skewed in a military direction because the United States spends twice as much per person on war as any other industrialized nation. As it struts the world stage, the US colossus, militarily speaking, is on steroids.

"We are at last beginning to understand the significance of the stockpiles," Senator J. William Fulbright remarked nearly forty years ago, during congressional hearings into the causes of the Vietnam war. He was referring to how the Cold War arms buildup, meant to deter a Soviet attack on Western Europe, helped propel the United States into fighting a war 10,000 miles away in Southeast Asia. The paradigm of this unintended causality was the B-52 bomber. A warplane designed to drop nuclear weapons on Soviet missile sites wound up raining conventional explosives down on thatched-hut villages in Laos. To the weapons, over the decades, has been added a stockpile of "defense intellectuals." Think of Cheney as a dirty bomb. Think of Wolfowitz as anthrax. Think of Rumsfeld, Perle, and the others as nasty little vials of smallpox. These weapons of mass destruction are never eliminated; they are just stored in their think tanks, consulting firms, and academic sinecures. Then someone like George W. Bush comes along, and throws the warehouse open.

What is the consequence of all this? Objectively speaking, the United States is the greatest threat to world peace, and has been for a long time, and not merely because it is the world's only superpower. Equally important, the United States is also far more disposed to use its power than any other powerful nation currently is. Though Americans are culturally and emotionally blind to the fact, the mere intrusion of US power is, in and of itself, destabilizing. Furthermore, there is no immediate likelihood of the worldwide imbalance of power being rectified any time soon.

A classical historian would perceive a different but not entirely unrelated theme in what has unfolded in Washington, at the United Nations, and in Iraq since George W. Bush took office: a cautionary tale Gibbon might have told of Rome. When a republic's most venerable institutions no longer operate as they were intended, it becomes possible for small cabals to usurp power, and, while keeping the forms, corrupt the function of those institutions for their own ends. Looking at things that way, the George W. Bush presidency has been both result and symptom of the decadence of America's constitutional mechanisms. The unremedied defects of the Electoral College, combined with the suborning of the Supreme Court by a partisan clique, allowed a Commander in Chief the American people had not chosen to be installed in the White House. By this light, the story of the George W. Bush presidency is the retelling of a tale well-known to Plutarch. We cannot know what catastrophes might have been averted had the Romans been more zealous in preserving the essence, and not just the appearances, of their republican institutions. We do know that in America—as in Rome in its decadence—once a group of quirky, adventurous extremists got their hands on the control levers of the world's greatest military power, bizarre things started to happen.

The Roman Senate endured in form long after its functions and powers had been usurped by the Caesars, a title which at the time was much closer in meaning to our own "Commander in Chief" than to "emperor." It is now unfortunately clear that in less than ten years, the United States has seen a kind of depravity creep into its own institutions. The impeachment power of the US Constitution was never intended to be used as tool of political warfare—as a device for defeating a president who could not be defeated at the polls. That, however, was what happened in 1998, when Bill Clinton was impeached.

The installation of George W. Bush was followed in Texas by

an effort, undertaken at the behest of Republican leaders in the US Congress, to redistrict out of office members of Congress who could not be defeated at the polls. That was followed, in California, by the removal from office of a governor who had won election less than one year earlier, and his replacement, through plebiscite, by an amiable movie star. The debates in the US Senate prior to the Iraq invasion were particularly revealing of a growing systemic dysfunction in America. The oratorical prerogative of every senator was scrupulously respected. Many beautiful speeches were given, some of them with philosophical as well as literary merit. This formality having been observed, the Commander in Chief launched his invasion.

What do these events demonstrate besides the fact that control of the Republican Party has fallen into the hands of unscrupulous radicals with no respect for the principles of democracy? They demonstrate what Lord Acton observed more than a generation after John Quincy Adams, in his own way, had made the same point: "Power corrupts, and absolute power tends to corrupt absolutely." There is nothing surprising about this. At least there is nothing surprising about it unless you happen to believe, as the majority of Americans do, that they and their country are exempt from the corrosive forces of history. From the viewpoint of a classical historian, it would be odd if America's stupendous worldwide power had not led to a corruption of its own internal political institutions—especially in an age when it is so easy to use nonconstitutional mechanisms (notably the manipulation of video images and the distribution of tax breaks, the current equivalent of circuses and bread) to manipulate opinion and generate money for political spending.

There is, of course, the technological explanation for why the

United States has such enormous unchecked power. Modern military technology means that if a US Commander in Chief gives the order, America can do in a matter of weeks or months what would have taken the Romans, the Persians, and even the great armies of World War II, years or even decades to do.

Technologically George W. Bush and Osama bin Laden are funhouse mirrors of each other. George W. Bush invaded Iraq because he could. That is to say—and here technology brings the moral inquest full circle—he invaded Iraq for the same reason Osama bin Laden destroyed the World Trade Center. Technology made it possible, so he did it.

Today small groups of individuals can unleash destructive powers nation-states did not have sixty years ago. This has served not so much to defeat US power as to make it irrelevant. George W. Bush has the power to conquer Iraq and Afghanistan. If he wanted, he could march US Marines down the Champs-Elysée and, in reprisal for his impertinence, take President Jacques Chirac prisoner and exhibit him in a cage on the Mall in Washington, D.C. But he cannot stop some Islamic fanatic—or just some homegrown anthrax loony—from exploding a nuclear bomb in New York harbor, or diffusing nerve gas through the White House air-conditioning ducts. One way of interpreting recent events is to view them as the desperate effort of the Bush Administration to convince themselves, if not the world, that smiting evildoers like Saddam Hussein still has some relevance to protecting American lives and property. The technological reality, however, is that the destructive powers these American war planners have spent their lives building up and angling to use are simply irrelevant in an age dominated, for both good and evil, by those two most American inventions: personal freedom and mass technology.

As the Iraq war and its aftermath have demonstrated, there is a worldwide imbalance of power. America's civil institutions are insufficient to check, or even balance, the power of an unelected president—and George Bush has proved himself to be unusually defective in moral as well as strategic vision. All of which proves that sometimes our own prophets are with honor.

Maybe what George W. Bush has proved, most of all, is that John Quincy Adams and Dwight David Eisenhower were right. Next time you have the chance, watch George W. Bush alight from Air Force One surrounded by his "security" men. Isn't what he emanates a "false and tarnished luster"? Certainly that is what people all over the rest of the world see in him. "Murky radiance of dominion and power" might as well be his middle name.

Is there anyone else who better personifies "the acquisition of unwarranted influence" than Dick Cheney? Combine the "tarnished luster" that George W. Bush epitomizes and the "unwarranted influence" of which Cheney is the paradigm with the American public's failure to heed Eisenhower's 1961 warnings, and you have almost a step-by-step description of what, forty years later, has happened to America and its government. What if we let the Dick Cheneys "in every city, every state house, every office of the federal government" usurp the decision processes of our democracy? What if we then let them install someone like George W. Bush in office? "The potential for the disastrous rise of misplaced power exists and will persist," Eisenhower warned.

"We must never let the weight of this combination endanger our liberties or democratic processes," he added. But what if such a combination did endanger our democratic processes, and the

American people still did nothing—not even when the democratic process in question was the choice of president of the United States? "Only an alert and knowledgeable citizenry can compel the proper meshing of the huge industrial and military machinery of defense with our peaceful methods and goals, so that security and liberty may prosper together," Eisenhower declared. What if, instead of heeding this warning, Americans took everything for granted? What if they weren't "alert and knowledgeable"? What if the American citizenry didn't do a damn thing as "the huge industrial and military machinery" usurped "our peaceful methods and goals"? Neither security nor liberty could prosper—and, under George W. Bush, neither has.

Conclusion
Unnecessary Evil

For Americans evil is a foreign menace, emanating from exotic locales. Its embodiments typically have mustaches and strut around in uniforms (Hitler, Saddam Hussein), though sometimes they are clean-shaven (Noriega, Qaddafi). You don't always have to be a military dictator, however. Democratically elected civilian leaders (Arbenz in Guatemala, Allende in Chile, Mossadeq in Iran) have at times also constituted evil so far as the United States is concerned. Then there are the villains who cannot be so easily labeled. Ho Chi Minh, Mao, even Stalin, all were too complicated, personally or historically, and too useful to the United States at various times, not to be embraced as friends of freedom, at least for a while. This did not keep them from being demonized when American attitudes toward them changed.

Mao Zedong, for example, started out (in American eyes) as an idealist fighting for agrarian reform and against corruption. During his guerrilla days, the Chinese leader very favorably impressed the American intelligence officers who got to know him. Mao also ended up much admired both by campus radicals and amoralists like Henry Kissinger, though for different reasons. President Richard Nixon especially revered Mao for his supposed grasp of realpolitik (though, by the end of his life, Mao's ideological blunders had turned China, strategically and economically, into a paper tiger). In the interval from 1950 to 1970, however, Mao, according to the official demonology of the United States was the most dangerous man on earth—a post previously occupied by Hitler and Stalin.

For twenty crucial years during the Cold War, this idea that the United States was engaged in a worldwide war with evil shaped everything America did. The war in Vietnam, remember, was started not just to "save" South Vietnam. It was fought, our leaders told us, in order to stop "the Sino-Soviet bloc" (itself an illusory entity) from overrunning Asia and "turning the vast Pacific Ocean into a red sea." This tsunami of evil was imagined to be so unstoppable that if South Vietnam were ever actually lost, even the state of Hawaii would topple. "We would be forced to pull our defenses back to California," Lyndon Johnson told John F. Kennedy, who himself averred that "behind the guerrillas subverting the brave people of South Vietnam are the evil rulers of Red China." Earlier, under Truman and Eisenhower, tens of thousands of Americans had been killed in Korea after Mao's decision to send Chinese troops there to fight US forces. Four American presidents and their advisers acted on the assumption that Communist China and its leader were not just rivals or adversaries, but implacable evildoers. Before that notion was abandoned—by Nixon, who had gotten his start in the anti-Communist witch hunts of the 1950s—more than 100,000 Americans had been killed in land wars in Asia.

We now see the Indochina war as strategic folly, but it is important to remember that Kennedy and Johnson sincerely believed in the domino theory. Why else would Kennedy have sent more than 10,000 US "advisers" to South Vietnam, or Johnson in his turn escalate the Vietnam conflict into a major war? The great revelation of the "Pentagon Papers"—the Defense Department's documentary history of the US buildup in Vietnam, which Nixon tried to keep secret—is that President Johnson and his advisers actually believed what they told the American public. What about George W. Bush? Is he, like Tony Blair, one of those politicians with a capacity to sincerely believe in whatever it takes to justify his predetermined course of action? Or has his war policy been propelled entirely by opportunism? We may never know. One of George W. Bush's first acts, upon entering the White House, was to make it even more difficult for future historians and the American public to gain access to papers documenting his decisions, even decades after leaving office. He will leave no tapes behind for analysis.

Along with Hitler and Stalin, Mao constituted a trinity of evil that from 1940 to 1970, justified and facilitated US involvement in three major wars (World War II, Korea, and Vietnam), as well as many smaller ones. Just like George W. Bush's wars today, these wars were justified not merely as defenses of America against evil. Each American war, in Franklin Roosevelt's words, was "a crusade for freedom." Abraham Lincoln once remarked that Americans were in sore need of a definition of freedom. The same is true of evil, all the more so when it becomes a key factor in deciding, or at least justifying, who the United States will go out into the world to kill. Evil, having been used for 150 years as the great justification for the United States standing aloof from foreign conflicts, suddenly became, starting fifty years ago, the great justification for the United States involving itself in foreign conflicts. But what is evil?

People will always argue about the nature of evil, but on two occasions in recent modern history, the world—including America—truly did confront it, first in the form of Hitler's Nazi Germany and then in Pol Pot's Cambodia. Hitler's "final solution" and Pol Pot's killing fields had something in common besides their horror. Even after the nature and the magnitude of the evil became known, the United States refused to help stop the killing. President Franklin D. Roosevelt, the "liberal" Democrat, refused to authorize air strikes to destroy Hitler's extermination camps. President Ronald Reagan, the "conservative" Republican, did FDR one better. He authorized clandestine support for Pol Pot and the Khmer Rouge—the better to fight the Soviet Union's "Evil Empire."

Looking at US actions over the past fifty years, it's impossible to discern any consistent definition of evil. It is much easier to correlate the imputation of "evil" with shifts in US foreign policy. Mao was "good" when what he was doing was perceived to be in keeping with American strategic or ideological objectives, such as reviving China and defeating the Japanese. Mao became "evil" when he had the audacity to claim—incorrectly as it turned out—that his ideology, not ours, was the wave of the future. Virtue was restored to Mao many decades later when Nixon decided that normalizing relations with China could help him both outflank the Soviet Union (which was true) and win the war in Vietnam (which was false).

Vacillations in the emotions and behavior of US officials do not reveal Mao's moral essence. They do hint at the realpolitik determinants of American political moralism. In fact, the most telling American responses have often been to foreign leaders who actually do try to conduct international affairs according to moral (or at least ethical) standards.

Mahatma Gandhi had no influence on the US approach to Asia in his time, just as Nelson Mandela has had no effect on George W. Bush's Africa policy. Instead, America has shown a consistent affinity for "strongmen"—the Shah, Ayub Khan of Pakistan, Chiang Kai-shek of Taiwan—who turn out to have feet of clay. At the height of the Cold War, Americans liked Kruschev; they were fascinated by Castro and Ho Chi Minh. Meanwhile Nehru, Nasser, and Sukarno all incurred the same hostility that in the run up to his Iraq war, George W. Bush directed toward Jacques Chirac of France and Gerhard Schröeder of Germany. George W. Bush's reaction escalated into one of grievous moral indignation when the United Nations and its various organs—including the Security Council and the International Atomic Energy Agency—failed either to support the war he wanted or to provide material justification for it. He then started to treat international peacekeeping organizations as though they were "evil" too. Steadily, his contempt for the supposed moral inadequacies of others extended to a widening circle of institutions, including NATO. It is as if the community of nations, not Saddam Hussein, has become George W. Bush's enemy. This isn't as paradoxical as it may seem. Saddam Hussein and Osama bin Laden bolstered George W. Bush's sense of political self-worth by making his "for us or against us" approach seem plausible. Chirac and Schroeder called into question his very legitimacy as a leader by arguing that it was his compulsive need to start a Middle East war—not the UN—that was bound to fail the test of relevance.

The leaders of France, Germany, and many other nations were only expressing the legitimate doubts about what George W. Bush wanted to do—doubts shared by the great majority of the people of the world. These ranged from close neighbors like

Canada and Mexico to vital allies in the real-world war against terrorism like Pakistan, Egypt, and Russia. It was easier, however, to deal with opposition to US policy by attacking the personal worth of the leaders who disagreed with the administration, and by belittling the institutions in which the criticism was expressed, than for George W. Bush actually to stop and consider whether such criticisms might possibly have merit.

It was time to fight evil, and the battle for hearts and minds was not just joined on the battlefield. FRENCH CHARGE DISINFORMATION CONSPIRACY, the *Washington Post* announced in May 2003. Asked if the United States really was mounting a psy-ops war against the French designed to make their failure to support the Bush war plans seem venal, Secretary of Defense Donald Rumsfeld, never one to keep cats in bags, responded as follows: "Certainly, there's no such campaign out of this building. I can't speak for the rest of government," he continued, "but I have heard of nothing like that."

By the time the bombs starting falling on Baghdad, Bush's original "axis of evil" had been expanded to comprise a much broader axis of annoyance. US citizens as well as allies were included. When one of America's own Africa experts, Ambassador Joe Wilson, pointed out that Tony Blair–generated tales of Saddam shopping for fissionable uranium in the Republic of Niger were nonsense, the administration's disinfo folks retaliated by blowing his wife's cover at the CIA, where she worked as an analyst. Had this been done by a non–George W. Bush administration, it would have constituted a violation of federal law.

The vilification campaign worked. Before you knew it, patriotic Americans were boycotting French wine and cheese. What H.L. Mencken called "the freedom blabber" filled the air to the extent it only does when US foreign policy gets really nutty.

French fries, for instance, were rechristened "freedom fries." That showed those Frenchies, but what about dealings with the monster of evil himself?

Thanks to the Bush-Cheney administration's utter mastery of spin, few Americans noticed it, but Saddam Hussein's own transformation into evil was quite a recent event so far as some of the capos of the administration were concerned—most notably Dick Cheney himself. His Halliburton Corporation continued profiting from business deals with Saddam Hussein right up to the moment he was picked to be the Republicans' vice presidential candidate in the summer of 2000, ten years after Saddam Hussein originally invaded Kuwait. Even after Americans had fought a war against him, and Saddam Hussein had become a legal as well as a moral pariah, Dick Cheney continued to do business indirectly with "evil." Cheney would have become even cozier with Saddam, if given the opportunity.

When it comes to assessing Cheney's actual as opposed to rhetorical response to evil—that is, to the question of how to deal with Saddam Hussein, two figures are relevant. One is $34 million; the other is $132 million. In summer 2000, when Cheney left Halliburton to become an "inhabitant" of Wyoming and George W. Bush's candidate for vice president, he walked away from Halliburton with a 34 million dollar gratuity. More than three years later, after the Bush-Cheney administration had awarded Halliburton billions in contracts for US-occupied Iraq, including more than 1 billion dollars on a noncompetitive basis, ABC news quoted American officials in Baghdad as saying the following: "Some $132 million of money that Saddam Hussein withdrew from the Iraqi Central Bank is believed to be funding the Iraqi insurgency against US troops."

The connection between the two figures is that part of

Cheney's $34 million, as well as part of the $132 million being used to kill Americans in Iraq, quite possibly derived from the same source: profitable deals Halliburton-owned companies made with Saddam Hussein while Cheney was CEO.

As Cheney himself constantly points out, Saddam Hussein was doing evil a long time before the United States invaded Iraq in March 2003. Saddam attacked Iran in 1979. He used poison gas against Iran in 1984, and then against his own people in 1988. He invaded Kuwait in 1990. Between 1991 and 2003, Bush, Cheney, and Rumsfeld apparently convinced themselves, Saddam Hussein compounded the evil he had earlier done by acquiring or trying to acquire a wide range of weapons of mass destruction, including chemical, biological, and nuclear weapons. He without doubt committed many other despicable acts, including attempting to have George W. Bush's father assassinated, after his defeat in Kuwait. None of this well-known nastiness, however, made Saddam Hussein evil enough for Dick Cheney not to want to do business with him.

The key strategic US objective in Iraq, once Saddam had been militarily contained after his expulsion from Kuwait, was to prevent him from becoming a danger again by getting hold of weapons of mass destruction. The keystone in the US effort to contain Saddam was the United Nations-authorized trade embargo.

The great allegation Bush and Cheney used to justify their Iraq invasion was that the sanctions had failed. Saddam already had weapons of mass destruction, they argued, waving Tony Blair's "dodgy dossiers" in the air to prove it. But the great revelation of their invasion—which so long Bush and Cheney refused to accept—is that the sanctions were a great success. This became evident as soon as the US invasion began. No

American troops were killed by poison gas. No missiles hurtled from Iraq to targets in Israel and Saudi Arabia, as they had during the first war against Saddam. Greatest blessing of all: No Saddam-crafted dirty nuclear bombs were set off. Had the Bush-Cheney-Rumsfeld allegations about Saddam and his WMDs been accurate, their invasion of Iraq might have led to millions of deaths in many countries. Fortunately, their fabricated "evidence" was wrong, and though they still deny it, their own actions proved it.

The trade sanctions against Saddam Hussein's Iraq saved countless lives. They also meant that so long as the sanctions remained in force, Cheney's Halliburton Corporation could make no profits in Iraq—not without violating US law, including the Trading With the Enemy Act. This interference with free trade did not sit well with the future vice president.

"We seem to be sanction-happy as a government," Cheney complained in 1996, referring to the Clinton administration's continuation of the strict US embargo that the first President Bush had imposed. This put the "conservative" Cheney in the same camp as loony lefties like former US Attorney General Ramsey Clark, whose opposition to the Iraq sanctions derived from their own peculiar "good versus evil" take on US-Iraq relations. Since US policy was bad, as they saw it, Saddam was good. Cheney's distaste for the sanctions was by contrast, motivated by love of money.

The United Nations sanctions permitted some trade with Iraq for nonmilitary purposes, but US sanctions, far tougher than the UN sanctions, barred American corporations like Halliburton from doing deals of any kind with Saddam. That didn't stop Cheney. "In 1998," according to the investigative reporter Jason Leopold, "Cheney oversaw Halliburton's acquisition of

Dresser Industries Inc., the unit that sold oil equipment to Iraq through two subsidiaries of a joint venture with another large US equipment maker, Ingersoll-Rand." According to UN statistics, Halliburton's European subsidiaries were selling spare parts to Saddam's government-owned oil monopoly as late as summer 2000, when Cheney was nominated for vice president of the United States. The Halliburton subsidiaries wanted to do even more business with Saddam, but those deals—for the kind of firefighting equipment and pipeline-repair materials that clearly had a potentially military impact—were blocked by the US government.

Somehow this information about Cheney's indirect business dealings with Saddam Hussein got even less attention, during the 2000 vice presidential campaign, than his military record did. However, seven months after the election, in June 2001, the *Washington Post* reported that while Cheney was at the helm at Halliburton, its subsidiaries had helped Saddam increase his petroleum exports from $4 billion in 1997 to $18 billion in 2000. Saddam's income from such deals had totaled $40 billion in all by the time the United States invaded Iraq. The $40 billion from the oil exports that the Halliburton subsidiaries had helped make possible was supposed to pay for food and medicine for the Iraqi people. US critics—notably neoconservative Republicans—accused the Clinton administration of using a humanitarian pretext to go soft on Saddam.

No doubt some of the money was skimmed. No doubt the best part of it went to Saddam, his clan, and the Republican Guards, including the marauders in brand-new imported pickup trucks who, starting in March 2003, first helped slow the US advance toward Baghdad, and since then have been zooming around Iraq killing hundreds of Americans. There's not much doubt, either, that at least part of the money used to kill Americans in Iraq got there thanks to Halliburton's involvement in trade with Saddam: It was precisely in order to stop something like that happening that the US sanctions had been made so tough. As for the relationship between Cheney's $34 million golden handshake and Saddam's $132 million warchest, Cheney's acquisition of Dresser Industries Inc., the company that sold oil equipment to Iraq, was a key part of his attempts to increase Halliburton's profits and, with them, his own "compensation."

If Saddam truly is evil—and if he doesn't meet the standard, who does?—then consorting with evil is a Republican tradition. A number of neocon think-tank strategists, including some active in the George W. Bush administration, welcomed Saddam Hussein's 1979 attack on Iran, even though, just like his attack on Kuwait later, it was a clear-cut act of military aggression. Their strategic analysis—off-base as usual—was that Saddam's dictatorship could provide a "secular" check on the power of Iran and fundamentalist Islam.

As usual, Saddam got it wrong too. First the Iranians repulsed his attack. Then, when the Iranians seemed on the verge of smiting Saddam Hussein himself, the Reagan administration rushed to his rescue. Saddam, as in Kuwait later, had lost his gamble that aggression would pay. His fallback strategy with Iran, as in Kuwait later, was to cling to power even in defeat, no matter how many Iraqis died. Feelers went out: Saddam was willing to do almost anything to stop the war, except inconvenience himself in any way.

In response, Ayatollah Khomeini of Iran expressed his willingness to end the war. All he demanded, in return for peace, was exactly the same thing that George W. Bush demanded, twenty years later, in return for calling off his own invasion of Iraq: regime change in Baghdad.

The Reagan administration was shocked at this grievous ethical lapse on the part of the ayatollah. "The United States finds the present Iranian regime's intransigent refusal to deviate from its avowed objective of eliminating the legitimate government of neighboring Iraq to be inconsistent with the accepted norms of behavior among nations and the moral and religious basis which it claims," the Reagan administration huffed. Exactly the same thing could have been said later about George W. Bush's own "intransigent refusal to deviate" from his "avowed objective of eliminating" Saddam Hussein. The crack about "moral and religious" pharisaism would have been especially appropriate in his case. However, as usual, the fact that George W. Bush did something transformed its moral significance. When he actually went ahead and did what the United States had condemned the Ayatollah Khomeini for wanting to do, it was transmuted into a triumph of good over evil.

According to a study by the National Security Archive at George Washington University, declassified US official documents show that the Reagan administration came to Saddam Hussein's rescue even though US intelligence had warned that Saddam "had long-range nuclear aspirations that would 'probably' include 'an eventual nuclear weapon capability.'" High officials in the Reagan administration also were aware that Saddam had "harbored known terrorists in Baghdad, abused the human rights of his citizens, and possessed and used chemical weapons on Iranians and his own people." None of this deterred Ronald Reagan from being Saddam's friend.

The National Security Archive report continues: "The US

response was to renew ties, to provide intelligence and aid to ensure Iraq would not be defeated by Iran." US support for Saddam also included the mother of all photo-ops: President Reagan sent "a high-level presidential envoy named Donald Rumsfeld to shake hands with Saddam (20 December 1983)." Photographs of the memorable occasion show Rumsfeld—dapper, ageless, and also as idiosyncratically askew as ever—grasping the hand of evil incarnate while smiling and making small talk. And it was small talk.

RUMSFELD DID NOT MENTION CHEMICAL WEAPONS, a later headline noted. This was partly because Rumsfeld hoped to jolly Saddam into letting the United States build a pipeline across Iraq. Seeing no evil, hearing no evil, and saying no evil, the same documents show, was also in keeping with "directives signed by President Reagan that reveal the specific US priorities for the region: preserving access to oil, expanding US ability to project military power in the region, and protecting local allies from internal and external threats."

Right-wing Republican zeal for defending Saddam's "legitimate government" continued after Reagan passed the torch to the elder President Bush. The United States refused to join the United Nations in protesting Saddam's forced relocation of about half a million people in northern Iraq. It refused to take any action against Saddam after he used poison gas. To the contrary, the United States sold Saddam nearly fifty helicopters, which the Iraqi military used both to continue the Iran war and crush internal resistance.

In spite of Saddam's well-known support of terrorism, Iraq also was removed from the State Department's list of terrorist nations. Saddam Hussein also got US government subsidies and loans as part of the Republican rescue mission. Saddam had "made it clear that Iraq was not interested in making mischief in the world," Rumsfeld later declared.

This support for Saddam had nothing to do with fighting "evil." Clearly, it did have a great deal to do with balance-of-power politics in the Middle East and, as always, domestic politics in the United States. The Iranians who were the victims of Saddam Hussein's aggression were the very same Iranians who earlier had taken the staff of the US embassy hostage—and in the process destroyed the Carter presidency. The ensuing "tilt" toward Saddam Hussein, under two Republican presidents, became more like an avalanche, as US supplies and arms cascaded into Iraq. The saddest thing about this depraved policy, which continued in force right up to the day Saddam Hussein invaded Kuwait, is that if the United States had truly used good and evil as a moral compass when it came to dealing with Saddam, two wars might have been averted.

There is a difference between doing harm and doing evil. Since becoming the world's greatest power, the United States has indisputably found itself face to face three times with true evil as almost all Americans understand it, whatever their politics or ideology. We have seen what happened in the case of Hitler and Pol Pot. In the case of Saddam Hussein, the United States became the actual accomplice of evil—until evil, in the form of Saddam's 1990 Kuwait invasion, bit the American hand that had fed it, petted it, and gave it the entirely justifiable impression that no act, however reprehensible, would ever incur so much as an American reprimand. (Even international condemnations of Saddam's use of poison gas had been toned down at US insistence.)

When Saddam Hussein truly was the Middle East's and perhaps the world's greatest threat to peace, the United States did nothing to stop him and much to encourage him. Only after Saddam was no longer a threat—after he had been as successfully contained as a genie in a bottle—did George W. Bush smash the vial, spilling poison all over the Middle East, proclaiming it a triumph of American good over evil. If there is a lesson to be learned here, about how the existence of good and evil affects the use of US power, it's certainly a bizarre one: Do such evil as you wish, but don't rule out the possibility that much later the same officials, or the children of the same American officials who once coddled you, will come back and smite you when you no longer pose a threat.

Contrasting what the United States has actually done about evil with what it purports to have done in the name of freedom, it's impossible not to agree with what Walt Whitman said back in the nineteenth century: "Such a thing means enough to make you laugh or cry. What a lot of nonsense has got current in the world with that word. It's been made to stand for the most devilish and most divine of human instincts." These endless American claims that everything Americans happen to do amounts to a triumph of freedom, or its defense, or its extension have always coexisted with an antipathy to introspection that George W. Bush epitomizes as well as any politician in US history. Since entering the White House, George W. Bush has found the time to stampede Congress into war, to antagonize the UN, to invade two Asian countries, and to raise nearly $250 million for the 2004 election campaign. But there never seems enough time for this unelected president to stop and sincerely consider the questions that mean the most to Americans, and to the efforts to protect them: How did I get the United States into its current strange situation? Could I have done my job better? To what extent am I responsible for the fact that on my watch a number of horrible things have happened? Instead George W. Bush goes on passing the buck for his screw-ups. New evildoers will emerge when and as the expediencies of the 2004 political campaign require.

We know what to think of Osama bin Laden, Saddam Hussein, and Kim Jong Il, but what are we to make of George W. Bush? Circle around recent events in America as many times as you wish. Approach the problem George W. Bush poses to any attempt to understand the present actions of the United States in the world from any direction. You will find yourself returning to the reality that with George W. Bush in power, the behavior of the United States has been increasingly aberrant. The easiest way to appreciate this aberrant quality is simply to ask ourselves how we would react if another leader of another country had acted as he has. Suppose President Putin of Russia had renounced the ABM treaty and invaded Iraq? Suppose, even worse, the Chinese had done all the things George W. Bush has done—including launching their own version of "Star Wars"?

More than most Americans—more than even most American presidents—George W. Bush purports to be doing God's work. Yet his main achievement has been to divide the world unnecessarily at a time when he—and we—had plenty positive to do in the world and needed more than ever to try to overcome—and if we could not overcome them, tolerate—the world's divisions and our own. Instead, George W. Bush has issued the world a kind of permanent ultimatum. He has demanded that people everywhere make their decisions not on the merits of any particular case, but on whether George W. Bush and those around him want to do something—whatever the merits of their arguments, and whenever, wherever, and for whatever reasons there happen to be.

By acting with such contempt for global institutions, and by insulting the intelligence of both friends and foes, George W. Bush has traumatized the world community and created new dangers for Americans and all human beings. Probably the greatest future harm will come from the fact that George W. Bush has destroyed belief in America's goodness and wisdom among hundreds of millions of people. As a result of doing that, he has created a crisis of American legitimacy in the world.

"You're either for us or against us" is the epitaph for the hopes and possibilities of an era in which, when America led, the rest of the world willingly followed because it trusted, respected, and admired the United States. George W. Bush for no valid reason has destroyed that trust, as well as those possibilities. When the time comes, his for-us-or-against-us remark should be engraved on his tombstone. It will ring down through the ages as the cry of a man who understood neither the world, nor human dignity, and had no desire to understand—who was impatient with understanding, angry at it.

The truth is, the rest of the world doesn't care about America's persistent obsession, so grotesquely personified by George W. Bush, with acting as though the world's a stage and all the actors on it are either for America or evildoers. Other nations and peoples do begin to get upset when America's delusional behavior starts to disrupt their own lives, hopes, and sense of reliable order in the world. Behind every successful nation's shining veneer of moral superiority lie dark crimes. America is no exception. The United States was founded in conquest. Slavery and genocide are at its roots. The United States is the only nation in history, at least so far, to use nuclear weapons against civilian populations. The crimes continue. In Indochina starting forty years ago, in Central America twenty years ago, and now, again, in the Middle East, America has gone on the rampage for no objectively verifiable reason.

The world knows all this and sees all this, even though most Americans don't, but until George W. Bush embarked on his global destabilization campaign, America's past crimes did not matter very much to the rest of the world. This was because America seemed, so triumphantly, to embody progress—moral, not just material progress. The dream of the third millennium—the promise of globalization—was that the whole world could become like America: free, prosperous, and good. The key word here is "become." People around the world loved America not because it incarnated "good" or had been singled out by God or "Manifest Destiny" to vanquish evil. They loved and respected America because, in spite of all its follies, faults, and crimes, it had become good, and seemed in the process of becoming better.

Americans themselves were so beloved because—unlike the British, the French, the Russians, the Germans, the Chinese, or the Japanese—the people of America were at once so very powerful and at the same time so accessible as human beings. What was most impressive to many people around the world was that Americans seemed able to learn from their mistakes. The American recovery after Vietnam and Watergate was stunning. In less than twenty years, a nation that had been militarily defeated in Asia and morally besmirched at home became the model for a whole new approach to the world. Inspired by the American example of freedom, which thanks to technology was now transmitted everywhere, people-power revolutions shook China and toppled the Berlin Wall. Most of the world seemed on the way to becoming like America—chaotic but functional, full of inequality but even fuller of hope, a place where, thanks to freedom and technology, dreams did come true.

In large part because of the way George W. Bush has used American power, this rosy vision of the world's future has proven to be overoptimistic. Of course, it was always incomplete. Many places and people—including most of Africa, and even some parts of America—were never part of it, so it was only to be expected that globalization would have its enemies, whether they were scruffy anti-WTO demonstrators in Seattle or Islamic fundamentalists in Afghanistan. It took George W. Bush's response to the challenges of globalization to turn the hopes of the third millennium, needlessly and gratuitously, into nightmare.

The gratuitousness of what George W. Bush has done brings us back to the question of evil. If being bad or doing harm were the same things as doing evil, that term could have an arithmetical definition. It is bad to kill one person; it is therefore a million times worse to kill a million people. At some point along the scale—like water changing from ice to steam according to readings on the thermometer—"wrong" would become "bad" and then "evil." However the numbers approach doesn't work. Many more people died because of Abraham Lincoln's actions while he was president than were killed because of Nixon's actions. Yet no one calls Lincoln evil. We don't even think of mass murderers like Genghis Khan as evil—even though the Mongol conqueror certainly killed more people in Iraq than George W. Bush ever will. This is because evil is, somehow, defined by its aberrance. Both Genghis Khan and Abraham Lincoln acted in context. What George W. Bush does keeps coming out of left field.

If there is an objective definition of evil, it has something to do with gratuitousness. Leaving Pol Pot aside, who else in very recent history would most people agree is evil? Slobodan Milosevic of

Serbia is probably the least controversial candidate. It is possible that, had he not been in power there, Yugoslavia might have made a peaceful transition from a Communist state into a collection of independent countries. Much more likely, there would have been a great deal of trouble, and considerable bloodshed, whoever was in power in Belgrade at that time.

What we do know is that Milosevic made things far worse than they needed to be. Contrast him to F.W. de Klerk in South Africa, and you see that the moral quality of individual leaders can make a difference for good, even when the regimes they lead have done many bad things. Refining things a little further, we can observe that intelligence, in addition to gratuitousness, must play a role in any successful definition of evil. Even though Czar Nicholas II of Russia and King Louis XVI of France brought catastrophe upon themselves and their people, history has decided they were too inept to be considered evil. At the same time you don't have to have been an A student at Yale to qualify. George W. Bush has no excuse not to have known better.

If evil has an objective meaning—if it is not an attribute that can only be applied to others—and if it is to be found in the world today, it most certainly is to be found in the White House in the person of George W. Bush. You have only to look at what he has done, and consider the gratuitousness and guile—as well as the consistency and determination—with which he has done it, to see that if the word "evil" applies to anyone, it applies to him.

There are gradations of evil, as there are of everything else, of course. But what causes most people to hang back from saying "George W. Bush is evil" is simply that he happens to be the leader of the United States of America, not some Balkan or Arab country. That in itself is a very odd application of a double standard. Should we not hold the leaders of a highly civilized country like the United States of America to a higher standard than the leaders of countries like Serbia and Iraq? We certainly should not excuse their actions because we continue to hope that America, at its heart, is still good. Instead we should apply to our own leaders at least the same standards we use when judging the presidents of Serbia or Iraq. That was what Henry Thoreau was urging back in 1848, when he called protest a patriotic duty, and added: "What makes this duty the more urgent is the fact that ours is the invading army." The fact that Polk's attack on Mexico brought great benefits to the United States can never make it right. To paraphrase Talleyrand, the fact that George W. Bush's Iraq invasion "was more than a crime, it was a mistake," does not transform the moral significance of what he has done to the world or to America, either. To the contrary, the fact that George W. Bush has acted foolishly makes what he's done even worse.

George W. Bush is a lesson to be learned, but who among Americans will teach or learn? Countries lose their way sometimes, and that's what history will have to record: At the beginning of the twenty-first century, at a moment when it held the world's respect and all the world's possibilities were in its grasp, the United States heeded a small and petulant voice that scorned the advocates of reason and sneered at the voices of wisdom. Turning its back on the real challenges it faced, America abandoned its honorable responsibilities and marched stubbornly, haughtily, into the wilderness.

In the end, it remains inexplicable—the anger, the antagonism, the need to break things. Maybe it is George W. Bush's "Americanism" that, in the end, makes him so un-American. We were supposed to have moved beyond all that destructive behavior. We were supposed to have "progressed." That is the paradox of him, and the American complaisance that has allowed him to act. He has changed the world more than any world leader since Gorbachev, but he has changed it for the worse, and that's not what Americans are supposed to do. He nonetheless remains living proof of that deepest and most idiosyncratic of all American beliefs: that one man truly can make a difference, if you give him enough freedom.

Index

Acknowledgments

RUTH BALDWIN, MY EDITOR at Nation Books, is the heroine of this endeavor. Since I have been forbidden to praise her to the extent, and in the manner I would wish in this instance, I will simply say: Thank you, Ruth. It has been privilege to work with you. You are truly admirable.

I must next thank my great friend from Bosnia war days, Chuck Sudetic. If it weren't for him, this book might never have had Ruth as its editor, though to this day they have never met. As is usual with war correspondents, there is a story: In early 2001, Chuck put me in touch with Bob Love, at that time executive editor of *Rolling Stone* magazine, and I was sent down to Colombia to check out the drug wars. After my series of articles, "Blowback," was whipped into shape by my editor at *Rolling Stone*, Will Dana, Ruth contacted me out of the blue. My contribution to the book she was editing at that time on the war on drugs, "Busted," was the beginning of a beautiful relationship.

The adventure of writing this book has run counter-clockwise to George W. Bush's misadventures. That is to say, I began it overseas, and finished it at home. Not only that, I wrote about half this book in my 800-year-old house in Lauzerte, France—

the very heartland of the country the radical Neo-Con unilateralists so detest. Most of the time I might have been writing anywhere, yet being in Europe in the immediate aftermath of the Iraq invasion was a revelation. The Bush-Cheney people don't seem to get it, but even the French don't dislike us, or even want to oppose us, but they do find American official attitudes awfully puzzling sometimes. This book would not be the same book, and it certainly would have been a late book, and an even longer one, were it not for the perspective and slight sense of distance from the American buzz scene that being in Lauzerte gave me. I must here thank my great friends. Patricia and Dominique Darniere, for more than a decade of friendship and help. Even to begin to acknowledge the help others in that part of the world have given me would necessitate naming practically everyone at the Saturday Lauzerte market, and also everyone who shows up at the Cafe de France in Montcuq on Sundays. Thank you, one and all. You know who you are.

I finished this book back in my apartment in New York, writing at a desk where every time I took my eyes off the computer screen, I saw the piece of empty sky where the Twin Towers of the World Trade Center once stood. The people who perished in that tragedy were with me every moment as I wrote. I hope, at the least, that this work does not dishonor them. Like America, they deserved better.

In New York, Vincent Douglas was of great help to me. Andrew Miller, my editor at Pantheon, generously gave me time off from another project, my forthcoming book on Florida, so that I could write this book. I only hint at the debt I owe Joyce Johnson in the dedication. Dr. ChengZong Sui was essential to the successful initiation as well as the successful completion of this project. It is a pleasure also to thank Tina

Brown for having sent me to Iraq for *The New Yorker* in the first place. The top-to-bottom background knowledge of Iraq I was fortunate enough to gain in the course of my travels there, from the Marshes in the south to Kurdistan in the north, and from the Jordanian desert to the former battlefields on the border with Iran, was essential to the writing of *Rogue State*.

I would never have written this book except that a fellow American I still have never met spoke to me one night around three AM. I was listening to the overnight repeat of Terry Gross's radio interview program "Fresh Air," while trying to write something on an entirely different subject. Her guest was John Brady Kiesling, the American diplomat who had resigned to protest the Iraq invasion.

She asked him a question I didn't quite hear, and his reply went as follows: "No, I don't consider what I've done particularly heroic." Then he gave me no alternative but to write this book, by adding: "I am sure any American who loves his country and who had the chance to speak out and be heard would do the same thing."

T.D. Allman
Lauzerte, France—Brooklyn Heights, New York
June 2003—January 2004